Timeline of American Aviation

1903	Wright brothers make world's first human-controlled powered flight.
1908	First airfield, Morris Field near New York City, built.
1908	Glenn Curtiss flies his *June Bug*, inviting a lawsuit from the litigious Wright brothers, who view the craft as an infringement on their patented airplane design. A judge agrees.
1908	First regulations passed restricting local aircraft operations in Kissimmee, Florida.
1908	Lt. Thomas Selfridge becomes first passenger killed in an airplane crash during a flight piloted by Orville Wright.
1908	First flight of a privately owned aircraft.
1909	First rotary-wing aircraft design wins patent.
1909	First commercial aircraft, a Curtiss pusher design, goes on sale.
1909	The U.S. Army buys its first airplane, a Wright A.
1910	First all-aviation exhibition, the Boston Aero Show.
1910	First pilot license issued to Glenn Curtiss.
1910	First flight at night, performed by Charles W. Hamilton over Knoxville, Tennessee.
1910	Blanche Scott becomes the first woman to fly an airplane alone.
1910	Curtiss's *Albany Flyer* becomes first plane launched from ship.
1911	Glenn Curtiss flies the first water takeoff and landing in his Curtiss Hydro.
1911	Post Office sanctions air delivery of mail.
1911	Cal Rogers, flying the *Vin Fiz,* completes first transcontinental flight, surviving 14 minor crashes, five total crack-ups, untold engine failures in flight, an in-flight scalding when an engine hose sprayed loose, and a head-on collision with a chicken coop.
1912	First parachute jump, performed by Albert Berry over St. Louis, Missouri. Tom Benoist and Tony Jannus win a patent for the parachute.
1912	Harriet Quimby becomes first woman to fly across the English Channel.
1914	First scheduled airline flight connects St. Petersburg, Florida, and Tampa, Florida.
1918	First transcontinental mail service inaugurated.
1918	First American pilots engage in air combat.
1919	First trans-Atlantic flight from Long Island, New York, to Plymouth, England, with stops in Newfoundland, Azores, and Lisbon.
1919	First scheduled international airline service joins Key West, Florida, to Havana, Cuba.

alpha
books

1920   Barnstormer Omer Locklear receives first criminal citation for "reckless aerial driving" in Los Angeles, California, costing him $25.

1921   Transcontinental air mail service flies between Mineola, New York, and San Francisco, California, in less than two days.

1922   First skywriting flight is made over New York, when Cyril Turner spells out "Hello USA."

1922   First aircraft carrier, USS *Langley,* created from an old coal ship, is commissioned.

1923   First nonstop transcontinental flight by Air Service officers Oakley G. Kelly and John A. Macready flying 2,500 miles from Roosevelt Field, New York, to San Diego, California, in 26 hours 50 minutes.

1924   First around-the-world flight involves four Douglas World Cruisers under the command of Army Maj. F. Martin and takes more than 15 days to return to Seattle, Washington. Only two airplanes finish the 26,345-mile journey, which was made at an average speed of 75 m.p.h.

1925   Contract Air Mail Act is passed, spurring passenger airline industry.

1927   Charles A. Lindbergh flies *The Spirit of St. Louis* nonstop across the Atlantic from New York to Paris in 33½ hours.

1928   Amelia Earhart becomes first woman to cross the Atlantic nonstop, though as a passenger.

1929   Adm. Richard Byrd, with pilot Bernt Balchen, flies over South Pole.

1931   First nonstop trans-Pacific flight, from Japan to Wenatchee, Washington.

1932   Amelia Earhart fulfills vow to be the first woman pilot to cross the Atlantic nonstop.

1933   Wiley Post becomes first to fly alone around the world, taking 7 days 19 hours.

1939   First successful flight of single main-rotor helicopter, performed by Igor Sikorsky.

1942   First flight of an American jet aircraft, the Bell XP-59A.

1943   Franklin D. Roosevelt becomes the first president to fly while in office. Presidential airplane soon followed.

1947   Air Force created as a separate military branch.

1947   Capt. Chuck Yeager breaks sound barrier at Muroc Dry Lake, California, by flying 700 m.p.h. in the Bell X-1.

1957   Jackie Cochran becomes first woman to break sound barrier, flying a Republic F-86 fighter.

1965   Lockheed SR-71 exceeds speeds of Mach 3 and altitude of 80,000 feet.

1977   Human-powered airplane piloted by Bryan Allen wins £50,000 Kremer prize by flying a specified figure-eight pattern.

1986   Jeana Yeager and Dick Rutan pilot the experimental Burt Rutan–designed *Voyager* on the first around-the-world, nonstop, unrefueled flight, taking more than nine days.

1999   Brian Jones and Bertrand Piccard complete the first nonstop, around-the-world flight in a balloon.

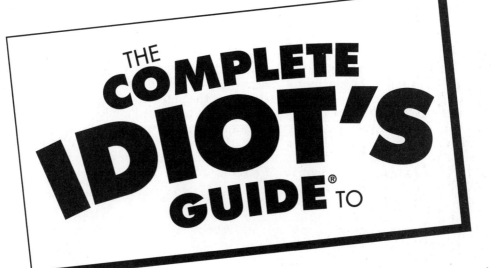

THE **COMPLETE IDIOT'S GUIDE**® TO

Flying and Gliding

by Bill Lane and Azriela Jaffe

alpha books

Macmillan USA, Inc.
201 West 103rd Street
Indianapolis, IN 46290

A Pearson Education Company

To Jennifer, who saw a further horizon than I and guided me to it.
—Bill Lane

Copyright © 2000 by Bill Lane and Azriela Jaffe

International Standard Book Number: 0-02-863885-9
Library of Congress Catalog Card Number: Available from the Library of Congress.

02 01 00   8 7 6 5 4 3 2 1

Interpretation of the printing code: The rightmost number of the first series of numbers is the year of the book's printing; the rightmost number of the second series of numbers is the number of the book's printing. For example, a printing code of 00-1 shows that the first printing occurred in 2000.

Printed in the United States of America

Note: This publication contains the opinions and ideas of its authors. It is intended to provide helpful and informative material on the subject matter covered. It is sold with the understanding that the authors and publisher are not engaged in rendering professional services in the book. If the reader requires personal assistance or advice, a competent professional should be consulted.

The authors and publisher specifically disclaim any responsibility for any liability, loss, or risk, personal or otherwise, which is incurred as a consequence, directly or indirectly, of the use and application of any of the contents of this book.

Publisher
Marie Butler-Knight

Product Manager
Phil Kitchel

Managing Editor
Cari Luna

Acquisitions Editor
Randy Ladenheim-Gil

Development Editor
Michael Thomas

Production Editor
Christy Wagner

Illustrator
Brian Moyer

Cover Designers
Mike Freeland
Kevin Spear

Book Designers
Scott Cook and Amy Adams of DesignLab

Indexer
Tonya Heard

Layout/Proofreading
Darin Crone
Svetlana Dominguez
Steve Geiselman
Ayanna Lacey
Eric S. Miller

Contents at a Glance

Contents

Appendixes

Foreword

Flying! Leaving the bonds of the earth behind and seeing the world from above! It's been our dream from the beginning of time. But only in the last 200 years or so—mere droplets in the great river of time—have humans realized this dream and enjoyed the wonderful exhilaration of flight.

We've reveled in our enjoyment of flying in every way imaginable. We've risen above the earth in balloons, airships, airplanes, helicopters, gyroplanes, and gliders—every contraption we can conceive of to take to the skies.

Bill Lane explores it all. Ever wonder what makes an airship or a helicopter fly? The answers are right here. Bill takes you from the ancient dream to modern-day reality and explains how each of these marvelous inventions works. In a delightfully playful and clear style he takes you beyond the mechanics of flight and shares his passion for every type of flying—letting you in on the behind-the-scenes jokes and stories that pilots usually share only with other pilots.

Bill is the perfect person to write this book. He comes by his love of flying naturally. His grandfather was a barnstormer who toured the country with an aerial circus. His father followed as a fighter pilot and then airline pilot. Bill himself learned to fly in high school and became a highly qualified flight instructor while obtaining his degree at Embry-Riddle Aeronautical University. After a career of sharing the gift of flight with others ranging from university students to fledgling airline pilots, Bill became a professional wordsmith, writing for newspapers and magazines on a wide variety of subjects—especially aviation.

With these special skills, Bill brings to you a clear view of the big picture of aviation. You will not only understand the deep satisfaction that pilots get from commanding an aircraft in flight, but you'll have a perspective on the inevitable risks involved. You'll realize that the habit all pilots have of talking about crashes among themselves comes not from a morbid preoccupation with death and destruction, but from a life-long desire to understand and carefully manage the risks of flight.

No matter what it is that fascinates you about flying—its promise of freedom, its beauty, its precision and science, or the prospect of adventure—you will find it all waiting for you in this book. Enjoy it! And who knows—you might just find, like thousands before you have, that you, too, become inescapably drawn to the sky!

John and Martha King
San Diego, December 21, 1999

(Photo courtesy King School, Inc.)

John and Martha King have, through the magic of video, instructed more pilots than anyone in the world. Known for their entertaining and personable onscreen style, the Kings have revolutionized the flight-training industry. They have pursued their enthusiasm for flying to the fullest, flying their Citation jet wherever they go and swapping captain and co-pilot duties on each leg. They are the first husband and wife to hold every class of pilot and instructor rating available. From airships and balloons to helicopters, gyroplanes, airplanes, and gliders, John and Martha enjoy them all.

Introduction

What is the appeal of aviation that draws thousands of new pilots to the skies every year? Is it the legacy of brave men like the earliest barnstormers and air mail pilots? Is it the legend of Charles Lindbergh or the mystery that haunts the memory of Amelia Earhart? Or is it the technicalities of flying, the simple forces of nature that enable tons of metal to lift free of the earth and behave like a bird?

By the time you finish reading *The Complete Idiot's Guide to Flying and Gliding*, you'll have a better idea about which aspect of aviation attracts you to this fascinating pursuit. This book is written for the prospective pilot as well as for the spectator who longs for a deeper understanding. The would-be pilot will find it an excellent introduction to concepts that he or she will soon understand in greater depth. And the spectator will come away with a greater appreciation for the sport that already gives him or her immense satisfaction.

What You'll Learn in This Book

In *The Complete Idiot's Guide to Flying and Gliding*, you'll learn everything you need to know about the history of aviation, the fundamental physical principles that make flight possible, what it takes to make a flight, the secrets behind the thrilling aerobatics that spice up air shows, and the mental and physical obstacles that face human beings when we go aloft.

Here's what you'll find in each part of the book:

Part 1, "Taking to the Sky: The History of Flight," traces the history of the human race's fascination with birds, the sky, and dreams of flight. You'll learn about the influence Leonardo da Vinci had on Renaissance thinking, the French ballooning craze of the eighteenth century, and the pioneers of airplanes, the glider pilots. You'll find out what drove the Wright brothers to develop the first successful flying machine, and follow the early aviators on their daredevil flights around the country to introduce a nation to aviation. You'll find out which airplanes and which pilots helped win the World Wars, how Charles Lindbergh and Amelia Earhart ignited the imagination of the traveling public, and how pioneering airplane makers gave the public safe, affordable planes in which to indulge in their new hobby—sport flying.

Part 2, "The Thrill of Flight," explores the nuts and bolts of flying, from the composition of a typical airplane to the physical forces at work to get it off the ground. You'll be introduced to the science of aerodynamics in simple, clear steps that will help you make sense of this complex subject. You'll learn about gliders and how they differ from powered airplanes, both in form and in function, and discover how glider pilots keep their craft flying for hours at a time without the aid of an engine. You'll understand how helicopters function and why they differ so starkly from airplanes, both in the way they operate and in the way they're put together. You'll be introduced to the placid, graceful world of hot-air balloons, which is full of fancifully shaped craft and tradition-bound pilots. Finally, you'll glimpse some of the oddballs of aviation, from airplanes that behave like helicopters to balloons that can circumnavigate the globe nonstop.

Part 3, "In the Cockpit," brings you to the front of the plane where the action takes place. For those who want to earn their wings, this part tells you how to achieve that goal. Here, too, you'll learn the principles of navigation, from the specialized maps used by pilots to the system of latitude and longitude that forms the basis for flight planning. You'll ride along on a flight and discover how pilots take off, navigate a course, interact with air-traffic controllers, and land their planes. Finally, you'll be introduced to modern stunt flying. We'll take a look at how aerobatic pilots execute their amazing maneuvers, from flying upside-down to the wild—and potentially dangerous—maneuvers that thrill crowds around the world.

Part 4, "Meeting the Challenges to the Perfect Flight," brings you face-to-face with the potential hazards of flying that all pilots must know about to make safe decisions. The weather, the most crucial factor in a pilot's planning, is explained in clear terms, from the structure of the atmosphere to the names and habits of clouds. You'll learn about how the body responds to high altitude and strenuous maneuvers, and how the effects of mental and emotional stresses can be amplified in flight conditions. We'll look at the last flight of John F. Kennedy Jr. and learn how his decisions before and during the flight created a chain of events that could have led to the tragedy. In the last chapter of the book, we'll take a look at the future of aviation.

Extras

Throughout *The Complete Idiot's Guide to Flying and Gliding*, you'll find four types of boxes that contain special information about aviation.

Plane Talk

These longer sidebars supplement your reading with bet-you-didn't-know facts and stories.

On Course

These sidebars contain tips and insights to make you more knowledgeable about flying.

Turbulence

These sidebars are warning boxes that alert you to potential problems or tell you about problems aviators have faced.

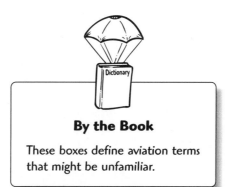

By the Book

These boxes define aviation terms that might be unfamiliar.

Acknowledgments

I wish to thank those who generously lent their time and energy in reading and advising on the manuscript. Special thanks to Shawn Arena, my cousin, a private pilot, airport manager at Phoenix Goodyear Airport in Goodyear, Arizona, and a fellow alumnus of Embry-Riddle Aeronautical University, who shares with me the inspiration and passion for flying passed on to us by our grandfather, Joseph Lacona, a flyer who first taught us to turn our eyes to the sky.

Very special thanks, too, to Sean Jeralds, a one-time classmate and now chief flight instructor at the finest flight campus in the country—Embry-Riddle in Prescott. Sean's joy of flying is perhaps equaled only by his joy of teaching it.

Thanks also to Bob Martel, who planted the hot-air ballooning bug in me.

Thanks to my co-author Azriela Jaffe, whose inspiration and encouragement helped ease me through the tough days.

For their generous offer of photographs, I thank Cessna Aircraft Company, Guenther Eichhorn, Allen Matheson, Groen Brothers Aviation, and Vince Miller.

Thanks to Heather Potter for her generous help in typing the manuscript.

And, most important, I thank my wife Jennifer, whose faith in me was often greater than my own.

Trademarks

All terms mentioned in this book that are known to be or are suspected of being trademarks or service marks have been appropriately capitalized. Alpha Books and Macmillan USA, Inc., cannot attest to the accuracy of this information. Use of a term in this book should not be regarded as affecting the validity of any trademark or service mark.

Part 1

Taking to the Sky: The History of Flight

In building the first airplane, the Wright brothers realized a dream that had captured the imaginations of people from the ancient Greeks to the Renaissance genius Leonardo da Vinci. In this part of the book, you'll follow each step in the evolution of airplanes from the dangerous playthings of daredevils to machines capable of crossing oceans. You'll also be introduced to the colorful personalities whose names have become aviation legends, from the barnstormers of an age gone by to heroes of today like Chuck Yeager.

Chapter 1

The Earliest Aviators

> ### In This Chapter
>
> ➤ The universal dream of flight
>
> ➤ The Greeks and early flying stories
>
> ➤ Leonardo da Vinci: the first aviation inventor
>
> ➤ Balloons "take off" in popularity
>
> ➤ The first airplanes: gliders

Human beings have always been flyers—all we lack are our own wings. From the time our ancestors carved pictures on the walls of caves, we have dreamed of what it might be like to soar with the birds.

For those of us with a passion for the sky, those dreams still fuel our imagination. Sigmund Freud might disagree, but it's possible that no other dream is as universal as the dream of flying. It's easy to understand why. Flying releases us from the grip of gravity and enables us to soar effortlessly above the ground, where everything from impassable terrain to bumper-to-bumper traffic hinders and frustrates us. Flying enables us to take our fortunes in our own hands and provides us with a tool that carries us—quite literally—to heights and destinations we might not otherwise have seen.

But many of us love flying for reasons that go deeper than its ability to move us quickly from one nation to another, or from our hometown airport to our favorite fishing lake. For us, flying is a way of expressing our spirit of adventure and our desire

Turbulence

Don't be fooled by bad science fiction movies that show screaming cavemen and cavewomen being carried to their doom by giant pterodactyls. Humans appeared about 194 million years too late to see a living pterodactyl. In any case, because the early species of pterodactyls grew to about the size of a sparrow, they would have had their claws full to carry much of anything.

On Course

The surest way to get hooked on flying is to spend an afternoon at your local airstrip watching the airplanes come and go. From a safe location outside the airport boundary, you'll begin to sense the pace and character of flying—and you'll fall in love with it. Warning: Aviation can be habit-forming!

to push ourselves to greater challenges. And to make it even more exciting, there is a thrilling hint of danger thrown in. Although statistics show that some forms of flying are safer than driving a car, no one can deny that flying carries with it some risk.

Tragedies like the death of John F. Kennedy Jr. in a flying accident in July 1999, remind us that flying can be unforgiving if we aren't careful. But the death of JFK Jr. also created more interest in flying because many of us read in news reports about how much he loved to be in the air. Kennedy loved flying and he flew his airplane whenever he could, taking friends and family along with him sometimes, just to share the fun.

What is it about flying that some people find so addictive? From the wise old pilots that hang around airports—the "hangar bums" or "ramp rats" as they are affectionately called—to the sounds and sights of planes arriving and departing from the landing strip, flying has an unmistakable mystique. In addition to the indescribable feeling of taking off into a beautiful spring sunrise or flying over the breathtaking landscapes of the Southwest or the great Smoky Mountains, there is a delightful social culture that makes every plane lover feel welcome, even if they haven't yet earned their wings.

In order to fully appreciate the culture of flying, let's take a look at how flying began and at some of the heroes who made it what it is today.

"If Man Were Meant to Fly ..."

For hundreds of generations, men and women have been obsessed with flying like birds, and maybe even *better* than birds. In fact, many ancient cultures seemed to acknowledge that flight is the most magical thing we could ever hope to do. Just look at their gods. The most revered figures in almost every religion and mythology were able to fly, and *aviation* myths form part of nearly every religion and culture—from the bird-man icons of the Egyptians to the Old Testament's much-debated account of the priest Ezekiel's encounter with a UFO.

Ancient flying tales range from the sublime to the considerably offbeat. For example, in China, storytellers pass down accounts of noblemen who were able to fly with the aid of large hats. These immense chapeaus caught the air and bore their wearers safely away from captivity and danger. These stories could be either the earliest accounts of people using parachutes or an ancient precursor to TV's *The Flying Nun!*

Did Icarus Beat Orville and Wilbur?

Perhaps the most detailed mythical account of early flight comes to us courtesy of the ancient Greeks. The tale of an inventor named Daedalus and his impulsive, thrill-seeking son, Icarus, has entered our cultural lexicon as a caution against daring to rise as high as the gods.

As the Greeks told the fable, Daedalus and Icarus fled from King Minos of Crete, who had ordered that the pair be arrested for an act of treachery. The two hid in a cave high up in the cliffs overlooking the rocky Cretan shoreline. From there Daedalus spent hours watching eagles soar in the powerful wind currents that pushed upward from the sea, and puzzled over how to craft wings that would enable him and Icarus to fly away from their pursuers. After experimenting with one material after another, Daedalus decided that he would fashion wings from the same feathers that helped the eagles fly.

Once he and Icarus had collected enough feathers—and given a whole new meaning to the term "bald eagle," no doubt—Daedalus began to press them onto two beeswax-coated, wing-shaped frames. Before their escape, and with King Minos's soldiers at the mouth of their cave, Daedalus gave his son a hasty preflight briefing: Fly halfway between heaven and the sea. Don't fly too low, he warned Icarus, or the wings could become soaked and heavy from the sea spray. And don't fly too high, or the heat of the sun might melt the wax and destroy the wings.

By the Book

Aviation is the word we use to describe almost any sport or occupation that takes place in the air. For example, sports like ballooning and gliding fall into the aviation category. Appropriately, the word derives from *avis*, the Latin word for "bird."

Turbulence

As it turns out, no matter how closely we try to watch birds with the naked eye, it is almost impossible to spot the incredibly subtle secret of their flying. It wasn't until slow-motion cameras were invented that we really began to understand how birds fly.

Plane Talk

Of course, it's not only feathers that enable birds to fly. They are fantastically evolved to combine strength with light weight. Birds' bones must be strong enough to withstand the enormous demands of rapidly flapping wings, but they must be light enough not to overload the muscles. The weight of man's bones and his large muscle mass force him to turn to technology in order to get off the ground.

Of course, we know how the story ended. Icarus ignored his father's warning and flew higher and higher, until the sun heated the wax and feathers and the boy fluttered into the sea. The Greeks read into the story a stern caution against arrogantly thinking that it is possible to devise tools that can reach the gods. (The rest of us hear a second message, too: Kids never listen to a thing their parents say.)

The myth of Daedalus and Icarus inspired centuries of aviation innovators, but, ironically, might have hindered our progress toward flight by encouraging generations of minds to focus somewhat slavishly on copying the wing structure and flying style of birds. The determination to mimic bird flight rather than invent our own form of flying delayed the progress of human flight until the eighteenth century.

Not So Mythical

As plausible as that story may have sounded to ancient ears, virtually all scholars and airplane designers agree that the story of Daedalus and Icarus has little or no basis in truth. One notable exception, however, was the renowned science fiction writer H.G. Wells, who insisted that the story was largely based on fact. His claim seemed to gain ground in 1900, when an English expedition uncovered evidence on Crete that possibly confirmed the details of the tale. Still, most pilots are skeptical that a man could have soared on wings made of pasted feathers.

For the Birds

The tale of Daedalus and Icarus is appealing because those of us who are crazy about flying wish that we could strap on wings made of eagle feathers and fly away. The story illustrates the deceptive simplicity of bird flight and the maddening ease with which birds accomplish what men and women have yearned to do for eons.

So how do the birds do it? In a few words, they combine up-and-down flapping movements with a front-to-back rowing motion. Together, the coordinated movement of the wings give birds upward *lift* as well as forward *thrust*. Add to that basic motion some intricate differences in each wing's independent motion—and mix in a timely flick of rudder-like tail feathers—and birds are capable of feats of maneuverability and aerobatics that have transfixed and baffled some of the greatest minds in history.

Even now, our rational understanding of the complex forces at work doesn't erase the sense of wonder we humans feel at watching birds wheeling and flitting through the sky.

Leonardo da Vinci, Aviation Pioneer

Here's a quiz: Which of the following applies to Leonardo da Vinci?

a) Designed the first machine gun.

b) Conceived a workable submarine.

c) Wrote in handwriting that had to be read using a mirror.

d) Designed an early version of a helicopter.

e) Designed a machine to manufacture gold sequins.

Answer: All of the above!

Surprised? No wonder. But the fact is that Leonardo da Vinci (1452–1519) was the epitome of the "Renaissance Man," and he generally was able to master anything he put his mind to. Leonardo brought an artist's keen eye to the pursuit of flight. He spent hours in the hills around the village of Vinci studying the motions of birds and visualizing the forces at work as they flew. He sketched what he saw, and when he died he left behind massive portfolios of sketches and notes that researchers continue to study and marvel over today.

By the Book

Lift is one of four forces of flight that we'll describe in more detail in Part 3, "In the Cockpit." It is the pressure created by airplane wings that counteracts the pull of gravity and enables planes to fly. In an airplane, **thrust** is the force, created by a propeller or jet engine, that produces speed.

Turbulence

If we had listened to Giovanni Alfonso Borelli, we might never have learned to fly. Borelli, a seventeenth-century aviation enthusiast, speculated that birds flew by combining the flapping of their wings with an intricate twisting motion of each feather. Because people could never duplicate the complicated motion, Borelli predicted we would never fly.

Leonardo designed some of the most ingenious devices of his age, including this "flying machine" that was to enable a man to fly like a bird. Unfortunately, it didn't fly.

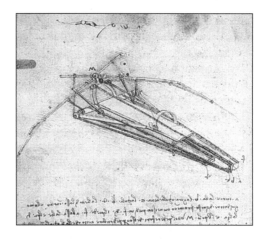

Leonardo was no idle sky gazer; he was a skilled engineer and inventor whose innovations included radically speculative creations such as a flapping-wing "ornithopter" and another contraption that resembled a cross between a screw and a parasol. Believe it or not, this was a primitive precursor to the modern helicopter. As if Leonardo's engineering and mechanical genius weren't enough to distinguish him, he also possessed a surgeon's understanding of the human body, not only in its physical form but in the mechanical demands that motion placed on its structure of muscles and bones.

And those accomplishments don't even touch on the artistic genius that some say made him the finest artist in all of Western history! Gee, was there anything this guy was *not* good at?

Leonardo's "ornithopter" was a complicated contraption that relied on a person's flapping a set of mechanical wings.

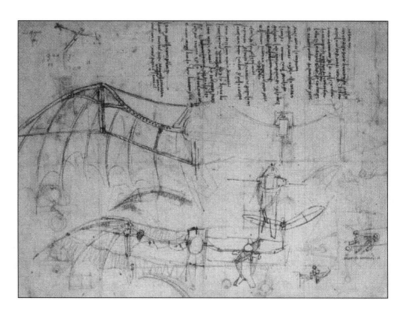

Leonardo and His Flying Machines

As Leonardo's understanding of bird flight grew, so did his visions of machines that would lift man off the ground and allow him to fly freely over the treetops. His flying machine featured complex wings and controls that fitted over the head and neck of the pilot. These cumbersome controls were meant to help a flyer control the sideways motion of the machine, much like a ship's rudder.

One of Leonardo's quirkier inventions was his take on the helicopter, whose design might not win any beauty contests but at least demonstrates that Leonardo understood the fluid properties of air. The main part of the machine, which never evolved beyond a drawing in a sketch book and a crude model, resembled a screw, a design that Leonardo had integrated into many of his mechanical inventions. Rather than wood or metal, the "thread" of this screw was constructed of heavy fabric that spiraled upward in a broad sweep around a vertical axle. As Leonardo sketched it, the helicopter was meant to be powered by human muscle; a pilot was to turn the central axle rapidly enough to force air down the sloping spiral of fabric, and therefore drive the machine upward.

Leonardo's machine was far too heavy to have been able to fly under human power alone, but it inspired a lot of imitators—including the Wright brothers, in an indirect way, as we'll see in Chapter 2, "The Bishop's Boys: Wilbur and Orville Wright."

Plane Talk

Leonardo designed an enormous device called an "ornithopter" that featured four flapping wings attached to levers. He intended the human pilot to pump the levers fast enough to lift the machine off the ground. Judging by the enormous physical demands Leonardo's machines placed on their pilots, the master engineer might have been better suited to a career as a designer of workout equipment!

The First Flight?

Legends have grown up around Leonardo that tantalize us even today, though his role as an aviation inventor has been overshadowed by his breathtaking paintings and his artistic studies of the human body. One legend that invites the wildest speculation is a story involving one of his many followers and students.

According to the tale, one of Leonardo's assistants was so impressed by the master's flying machine that he strapped himself to it and leaped from a tall cliff. There is no account of the flight—if it can be called that—but only of the outcome: The would-be flyer hit the ground hard and was seriously injured. It's interesting to think that if the story is true, and if the flyer glided even slightly outward, then the tiny village of Vinci became on that sunny Florentine morning the site of the first human flight.

Leonardo's wing designs show an amazing level of detail, and strongly resemble bat wings.

Plane Talk

If the legend of Leonardo's impetuous test-pilot assistant is true, the young man might have appreciated another of Leonardo's inventions—the parachute. Or maybe not. In his notebook, Leonardo drew a detailed sketch of a pyramid-shaped apparatus that dangled its wearer below it just as modern parachutes function. But rather than the light, billowy hemisphere of fabric used in parachutes of the twentieth century, Leonardo's parachute featured a sturdy pyramidal wood frame covered with heavy fabric. The whole thing was gigantic, meaning that it would have been absurdly heavy. No one is known to have tested the parachute, and considering Leonardo's scant success with his flying inventions, it's probably a good thing.

All in all, Leonardo's aircraft designs were startlingly fresh and innovative. But it was the world's ill fate that Leonardo was born too soon. Europe of the fifteenth and sixteenth centuries based its industry on wood and metal. Manufactured goods may have been durable, but they were also heavy. Leonardo must have known that each of his flying machines would ultimately fail. We can only imagine the frustration he must have felt; he was perhaps the first man ever to possess the engineering genius that could have permitted people to fly, but he was trapped by relatively primitive earth-bound technology. He died without ever seeing his inventions work the way he imagined they would.

Aeronauts and the Balloon Revolution

For millennia, men and women crowding around crackling fires and steaming pots noticed a universal constant: Smoke rises. That principle is so simple that it's not clear why humankind waited until the eighteenth century to create a hot-air balloon and try to take to the skies. In fact, the simple fabric that the first balloons were made of has been available since the time of the ancient Sumerians and Egyptians.

A Lot of Hot Air

In 1783, two French brothers named Joseph and Etienne Montgolfier made what is considered to be the first vehicle to achieve sustained flight—a hot-air balloon.

The brothers, who were inventors, were experimenting one day at their paper factory when they noticed that a paper bag rose toward the ceiling when it was filled with hot air. They tried filling another bag with steam, but the water vapor soaked the paper and weighed it down. They held bags over a fire and found that the bags rose quickly and remained aloft as long as the air inside stayed hot.

Turbulence

It took people until the 1700s to invent the hot-air balloon, but that doesn't mean people weren't thinking about it long before then. A Jesuit priest named Francesco de Lana wrote in 1670 that four copper spheres with most of the air sucked out of them would become buoyant, and could be tethered to a gondola equipped with a sail.

The Very First Aviators

Knowing they were on to something big, the brothers announced they were ready to publicly display their invention. On June 4, 1783, the Montgolfiers staged a Paris demonstration for Louis XVI and Queen Marie Antoinette, and their full-size balloon created a Gallic sensation. Worried that the air a few hundred feet off the ground might be too thin to breathe, the brothers didn't actually participate in the ascension—they left those honors to a sheep, a chicken, and a duck. While an enormous crowd watched, the animals slowly ascended 1,700 feet into the sky. The sheep and duck were unharmed in the return to earth, but the chicken broke its neck on landing and wound up that evening as part of a family's dinner.

Hot air kept early balloons aloft, and the on-board fire that provided the heat kept pilots on the alert for embers that could ignite the delicate paper the first balloons were made of.

The first human balloon flyers, or *aeronauts,* in history were not the Montgolfier brothers, but two French courtiers named Jean-Francois Pilatre de Rozier and Francois Laurent, the Marquis d'Arlandes. They stoked a fire in the balloon the Montgolfier brothers had built and lifted off from the verge of the Boulogne forest near Paris and drifted to a safe landing five miles downwind. The two men set a number of "firsts" in aviation history, including sustaining a prolonged flight in a craft they powered themselves—in this case by keeping a fire burning under the balloon's envelope.

The Race Is On!

From the first flight by human passengers in October 1783, adventurers quickly vied to out-climb, outrace, and outthrill each other and their adoring fans waiting on the ground or chasing the "aerostations," as the French called them, all over the countryside. The Montgolfiers didn't have much to do with the new wave of flying mania, however. Only one of the brothers, Joseph, ever flew in a balloon, and he did it only once. Having given aviation a single important push, the Montgolfiers went back to making paper and left the flying to a new breed of adventurer.

By the Book

If the word **aeronaut** sounds vaguely familiar, it should. Aeronaut, the name balloon flyers call themselves, derives from Greek words meaning "voyager of the air." Likewise, "astronaut" means "voyager to the stars," while the Russian word "cosmonaut" means "voyager to the universe."

Plane Talk

Not everyone took kindly to the new-fangled flying machines of the Montgolfiers and others. The first untethered hydrogen balloon flight, which was mercifully unmanned, drifted some 15 miles away from its launch site, where it came to earth in the hamlet of Gonesse. Unaccustomed to seeing giant gas bags plopping down in their usually quiet streets, the panicked inhabitants set upon the balloon with knives and stones, slashing the rubber-coated silk envelope to shreds.

As other flyers took to the air, it became clear that aviation was to become a nearly unending chain of men and women pushing the boundaries of human flight. Just a week after the flight from the Boulogne forest, two men lifted off from the Tuilleries in the heart of Paris in a balloon filled with hydrogen rather than heated air. They floated more than 20 miles to the town of Nesles. More than 400,000 cheering people witnessed the takeoff, including Ben Franklin (who seems to have been everywhere in Paris).

The balloon technology race had been launched. Aeronauts were quick to reach greater heights and farther distances. Naturally, the English Channel, which separated England from the continent, was among the first challenges to be conquered. And using hydrogen, other aeronauts were reaching altitudes above 10,000 feet. In the 1800s, some even attempted to motorize the giant ships with primitive gasoline engines, though those efforts would not succeed on a major scale until much later.

Plane Talk

A spectator at one of the early French hydrogen balloon demonstrations was Benjamin Franklin, who was then acting as American ambassador to Versailles. In one of those almost-too-perfect-to-be-true stories with which Franklin's mythology is peppered, a nearby balloon watcher was heard to ask skeptically, "What good is it?" Franklin replied, "What good is a newborn baby?"

A brief political dispute known as the French Revolution sharply reduced the number of flights in Europe during the last decade of the eighteenth century. But in America, the pace picked up. The first person to fly in a balloon on American soil was Jean-Pierre Blanchard, whose 1793 flight in Philadelphia was witnessed by George Washington and four future presidents: John Adams, Thomas Jefferson, James Madison, and James Monroe.

Though the French made use of the infant balloon technology during their Revolution, it wasn't until 1862 that Americans turned toward balloons for military purposes. During the Civil War, tethered balloons were used for reconnaissance of enemy troop movements—and probably as practice targets for bored enemy soldiers. In the Spanish-American War of 1898, a tethered balloon was used by American forces to direct artillery fire during the Battle of San Juan.

Plane Talk

Francois Pilatre de Rozier, the first man to fly in an untethered balloon, also suffered the distinction of being the first man to die in one. During an attempt at a high-altitude crossing of the English Channel from France to England, his hydrogen balloon exploded and he was killed. De Rozier's wife, who later became a noted aeronaut in her own right, was also killed in a ballooning accident in 1819.

Gliding Pioneers

Even before the Wright brothers flew at Kitty Hawk, North Carolina, aviators at the end of the 1800s knew that motorized flight was the wave of the future. They mounted motors to frame-strengthened balloons, called "dirigibles," but the giant craft were slow and ungainly. Still, those brave innovators succeeded at making the sky a familiar, if not a comfortable, place to be. The stage was set for the next stage in human flight—gliding.

Although centuries had passed since the days of Leonardo, the master engineer was viewed as prophetic in the late nineteenth century when gliders began to replace balloons as the next major advance in aviation. Designs for the early gliders bore a striking resemblance to the articulated wings that Leonardo had sketched in his notebooks. But now science was coming to the aid of fancy, and engineers were puttering around with wing designs that took advantage of some of the new discoveries about the physical properties of air and the effect it can have on objects like wings. The newly fashionable science was called *aerodynamics*.

Sir George Cayley

The theoretical capabilities of gliders became apparent as early as 1804, when Englishman Sir George Cayley foreshadowed many of the later

By the Book

Aerodynamics is part of an arcane branch of physics called "fluid mechanics." In the case of aerodynamics, scientists and engineers study the motion of air, including the forces it exerts on objects that move through it. Aerodynamicists study wing shapes, jet propulsion, and the extreme conditions of high-speed flight, among other things.

discoveries of glider and airplane builders, earning himself the honored title of "father of aerial navigation." Cayley's greatest contribution to human flight was his understanding that, in order to sustain an aircraft in heavier-than-air flight—meaning without hot air or other gases to keep it buoyant—a designer had to create a structure so large that the force of air resistance on its wings was greater than the craft's weight.

But Cayley's insights went much further than describing the fundamentals of flight; he put into writing many of the very principles that we continue to practice today when we design safe, stable aircraft. The remarkable thing is that Cayley did it a full century before the Wright brothers were able to fly the first powered plane!

What's more, based on the same naked-eye observations that Leonardo had made when trying to divine the secret of how birds fly, Cayley hypothesized correctly that birds produce lift in part thanks to the natural "camber," or curve, of their wings. He also declared correctly that a bird's outermost feathers provided a sort of propeller action that pushed it forward and gave it the necessary speed to provide adequate lift. (The mechanics of flight are something we'll discuss later in Chapters 7, "How Airplanes Fly, Part 1: The Parts of a Plane," and 8, "How Airplanes Fly, Part 2: The Aerodynamics of Flight.")

Plane Talk

Sir George Cayley was an impressively accurate prophet. In 1809, he wrote, "This noble art will soon be brought home to man's convenience and ... we shall be able to transport ourselves and families, goods and chattels more securely by air than by water, and with a velocity of 20 to 100 miles per hour."

Cayley even mapped out, in 1804, an airplane design that is basically indistinguishable from the design of those we fly today, with wings in front and tail surfaces in back. As we'll see, even the brilliant Wright brothers didn't put those structures into their configuration until long after their first powered flight.

For all his theoretical genius, Cayley never flew. But he inspired the very first glider daredevils, including Jean Marie Le Bris, who used a horse to tow a glider a few hundred feet in the air. Le Bris didn't follow up on his experiments, however, and history mostly forgot him.

Otto Lilienthal

Though increasingly daring—and dangerous—experiments through the mid-1800s helped to refine gliders, by the 1890s they remained heavy and primitive contraptions. But it was the important advances by these glider pioneers that gave Wilbur and Orville Wright a leg up on their first sustained, powered flight.

One of the most dedicated of the glider pioneers was a Prussian-born inventor named Otto Lilienthal. Lilienthal blazed some of the design trails that the Wrights would later follow in designing the earliest airplanes. In fact, the Wrights corresponded with Lilienthal, whose designs influenced the makeup of their first successful airplane.

But Lilienthal was not to live to see the fruits of his work. After returning to Berlin from Egypt, where he built a miniature pyramid to use as a launch pad for his glides, Lilienthal made the last of his 2,000-odd glider flights. Although Lilienthal was a superbly skilled flyer, something went wrong that day in August 1896. The glider pitched up, then fluttered to the ground. Lilienthal suffered a broken spine and was rushed to a hospital. He survived for one more day, enough time to weigh the risks he had taken against the advances he was able to make toward controlled human flight. In the end he approved of the balance he had struck, and with his dying breath was heard to say, "Sacrifices must be made …."

Lilienthal was not alone in his fondness for gliders and his conviction that gliders could help speed the development of powered flight. In America, a French-born engineer named Octave Chanute was inspired by Lilienthal's life and courageous death. In 1896, at the age of 64, Chanute began experimenting with gliders and wrote books about his findings. This research was to help a pair of brothers from Ohio to launch a revolution that would change the lives of every person on earth.

The Least You Need to Know

➤ The dream of flying is universal to all cultures.

➤ Leonardo da Vinci was a Renaissance genius whose sketches were prototypes for later aviation inventions.

➤ The desire to imitate birds and base designs on their wing structures ironically hindered the progress of aviation.

➤ Like the Space Race, intense competition among balloonists accelerated technical advances in aviation.

➤ The insights and exploits of gliding pioneers, such as Englishman Sir George Cayley and Prussian-born inventor Otto Lilienthal, set the stage for the Wright brothers.

Chapter 2

The Bishop's Boys: Wilbur and Orville Wright

> ## In This Chapter
>
> ➤ The Wright brothers: born to fly
>
> ➤ The faltering first flight
>
> ➤ Did someone else beat the Wright brothers?

At the turn of the twentieth century, flying was about to take a giant step forward. As we saw in the last chapter, the science of flight began to take off in the last few years of the 1700s, when daring experimenters pushed the boundaries of ballooning by flying to higher and higher altitudes. In the late 1800s, some even attached early internal combustion motors to the balloons to create a sort of early blimp.

In the late 1800s, groups of pioneers began to do their own experimenting by strapping homemade wings to their backs and soaring off cliffs. These first bird-men, building better and better gliders, paved the way for a new breed of flyer that was about to emerge. The early glider pilots worked mostly in Europe, but something was brewing in Dayton, Ohio, that would give a couple of restless Midwest boys their own chapter in history.

The Bishop's Boys

In 1878, Reverend Milton Wright brought home a little rubber band–powered toy for his sons Wilbur and Orville. Wilbur, who was 11 at the time, and Orville, who was 7, took turns winding it up and sending it flying off around the room. The toy, which resembled a helicopter, was delicate and it wasn't long before it was damaged beyond repair. But those few hours the boys spent flying a toy around their house was enough to set them off on a career that led to man's first heavier-than-air flight.

Later, the brothers dropped out of high school and started a couple of businesses that made them enough money to support their hobby of building gliders, as other experimenters were doing. Eventually, they started fiddling around with an engine, propellers, and the complicated systems that would enable them not to glide, but fly.

Turbulence

Toy makers were delighting children with helicopter-like flying toys long before the Wright brothers came along—but don't be fooled into thinking that the helicopter was invented before the airplane. The first American helicopter didn't fly until 1939.

The Race to Fly

The brothers read everything they could lay their hands on about other would-be flyers and the glider experiments going on in Europe and America. They were latecomers in a race that seemed to be already out of their reach. But the bicycle makers from Dayton had a personal chemistry that enabled them to catch up with and then surpass their competitors.

Still, when Wilbur and Orville finally made history's first sustained, controlled flight in December 1903, the event was almost anticlimactic. Just look at the setting where the pivotal technological feat of the first half of the century took place: a deserted, windblown beach on the North Carolina coast, where the brothers worked in near isolation.

This kind of roughing-it aviation had a whole different flavor from what was going on then in Europe. On the Continent, would-be flyers gathered in clubs and salons to hear lectures while they sipped wine and cordials. And while some members of the European intelligentsia debated whether controlled, heavier-than-air flight was even possible, the Wrights tinkered with their hand-built engine and sanded their self-designed propellers in that drafty shack on Kill Devil Hill.

The somewhat primitive conditions the Wrights chose to do their research and conduct their early flights in are deceptive: What Wilbur and Orville did on that sandblown beach was years ahead of its time. In fact, although the Wrights would continue to refine and improve their planes as soon as they finished their first powered flight, it wasn't until 1906 that anyone else was able to make even as small a flight as the brothers' initial 12-second hop. And it took even longer for another American to match the feat. Glenn Curtiss managed to fly his *June Bug* in 1908; by which time the Wrights had already flown hundreds of times in trips of dozens of miles at a time. While major technological breakthroughs typically inspire wild flurries of imitations and discoveries, the Wrights' flight was so advanced that the brothers had no competitors for years.

The Wright brothers, Orville (left) and Wilbur, were inseparable for most of their lives. They were in a number of businesses together, including the airplane and engine company that made them rich.

Getting Off the Ground

The Wright brothers' first flight at Kill Devil Hill in December 1903 was as much an exercise in audacity as it was a test of flying know-how. The brothers, who ran their own bicycle shop and who had taught themselves how to build everything from printing presses to airplane propellers, braved something that more timid souls at the time thought was suicidal folly: They strapped themselves to a craft that was little more than an oversized kite and lit the fires of a temperamental motor that spun a pair of homemade wooden propellers. If nothing else, Wilbur and Orville Wright were brave!

But the Wrights were also brilliant. They were voracious gatherers of new information and fresh news about the technology of flight. They stayed in touch with the most advanced experimenters and incorporated the best results of competitors' work into their own, then added a dash of their own genius to the mix.

And they were unparalleled tinkerers. Together, there was almost no machine they needed that they couldn't fashion out of spare parts and rubbish they found lying around their shop. Once, in 1892, the brothers used a broken tombstone and some spare buggy parts to cobble together a printing press that they used to start a printing business and to print their own newspaper.

Before they put a motor and two propellers on their airplane, the Wrights spent years refining their piloting instincts by flying gliders off any hillside they could find.

In 1896, while Wilbur was housebound recovering from an injury, the brothers read about the tragic death of glider pioneer Otto Lilienthal. (Read more about Lilienthal in Chapter 1, "The Earliest Aviators.") Right away, they began devouring every book they could find about Lilienthal, his gliders, and the newly born science of aeronautics. It wasn't long before the brothers concluded that much of Lilienthal's findings were wrong and they began conducting flight tests using gliders of their own design.

Life wasn't very sweet on the cold, windswept dunes of Kill Devil Hill, North Carolina. The Wright brothers and the few locals who helped them work on their airplane often had to duck into a shack for shelter from the piercing wind that seemed to blow continuously.

While they were testing Lilienthal's research, the Wright brothers happened upon a 30-year-old technology called the *"wind tunnel,"* which helped them put theoretical aerodynamics to the test. Their wind tunnel was the first ever built in the modern style, using a large mouth to draw air in, then accelerating it through a narrow throat. Even without their later successes in controlled powered flight, their wind-tunnel innovation alone would have placed the Wrights firmly among the pantheon of aviation pathfinders.

Lilienthal, Chanute, and Langley

For all their independent thinking, the Wrights relied heavily on the groundbreaking experiments of three creative geniuses who formed a small group of competitors vying with each other to make the first controlled, powered flight. In addition to studying the work of Lilienthal, the brothers stayed in touch with Paris-born engineer Octave Chanute and intellectual gadfly Samuel Pierpont Langley.

Chanute was working in the United States on the same thorny problems of aerodynamics, stability, and aircraft control that Lilienthal faced in Germany. He was too old to do any of his own flying, being in his 60s when he came into aviation, so Chanute hired pilots to do the actual air work. Chanute had an engineer's mind and a keen sense of the forces at work in flight. The Wrights relied heavily on his research, and it was actually Chanute who convinced the bicycle-building brothers to design their flyer using the sturdy strut-and-wire design; Wilbur and Orville had been inclined to rely on the more delicate bat-wing design favored by Lilienthal.

So in a way, Octave Chanute, who has been largely pushed aside by history, is responsible for the evolution of aircraft design. The *truss construction* he advocated continues to play a role in airplane design to this day, and is still used in modern biplanes made for stunt pilots.

By the Book

The Wright brothers' **wind tunnel** was a long wooden box that used a motorized propeller to accelerate air into one side and out the other. Researchers insert a wing or other aircraft surface into the high-speed air stream to study its aerodynamic reactions.

On Course

Why Kitty Hawk? Why didn't the Wright brothers conduct their aeronautical experiments closer to their hometown of Dayton, Ohio? The answer, my friend, is blowing in the wind—literally. The brothers researched the country's windiest sites, and learned that the low-lying and nearly deserted beaches around Kitty Hawk enjoyed the steadiest winds anywhere. The winds of Kill Devil Hill, near Kitty Hawk, were critical to the first successful flight.

Plane Talk

Glenn Curtiss, the pride of Hammondsport, New York, was another bicycle maker who turned to aviation. After setting land speed records on motorcycles, Curtiss was backed by inventor Alexander Graham Bell in building the *June Bug*, which the Wrights saw as a theft of their patent on the airplane. Later, Curtiss and a partner started the first commercial airplane manufacturing company, but the partnership split up over patents and Curtiss retreated to Florida, where he become one of the state's first real estate developers.

The third member of the inspirational trio that lit the way for the Wrights' first controlled flight was a mostly self-taught engineer and architect from Roxbury, Massachusetts, named Samuel Pierpont Langley. When he wasn't conducting groundbreaking astronomy research or heading up the Smithsonian Institution, Langley made important discoveries in aerodynamics and aircraft design.

In fact, Langley came within days of beating the Wrights to the Holy Grail of the first powered, controlled flight. In November 1903, a month before the Wrights' success in North Carolina, Langley's single-wing aircraft, or "monoplane," was twice launched from a houseboat floating in the Potomac River near Washington, D.C. In both attempts, the airplane, which Langley called the *Aerodrome*, fell into the river and cracked up; the pilot, a young Cornell University student named Charles Matthew Manly, nearly drowned both times.

Manly, incidentally, may have been a flop as a pilot, but he had a certain magical gift for designing engines, the technological hurdle that, more than anything, delayed the Wrights' first flight. In fact, Manly designed an engine for Langley's *Aerodrome* that produced between 40 and 50 horsepower, making it a remarkably powerful motor for the time.

By the Book

Truss construction, while making a plane somewhat heavy, is enormously strong, a key for the Wrights' *Flyer*. Many modern airplanes have replaced the heavy trusses, which gained their strength from exterior cross-members that ran vertically and diagonally between the upper and lower wings, with a type of construction called "monocoque," which puts the strongest parts inside the plane's body and uses the plane's "skin" to add strength.

For the Wrights, it was the engine questions, more than the design of their airplane, that kept them awake at night. They needed to reach a workable compromise that yielded light weight but also enough horsepower to propel the craft on its rails. The airplane, dubbed the *Flyer*, had no wheels, which was not surprising considering that none of their test gliders featured wheels. It took off from a wooden monorail track and landed on wooden skids. The weight of wheels, tires, and all the suspension gear that goes along with them was simply too heavy for those early flights.

"Turning" Point

Although researchers like Chanute, Langley, and Lilienthal deserve a portion of the credit for inspiring the structure and design of the *Flyer*, one of the plane's most important innovations

Turbulence

Do you think the Wright brothers named their plane the *Flyer* because they were certain it would fly? Think again. The plane, which now resides in the Smithsonian Institution's National Air and Space Museum, was named for one of the models of bicycle the Wrights manufactured in their Dayton shop.

was something the Wrights figured out without anyone else's help. Before their successful flight in 1903, the Wrights suffered the same problems the other pioneers did when trying to control the plane's direction in flight. No one had figured out a good way to turn the airplane. But while fiddling around with a long cardboard box, the brothers experienced an epiphany that was to provide the margin by which they won the race for the first flight.

The brothers noticed that if they twisted the long box, one end would turn upward while the other would turn downward. They quickly devised a method to twist, or warp, the wings of their flying machines, which diverted the air passing over the wings and enabled a pilot to bank the wings. Now, the Wrights would be able to make controlled turns during flight, something that baffled the other experimenters. Together, the warpable wings, movable rudder, and front-mounted elevator to point the nose up or down allowed the *Flyer* to maneuver.

Ready for Takeoff

By the end of 1903, after years of testing wings and models in wind tunnels and of jumping off sand dunes strapped to their gliders, the brothers were ready to try to fly. They had combined an airframe, an engine, and two propellers that they hoped would do what they wanted: maintain level flight in a machine they could steer and control. Even if they had no idea how to land the thing, the Wrights would at least start learning to control it in the air.

Plane Talk

Three sets of control surfaces combine to allow pilots to smoothly maneuver in the air. Ailerons, the hinged vanes near the tip of both wings, move in opposite directions from each other and are responsible for turning the airplane left or right. The elevators, the hinged vanes on the rear edge of the horizontal stabilizer, allow the pilot to move the nose up or down. The rudder, which is attached to the vertical stabilizer, helps pilots control the direction the nose points in and, in coordination with the ailerons, has a subtle role in turning the plane. We'll learn all about these different control surfaces in Chapter 7, "How Airplanes Fly, Part 1: The Parts of a Plane."

The first attempt to get the *Flyer* off the ground came in mid-December 1903, and ended in a crack-up. Wilbur won a coin-toss for the chance to make the first flight in the *Flyer*, which the brothers had equipped with a 12-horsepower motor that turned two handmade propellers. Wilbur climbed in and layed flat on the bottom of the plane's two wings, and Orville pushed the plane along the monorail track built on the sand. The plane lifted off the ground, but it stayed in the air for just a couple of seconds before it crashed into the sand. Wilbur wasn't injured too badly, but the airplane needed two days' worth of repairs. When it was finally put back together, it was Orville's turn at the controls.

On the next flight attempt, Orville pushed the Wrights' home-built engine to full throttle, and with Wilbur at the wingtip to steady the plane, rolled off down the monorail track. Almost exactly where the brothers calculated it would, the 700-pound *Flyer* lifted off the rail and flew unsteadily into a 20 m.p.h. wind. Orville controlled the plane's bank by warping the wingtips using cables connected to a sort of steering wheel. And he kept it straight and level using a combination of rudder and elevator.

Twelve seconds later and 120 feet down the beach, Orville let the *Flyer* settle back to the sand, bringing an end to the first controlled, heavier-than-air flight and sparking a technological revolution that would change the world.

The Wrights sent their family in Dayton a telegram announcing their success. It was sent without punctuation and with some eccentric capitalization: "Success

On Course

The world's first flight was a short one, covering about half the length of a Boeing 747.

four flights thursday morning All against twenty one mile wind started from Level with engine power alone speed through air thirty one miles longest 57 second inform Press home Christmas."

With local resident J.D. Daniels manning the camera, Orville Wright becomes the first human to make a sustained, controlled flight, while his brother Wilbur helps steady the wings.

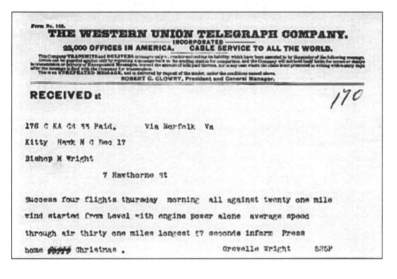

The Wrights were no fools. They established concrete proof of their history-making flight by dashing off a telegram, which set them firmly in the history books, but didn't exactly impress everyone back home in Dayton, Ohio.

Proof Positive

The Wrights were prepared to prove their claim to be the first people to fly. They set up a camera and asked one of the members of the local rescue squad, or "Life Saving men," as Orville called them, to snap the shutter once the *Flyer* flew off the ground. The man who snapped the picture was J.D. Daniels, and here's what Orville wrote about that moment: "One of the Life Saving men snapped the camera for us, taking a picture just as the machine had reached the end of the track and had risen to a height of about two feet. The slow forward speed of the machine over the ground is clearly shown in the picture by Wilbur's attitude. He stayed along beside the machine without any effort."

Daniels had still more excitement ahead of him that day. Around noon, after the brothers had already made three more flights, the longest covering 850 feet in 59 seconds, a gust of wind began to overturn the *Flyer* while it was resting on the ground. Orville and Daniels raced to one rising wing and tried to hold it down. Orville lost his grip, but Daniels held on as the *Flyer* turned over and tumbled across the ground several times. Daniels was all right, but the *Flyer* was banged up so badly the brothers didn't make any more flights that year.

Plane Talk

The Wright brothers may have been the first to fly, but don't think they received any special treatment when the government began issuing pilot certificates in 1910. Certificate no. 1 went to daredevil and speed racer Glenn Curtiss; no. 2 went to balloonist and military officer Frank Lahm; no. 3 was assigned to balloonist and self-taught endurance flyer Louis Paulhan; and finally, nos. 4 and 5 were given to Orville and Wilbur Wright, respectively. Why push the Wrights to the back of the line for the first certificates? Given the small number of trained pilots at the time, bureaucrats opted for simplicity: They handed out the certificates in alphabetical order.

Who Was Really First?

Almost from the time they first flew, it has been fashionable for iconoclasts to pooh-pooh the Wright brothers' achievement in designing, testing, and flying the first airplane. Conspiracists, mostly in the camp of a German-born flying enthusiast named Gustave Whitehead, rail and protest against the bicycle makers, insisting that any number of other people deserve the title of "first aviator." Undoubtedly, a lot of the spite directed against the Wrights stemmed from the brothers' 1906 patent of the *Flyer*, a move that many of their competitors saw as disrespectful of other pioneers whose research contributed to the Wrights' success.

The most credible and dogged effort to dislodge the Wrights comes from Connecticut and the descendents of Gustave Whitehead. But why don't you be the judge?

Gustave Whitehead

Could a flyer have beaten the Wrights into the air by as much as four years? Hard to believe, but that was the claim of a German sailor turned concrete salesman named Gustave Whitehead. After shipwrecking in the Gulf of Mexico as a young man, Whitehead made two key decisions: to give up his job at sea and to settle in America. After wandering through Pennsylvania and the Northeast, Whitehead landed in Bridgeport, Connecticut, where he worked as a mechanic and tinkered with flying machines. Whitehead had a talent for building engines, including the 10-horsepower acetylene motor that helped him make history's first flight—if his story is to be believed.

Plane Talk

Gustave Whitehead was so crazy about flying and parachuting even as a boy that he early on earned the nickname "The Flyer." The nickname is ironic, considering that the airplane that he thought helped the Wright brothers steal his place in history was also named the *Flyer*.

In 1901, Whitehead claimed, he flew for the second time (that's right, second time), a half-mile jaunt that came off uneventfully, or so *The New York Herald* reported shortly after the August 14 flight. On the same day, *The Boston Transcript* reported the very same flight, citing details that were nearly identical to those reported in *The Herald*. News reports published five days after the Bridgeport flight summed up the event: "Last week Whitehead flew in his machine half a mile." According to the newspaper, the flight was flawless.

German-born Connecticut mechanic Gustave Whitehead claimed to have beaten the Wright brothers into the air by several years, and he still has plenty of believers.

Plane Talk

The newspaper accounts of Whitehead's pre-Wright flight were full of wonder and praise, but they are also puzzling. For decades, Whitehead proponents have pointed to the news account, and to later stories in *Scientific American,* as proof of their claims. But the fact that the news stories weren't written until five days after the reputed flight casts the whole matter in a less certain light. After all, manned heavier-than-air flight was at the time the most debated and controversial topic of discussion among scientists and engineers. What reporter, who had witnessed the flight, could have resisted writing the story immediately and beaming the news via telegraph to every newspaper in the country? Why wait five days?

Whitehead's first flight, he claimed, had taken place two years earlier, in 1899. If the claim is true, the flight must have been spectacular, not only for the wild crash that brought it to an end but also because it was so far ahead of its time.

The best testimony we have about the flight comes from Louis Darvaritch, who said he was the lone passenger on that flight in his role as stoker for the steam engine that powered the craft. Darvaritch recounted the details of the 1899 flight in an affidavit he gave in 1934. But he was also a friend of Whitehead's, a fact that pro-Wright forces marshal in refuting the claim.

According to his sworn account, Darvaritch went along on the half-mile flight, which at times reached altitudes of 20 to 25 feet. But a mansion loomed and Whitehead wasn't able to maneuver around it. The plane struck the building three stories above the ground. Whitehead wasn't hurt in the crackup, but Darvaritch was badly scalded by the hot water in the steam engine and was taken to a hospital for a few weeks. (The hospital records have since been lost.)

The arguments against this account are legion. For starters, it's hard to imagine an accident as spectacular as this one, complete with a burst boiler, horrific burn injuries, and a smashed-up flying machine on the ground beneath a plainly visible impact mark on a mansion wall. Can you imagine anything that would attract more attention, not only from local civic officials but also by sensation-hungry reporters? And it is a rare homeowner who would not go to court to make an example out of a local eccentric who had smashed into his wall, presumably costing a good deal more to repair than the itinerant mechanic laborer could afford to pay. Documents should show records of a hefty lawsuit, but none has been discovered. A complaint describing the damage to a wall 25 feet off the ground by a flying contraption would all but seal the first-flyer debate in Whitehead's favor.

Finally, there are few engines that need more pounds of machine for each horsepower than a steam engine. Perhaps a mule driving a mill wheel is slightly less efficient, but not by much. The weight of an engine powerful enough to carry the plane, two passengers, a stash of fuel for stoking, not to mention the engine's own weight, would be far too heavy to have succeeded. In 1986, when Whitehead backers successfully flew a rough approximation of one of his later models, they did nothing to prove the feasibility of Whitehead's motors. They only set out to test the design, which they learned was just barely up to the task.

Whitehead may or may not have been first in the air, but he certainly deserves credit for his creativity. It's been said that to a man with a hammer,

On Course

Do you think Whitehead's claims deserve more investigation? Call the National Air and Space Museum at 202-357-2700 to press your case. So far, museum administrators have refused to consider the case, and consider the Wright brothers the world's first flyers.

every problem looks like a nail. Well, for Whitehead, a gifted mechanic and engine designer, the problem of flying could be solved by throwing in as many engines as possible. To him, that meant using one engine to accelerate his bat-winged craft on the ground, then two more to keep it aloft. The wing-mounted engines each turned their own propeller, and Whitehead planned to use a difference in the power of each engine as his rudder: A faster-racing engine on the left wing, say, would propel its side faster than its counterpart on the right wing, turning the plane to the right.

The Flight That Wasn't?

In the end, the fabric of Whitehead's case is left in tatters. If nothing else, Whitehead failed as a publicist, something at which the Wrights excelled. After all, Wilbur and Orville's very first telegram announcing their successful first flight included just one command: "Inform press!"

Years after his purported history-making flight, Whitehead supporters pieced together a machine they believed duplicated the inventor's, even though Whitehead left precious few instructions or printed plans. Later, one of these models, equipped with modern engines, actually flew.

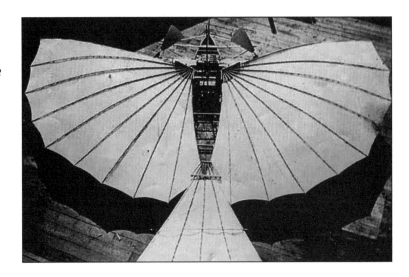

Whitehead supporters haven't let the issue rest. For years, they have pestered officials at the National Air and Space Museum in Washington to probe into the Whitehead case until evidence turns up to back their claim. Museum curators flatly refuse to open the case, and Whitehead's case, to say nothing of his original airplane, has no chance of getting off the ground.

Plane Talk

The who-was-first battle is considered far from over by Whitehead supporters. One of the most prominent forces arrayed behind Whitehead is a retired naturopathic physician and Connecticut state senator who pushed through a law forcing the Smithsonian Institution to hold hearings on the Whitehead claims. So far, the Smithsonian has refused, fueling charges among Whitehead zealots of a pro-Wright conspiracy and coverup in the halls of the national museum.

The Least You Need to Know

➤ The Wright brothers applied their mechanical brilliance to their passion—gliding.

➤ The Wrights combined painstaking research with engine know-how to make the first successful airplane.

➤ Gustave Whitehead and his supporters contest the Wrights' claim as the first to fly, but the best evidence remains in the Wrights' favor.

Chapter 3

Barnstormers and Other Risk Takers

> **In This Chapter**
>
> ➤ Early pilots who tempted fate
>
> ➤ The most daring men: barnstormers
>
> ➤ Air mail takes its first dangerous steps

As with any technological revolution, aviation in its adolescence had its share of dare-devils who probed its boundaries. Those death-defying pilots of the early Air Age not only discovered some unforgiving barriers—namely the ground or a building—but they also succeeded in bringing the new pursuit of flying to a curious public.

Harriet Quimby

Harriet Quimby was one of the early thrill pilots—and one of the first to "buy the farm." The Manhattan secretary and former drama critic with beauty-queen looks was the first woman to earn an American pilot's certificate, and she hoped to win world fame with it. She figured that she could quickly make a name for herself if she was the first woman to fly across the English Channel. In April 1912, she did just that, departing from Dover and landing safely on the Normandy coast. But unfortunately for her, the historic flight was pushed out of the headlines for a slightly bigger story: The "unsinkable" *Titanic* had gone to the bottom of the icy North Atlantic the previous night.

Plane Talk

Early pilots were not only cheating death, they were defying science. At the time, scientists thought that flying over 60 miles per hour would be deadly because the wind would be so strong it would suck the air right out of a pilot's lungs.

Undeterred, Quimby sailed back to the United States with plans to make real headlines. She entered the Boston-Harvard air meet, where she intended to set a speed record. Just before her attempt, she took her Bleriot two-seater up for a warm-up flight, carrying a passenger along for the ride. When she had flown out over Boston Harbor, spectators on the ground saw the plane make a sudden dip and saw the passenger fall from the plane and plunge hundreds of feet into the water. Harriet managed to recover control, but a few moments later, the plane again dipped, this time tossing Harriet to her death.

Plane Talk

Boston and other areas in the Northeast were a center of flying enthusiasm in the early days of aviation, probably because the Hub was home to some of the brightest engineering minds in the country. Over the years, however, better weather elsewhere, particularly in the South and Southwest, spread flying fever throughout the nation.

Lincoln Beachey

Lincoln Beachey was another daring young pilot who didn't survive to be a daring old one. Beachey was the first, and perhaps greatest, pilot of the "flying circuses," as people called the barnstorming shows that traveled across the country. Beachey helped define the daring art form by creating some of its best-loved stunts. He was the first to loop an airplane by flying in a vertical circle. He was the first to fly upside down. He even flew "under" Niagara Falls by plunging down over the brink of the

American River and into the mist before reappearing near the water's surface below. And Beachey created his signature "dip of death"—a stunt that was eventually to be the death of him.

In 1915, while performing an air circus act in his hometown of San Francisco, something went wrong during the "dip of death," in which Beachey rocketed toward the ground at terrifying speed, then pulled up at the last moment. The stunt was a heart-stopper, and it was known to make spectators faint in fear.

During his last stunt, though, his speed, which usually approached a then-blistering 90 m.p.h., got out of control at 103 m.p.h. Before he neared the ground where he could level off, the wings of his airplane crumpled, and he crashed.

Plane Talk

Stunt flying continues to take its toll today, sometimes even in Hollywood. One of the most famous movie mishaps took the life of legendary stunt flyer Art "The Professor" Scholl, a disciplined flyer with an engineer's mind who flew his stunt routines with his little dog Aileron as copilot. While flying a dangerous inverted flat spin during the filming of the movie *Top Gun*, something went wrong that no one yet understands. The stunt, though dangerous, was one that Scholl knew well and had performed safely hundreds of times before. On his final flight, though, Scholl didn't recover from the spin, and radioed his ground crew, "I've got a problem." A few seconds later, he radioed again for the last time: "I've really got a problem."

The Wrights' Deadly Circus

Many pilots in aviation's rollicking early years earned fame by flying on an air circus circuit organized by the Wrights. The famous inventors took to the road in 1910 with a stable of young pilots who were eager to perform and earn the top-dollar salary that the Wrights paid them. Wilbur and Orville paid their air circus pilots $20 per week in base pay, and another $50 for every day they actually flew. That could amount to $7,000 per season for some pilots, and that was enough incentive to convince performers to fly some hair-raising stunts.

One of the pilots who flew with the Wright Exhibition Company was Arch Hoxsey. Hoxsey was a daredevil who tried to outperform his fellow pilots by pushing his speed a little higher than theirs or by zooming lower to the ground than they did. He was a bit too reckless for the Wrights, who once grounded him in hopes of cooling his love for danger. But the brothers trusted Hoxsey's skill enough to assign him to pilot a flight with ex-President Teddy Roosevelt as his passenger.

Plane Talk

The Wright brothers earned a good living, too. In the few years their air circus was in business, they took in about $1 million a year.

Hoxsey's specialty was performing in a kind of aerial battle with fellow pilot Ralph Johnstone. The two created the myth in the local papers that they disliked each other and were actually trying to hurt each other in the air. In reality, the pair were friends, but their act never failed to thrill spectators.

Hoxsey didn't reserve his hazardous flying to his air circus performances, however. He liked to attempt to fly to higher and higher altitudes, and during one of those attempts at a California show, he either lost control of his airplane or something broke. Whatever the cause, Hoxsey's plane spun thousands of feet from the sky and crashed, killing him.

Ralph Johnstone

Ralph Johnstone, the performer who engaged in mock air battles with Arch Hoxsey, was a veteran performer, having toured America and Europe as a trick cyclist on the Vaudeville circuit. Although he was a far more cautious pilot than the brash Hoxsey, Johnstone also knew how to thrill audiences with his flying skill. Johnstone met a grislier end than most of his comrades who died while performing aviation stunts.

During a 1910 show in Denver, Johnstone was flying about 800 feet above the ground when his airplane broke up. As he struggled to gain control of the plane, he was tossed from his seat, which, like all airplane seats at the time, wasn't equipped with a seat belt.

Johnstone's luck held, however, at least for the moment. As he was falling overboard he stopped his fall when he reached out and grasped a strut. He hung on desperately as the plane sped toward the ground and crashed. The spectators were horror-struck, but recovered their senses in time to rifle the bloody body for souvenirs of gloves and pieces of clothing.

The *Vin Fiz* Falls Flat

With their breakneck antics, the early *barnstormers* managed to plant seeds in our collective psyche that made flying appear to be a life-and-death struggle with the elements. Though that may have been an accurate description in the early years of aviation, flying today is far from the dangerous pastime that it once was, and modern pilots are a bit less swashbuckling.

There may never have been a pilot more dashing than Cal Rodgers, but as most of those who shared the skies with him, he died young and he died in an airplane. Still, it was Rodgers who first proved to a skeptical American public that flying could progress beyond a death sport to become a viable way of getting from one side of the continent to the other.

By the Book

Barnstormer was the name given to the swaggering and sometimes unsavory pilots who swooped down past barnyards and farmhouses to signal to everyone for miles around that airplane rides were being sold.

Spurred by a $50,000 prize offered by publishing magnate William Randolph Hearst to the first flyer who could complete a coast-to-coast flight, Rodgers and a handful of other pilots signed up in 1911 to hopscotch across a country where airplanes were almost as unfamiliar as flying saucers and where airfields were all but nonexistent. The Hearst prize imposed a 30-day time limit, a daunting challenge in 1911.

Part of Rodgers' appeal during his grueling cross-country race was the name of his Wright EX (for "Experimental") biplane: the *Vin Fiz*. In exchange for emergency money—and he'd need all of that—Rodgers agreed to advertise Armour's new grape soda on his plane by painting *Vin Fiz* across the bottom of his wings. As it turned out, the *Vin Fiz* people might have got a better value for their marketing dollars if Rodgers had emblazoned the slogan on the sides of his plane; he spent far more time grounded than he did aloft.

All told, in his trip across the country, Rodgers survived 14 minor crashes, five total crackups, uncounted engine failures in flight, an in-flight scalding when an engine hose sprayed loose, and a head-on collision with a chicken coop. Finally, with the Pacific Ocean finish line in sight after 49 days of misery and near-fatal accidents, he crashed again on the final leg from Pasadena to the beach. This time he crushed the bones in his ankle; the injury required a month to heal.

At last, 84 days—nearly three months—after leaving New York, Rodgers rolled the wheels of the *Vin Fiz* into the surf of the Pacific Ocean, carrying only a rudder and an oil pan from the original plane. Everything else had been destroyed and replaced en route.

Cal Rodgers (right) completed a grueling cross-country flight in 1911 in hopes of winning $50,000. He didn't even come close to completing the flight in the allotted time, but he was the only flyer to actually finish the flight. He died in a plane accident shortly afterward.

Because he badly overshot Hearst's 30-day deadline, Rodgers was left empty-handed in Los Angeles. But he had movie-star looks and enough personality to charm a curious nation. Even if technically Rodgers's flight was a failure, it was successful in that it—and Rodgers—turned America's eyes toward the possibility of commercial aviation.

Four months after finishing the *Vin Fiz* tour, and almost on the very spot where he made his final landing at the end of that adventure, Rodgers flew his Wright EX into a flock of gulls—apparently in a deliberate show of bravado. One of the gulls jammed his rudder and caused the plane to fall out of control. Rodgers died of a broken back and a broken neck.

His tombstone reads, with characteristic flair: "I endure—I conquer."

Defying Death

Rodgers was cut from the same cloth as hundreds of other daredevils who criss-crossed the country in those early days of aviation, wowing crowds with dangerous stunts and taking thrill-seeking passengers on $15 sight-seeing jaunts. If a passenger plunked down another $10, a barnstormer might perform a loop-the-loop, where the pilot pulled the nose of the plane higher and higher until it was upside down before continuing in a vertical circle back to level flight.

But when there were no passengers aboard, nothing was too dangerous for daring barnstormers to try at least once. Photographs from the era show wing walkers trotting cavalierly about the airplane and scrambling from bottom wing to top wing and from cockpit to tail. One publicity photo even shows two wing walkers facing each other along the length of the top wing of a vintage biplane, each brandishing a racquet and pretending to play tennis. It was common for wing walkers to not only move around the wings during flight, but also to dangle beneath the wings and even drop from the bottom wing of one plane to the top wing of another while flying thousands of feet in the air—all without a parachute.

It was also typical for pilots to fly without a parachute. In those days parachutes were bulky contraptions that were as likely to tangle as to open safely, and even if the canopy did open, the descent speed was still fast enough to break a few bones. Besides, barnstormers and stunt pilots had more daring than sense.

On Course

Want a "crash" course on barnstorming and the days of flying circuses? Rent or buy a videotape called *The Great Waldo Pepper*, starring Robert Redford. The film, co-written with director George Roy Hill, may capture the rip-roaring spirit of the day better than any other movie. Watch for the real-life life-and-death wing walking stunts by stunt flying legend Frank Tallman.

Plane Talk

Barnstormers weren't the only daring flyers in the sky during aviation's early years. Hollywood's hunger for cinematic thrills gave birth to a new specialty vocation—the movie stunt pilot. One group of pilots who specialized in onscreen flying thrills called themselves "The 13 Black Cats." They published a "menu" of stunts they would perform on film along with a price for each:

> "Crash ships into trees or houses: $1,200
> Loop with man standing on center section: $150
> Drop from airplane to train: $150
> Blow up plane in mid air, pilot parachutes out: $500."

"The 13 Black Cats" were expensive, but so was life insurance.

Beginning of the End

The golden era of barnstorming started coming to a close in 1927. That year, a former barnstormer shed forever the carefree life of thrill flying to break a geographic boundary that some thought would never be breached: Charles A. Lindbergh crossed the Atlantic Ocean nonstop, and in the process achieved worldwide fame that "Lucky Lindy" could never shed, no matter how he tried. Lindbergh also proved to a skeptical world that the continents were no longer separated by impenetrable barriers but now could be easily visited by friends—or menaced by enemies.

Also that year, air mail began to enter the American lexicon as government backing helped spur the very earliest airlines toward profitability. Starting as early as 1918, Congress and Washington bureaucrats foresaw that the future of transportation lay in the skies. It was in 1918, when America was fighting World War I, that the first government air mail route was inaugurated between Potomac Park in Washington, D.C., and a makeshift landing field at Long Island's Belmont Park race track.

Flying by the Pound: Air Mail

The letter-writing public didn't think much of air mail when it was first offered. In the early 1920s, airlines consisted of oil-streaked planes flying mostly empty mail sacks, which often contained only a smattering of letters and a smuggled brick used to tip the scales a little heavier when it came time for the Post Office to pay—by the pound. But the federal government and a few entrepreneurs were convinced they were onto a winning way to move mail, as well as a host of other goods, by air, and Washington, D.C., offered enough financial incentives to keep the fledgling airlines from drowning in red ink.

Air Mail Pilots

When reading about the early history of flying, it sometimes seems as if no one who did it for very long managed to make it out alive. If we look closer, we find that most pilots lived through those heady days long enough to join the nascent air mail business—where those who survived barnstorming often perished.

Flying hastily built airplanes that leaked gasoline and reading road maps that usually led pilots off course, the United States Aerial Mail Service took off with mixed success. The pilot of the first flight didn't quite make it to a refueling stop in Philadelphia before he ran out of gas. In the crash landing that followed he rolled his biplane onto its back and was forced to lug his bag of airmail back to Washington to await the next day's flight. It was an inauspicious start, but the experiment was a success.

George L. Boyle (left) flew the first air mail shipment between Washington and New York via Philadelphia.

Air mail pilots were a colorful bunch, and Fred Kelly of Western topped them all. He was a college football and track star who set a world record and won a gold medal in the Stockholm Olympics in 1912. In 1916, while learning to fly near New York City, he *buzzed* President Woodrow Wilson's yacht, then flew under every bridge along the Hudson River before returning home to a seething commander. "I just wanted to say good-bye to the President," a sheepish Kelly said.

The Birth of the Airlines

Though pilots sometimes carried sacks of mail that were "more sack than mail," visionary airline executives like "Pop" Hanshue of Western Air Express—later Western Airlines—and Juan Terry Trippe of Pan American World Airways took leaps of faith on an industry that seemed to have no chance of success. After all, carrying two passengers at a time in temperamental airplanes that seemed to crash as often as they managed to reach their destinations was no way to run an airline.

By the Book

Buzzing is a dangerous business that has claimed hundreds of pilots through the decades. Against all warnings, pilots continue to tempt fate by flying at treetop level. Even my father, in a moment of youthful indiscretion, once buzzed the tiny town of Hermosa, South Dakota, in a Korean War–era military jet, scattering frightened cattle and becoming a part of local legend.

Turbulence

Passengers endured the same dangers and discomforts as pilots, braving accidents and frostbite in icy flights over dangerous territory, all while seated atop lumpy sacks of mail with no more than a sandwich and a Thermos bottle of orange juice.

Most modern airlines have their roots in those early days of seat-of-the-pants air mail flying. The airline that can trace its roots back the farthest in a direct line is Western Airlines, the company that coined the term "The only way to fly." Legend has it that 1920s air mail pilots for Western also coined another phrase: "He bought the farm." The reference was to the practice of paying for crop damage or damage to a barn caused by an airplane crash. If a crash was bad enough to kill a pilot, his friends sometimes said he had "bought the farm."

Daring pilots who died while plying their dangerous trades have become the stuff of legend. The barnstormers, both of yesteryear and today, seem to thrive on life-and-death risks. Through its first few decades of growth, aviation was the right hobby for men and women who craved danger: It would be years before the send-off "Have a safe flight" would be much more than whistling in the graveyard.

The Least You Need to Know

➤ From its earliest days, aviation has attracted thrill-seekers and others who crave danger.

➤ Despite huge risks to life and limb, barnstormers introduced aviation to a curious America.

➤ Air mail piloting in the early days of the air mail service was sometimes a deadly profession.

Chapter 4

Great Flyers of the World Wars

In This Chapter

➤ Aviation enters World War I

➤ "Eddie" Rickenbacker: America's Ace of Aces

➤ The bloody Red Baron

➤ The bombers that won World War II

➤ The P–51 Mustang and Chuck Yeager: two aviation legends

In the years between the Wright brothers' first flight in 1903 and the spark that ignited World War I, aviation grew through an awkward adolescence. Fragile American biplanes that had been viewed mostly as adventurers' playthings were, after barely more than a decade of refinement, gradually being pressed into military service.

The First Military Planes

In one of America's least-remembered conflicts, in April 1914, President Woodrow Wilson ordered navy *seaplanes* into action in a military dust-up with Mexico. The planes were lowered from ships into the Gulf of Mexico and taken aloft on mine-spotting missions.

Later, generals put the planes to work in reconnaissance missions over the mainland. Enemy soldiers took pot shots at the lumbering craft, but didn't manage to bring any of them down. Still, story-hungry newspaper reporters covering the hostilities quickly transformed the bullet holes in the floatplanes' skin into the first "shots fired in anger" against an American air force.

Airplanes were flown into action again in March 1916, when General John "Black Jack" Pershing went gunning for Mexican revolutionary Pancho Villa, who had invaded New Mexico. Wooden propellers cracked and peeled in the dry desert heat, fuel was frequently contaminated, and the horse-savvy officers in charge of the campaign had no idea how to put the airplanes to work. You might say the airplane had failed its first real military test. Nevertheless, the experiences of the First Aero Squadron gave the military its first taste of airborne war tactics.

By the Book

Shortly after pilots and designers learned how to build and fly airplanes from dry ground, they turned their attention to the water. Glenn Curtiss (see Chapter 2, "The Bishop's Boys: Wilbur and Orville Wright") designed a **seaplane** in 1911 that could take off and land on water; it didn't require dry land at all. The idea was a natural for Curtiss, who grew up near New York's Finger Lakes, which became miles-long runways for his daring inventions.

World War I: Aviation's Fiery Trial

At about the same time Pershing's men were trying to keep planes in the air in the American Southwest, a more serious confrontation was taking place in Europe. In the eighteen months since the start of World War I in July 1914, air battles between warring European pilots had turned from gentlemanly encounters between enemy scouts—in the first days of the war, enemy reconnaissance pilots often waved greetings at each other as they passed over each others' front lines—into battles to the death.

When the first defensive flights took to the air, pilots and backseat observers were armed with only pistols and rifles, but soon pilots were mounting machine guns in front of the cockpit. The machine guns were fixed in place, however, so the pilots had to use the whole airplane to point the machine gun.

At first, pilots thought they could use the wing-and-a-prayer method of machine gunning through the spinning propeller, relying on the odds that most bullets would miss the wooden blades. In the first experiments, the few bullets that did strike the wooden blades were enough to do considerable damage. So engineers attached a strip of metal to the leading edge of each propeller blade in hopes that most of the bullets would be deflected. The idea worked well enough for a time. Then an engineer for the British- and French-led Allies and the German-led Central Powers devised a timing device for machine guns that enabled the machine guns to fire between the blades.

Rickenbacker: From Chauffeur to Fighter Ace

Some American pilots, eager to put themselves to the ultimate test of airmanship, the *dog fight,* were growing weary of America's reluctance to enter World War I. The most famous of the impatient group was a champion auto racer named Edward V. "Eddie"

Rickenbacker. He and other mercenary flyers helped the French battle the German aces who were cutting a bloody swath through Allied skies. Their deadliest enemies were a sharpshooting band of German pilots called the "Flying Circus." We'll get back to them shortly.

"Eddie" Rickenbacker, loved by millions as "Captain Eddie," emerged from World War I as America's greatest hero, and went on to become a corporate leader.

Rickenbacker—born Richenbacher, he Americanized it in response to anti-German wartime propaganda—arrived in Europe in 1918. His expertise with auto engines won him a job as General John "Black Jack" Pershing's personal chauffeur. In a moment of historic happenstance, Rickenbacker's mechanical skills were also the key to getting him into the cockpit of a fighter plane, launching him on a career that made him one of the greatest of American heroes.

One day in 1917, Rickenbacker stopped to help the driver of a Mercedes that had stalled on the side of a French road. The driver was legendary military firebrand Col. Billy Mitchell, an officer in the infant Air Service. In thanks for the roadside help, Mitchell agreed to transfer Rickenbacker to a flying squadron where he could learn to fly.

Rickenbacker Throws His "Hat in the Ring"

When the United States entered World War I in 1917, Rickenbacker and a small group of daredevils joined the "Hat in the Ring" squadron. The name reflected the cavalier attitude many pilots took toward their deadly adventures. As if barnstorming—or in Rickenbacker's case, auto racing—wasn't dangerous enough for these flyers, they were about to go nose to nose with pilots who had years of combat flying experience and who had mastered the art of airborne sharpshooting.

Rickenbacker didn't take to the sky naturally. In his early months as pilot, he battled severe airsickness, and when it came to shooting down enemy planes, he was not an overnight success. But he had a competitive spirit and he worked harder than other pilots. He was one of the few pilots who liked to fly solo missions along the front lines, something that most flyers regarded as akin to a death wish. His independent habits served Rickenbacker well and contributed to his kill total of 26 enemy planes by war's end.

By the Book

What is a **dog fight?** When two packs of enemy pilots battled to the death in aerial combat, it reminded observers of a fight between savage dogs. After all, in both cases combatants circle for advantage, chase and dodge, and tear into each other with every weapon they have. The term "dog fight" perfectly described the chaos of an air battle, so it stuck.

Plane Talk

After the war, Rickenbacker revealed the secret to his airborne success: "In addition to leading my flight on routine patrols, I emulated (French fighter ace Raoul) Lufberry's example and flew my own lone-wolf missions over the lines. He always said that it was impossible to shoot down German planes sitting in the billet with your feet before the fire. I heeded this advice so well that I had more hours in the air than any other American flier."

The Fastest Gun in the Sky

Rickenbacker might have racked up his kills at a faster pace than anyone who flew in the Great War. His first combat mission was in March 1918, and his first kill came the following month. Between April and the end of the war in November, Rickenbacker shot down 22 airplanes and 4 balloons, a remarkable tally in a seven-month stretch. But the total is even more amazing when you take into account the two months that Rickenbacker spent in the hospital after surgery on his shoulder. Had he started flying earlier in the war, and had he been able to keep up that amazing pace, Rickenbacker probably would have been the highest-scoring ace in the war. As it was, Rickenbacker was promoted to commander of the "Hat in the Ring" squadron, and earned the title of America's "Ace of Aces."

Plane Talk

Billy Mitchell may have sensed the seeds of aviation greatness in "Eddie" Rickenbacker. After all, Mitchell had a gift for seeing the future. In the early 1920s, he predicted the Japanese would strike America with an attack at Pearl Harbor. He forecast that the blitz would come from the north using fighters that had been launched from aircraft carriers. He even predicted the attack would come on a Sunday morning. All of it, unfortunately, came true.

Rickenbacker's heroics led to peacetime fame once the Armistice was signed in November 1918. Because he was one of the few combat aces to survive the war, Rickenbacker returned to the United States to a hero's welcome. He bought the Indianapolis Speedway and managed it from 1927 to 1945.

Plane Talk

For his heroism in attacking a formation of five German planes, downing two and chasing the others away, Rickenbacker received the Congressional Medal of Honor. He also received the Distinguished Service Cross and the French *Croix de Guerre*.

He put his automotive know-how to work when he created the "Rickenbacker car," which featured a brake for each wheel. No competing carmaker offered this feature and it led one of them—no one has proven which company was responsible—to

Turbulence

World War I pilots suffered some indignities along with the adoration they received from the starstruck public. For example, airplane mechanics found that the only reliable way to thin the engine oil in the bitter European winters was to mix it with cod liver oil, a popular folk remedy for constipation. In flight, as the oil mixture vaporized in the engine cylinders, pilots inhaled the fumes. The result was predictable, and one which humbled the war's greatest flyers.

spread rumors that the brakes led to crashes. In reality, the cars didn't crash, but Rickenbacker's company, thanks to the malicious rumors, did. It took Rickenbacker years to pay off the debts that had piled up, but he eventually paid back every penny.

In 1938, Rickenbacker became president of Eastern Airlines, and in his very first year on the job he made the company profitable—something that no airline executive had yet managed to do. He moved into the chairman's seat in 1953, and stayed there until he left the airline—and left it profitable and respected—in 1963.

"Captain Eddie" Becomes Captain of Industry

When "Captain Eddie" became a captain of industry, his life of adventure was far from over. Early in America's participation in World War II, Rickenbacker signed on for two secret government missions, one to Russia and the other to the South Pacific. The Russian mission was uneventful, but Rickenbacker's October 1942 B-17 flight to New Guinea was a hair-raiser. En route, his airplane crashed into the Pacific Ocean and he and the crew were forced to scramble onto life rafts. Rickenbacker, who was now in his early 50s, drifted in the middle of the ocean for 22 days before being rescued. On his arrival back in the States, he received the same welcome he enjoyed in 1918 when he returned from Europe as America's greatest airman.

Rickenbacker died October 24, 1973, in Switzerland, and is buried in his hometown of Columbus, Ohio.

Plane Talk

In yet another piece of good luck, in May, 1918, "Eddie" Rickenbacker managed to get back to his home base in one piece after the fabric covering the upper wing of his Neuport 28 biplane peeled into shreds during flight. The flight was a testimony to his expertise in the cockpit and to his ability to keep a cool head in the face of disaster.

The Dreaded Red Baron

"Eddie" Rickenbacker's World War I kill total ranked him as America's top pilot. But even a tally of 26 enemy aircraft kills places him far down on the list of pilots that includes aces from other countries. For example, England's Maj. Edward Mannock downed 72 enemy aircraft, and Belgium's Capt. Willy Coppens posted 36 kills.

But the greatest aces of the war, by far, were German flyers. Ernst Udet, who was immortalized in the Robert Redford film *The Great Waldo Pepper,* shot down 62 enemy aircraft, then went on to play a major role in leading Germany's air force during World War II. And when he wasn't writing the rules of air combat for German fliers, Oswald Boelcke found time to shoot down 40 enemy aircraft.

But by far the deadliest ace of them all was Manfred von Richthofen, the renowned "Red Baron." Richthofen (pronounced *RIKT-hoffin*) was a dashing character who became so famous in Germany during the war that he outshone even the brightest stars of the theater and cinema. And he flew in the face of modern stealth tactics by painting his Fokker triplane a bright, menacing red.

Manfred von Richthofen was the deadliest pilot in the skies during World War I.

From White-Knuckle Flyer to Red Baron

Richthofen didn't start out as the dashing aviator he eventually became. As an airborne observer early in the war, he was a white-knuckle flier. Richthofen overcame his fear and asked to be assigned to flight training, where he proved relatively inept and crashed several times. He barely managed to graduate from the training program. His instructors undoubtedly expected that he would be machine gun fodder for enemy pilots.

After his first combat mission, his instructors' worst fears seemed destined to come true. Richthofen took off for a mission over the Western Front, but the untested pilot got turned around and became lost. To find his way home, he was forced to land and ask directions!

Turbulence

Those long silk scarves looked dashing as they trailed in the wind behind the daring young men in their flying machines. But the gallant accessory was actually born of necessity. As pilots swiveled their heads to keep their eyes on the enemy, the scarf prevented the heavy fabric of their flight suits from chafing their necks. Flying scarves continued to be used as standard pilot issue even past World War II.

Turbulence

The Red Baron might not have been in fighting condition during the weeks before his death. In addition to shattering his sense of invincibility, his head injury affected his reflexes, perhaps contributing to his demise.

Richthofen soon flourished in the air, however. Under the tutelage of German air hero Oswald Boelcke, Richthofen gained confidence and quickly began to amass an impressive kill total. Later, when Boelcke (pronounced *BELL-key*) perished in a midair collision, Richthofen took over the flying unit, which had earned the nickname "Flying Circus" because of the gaudy markings and colors of its planes.

Richthofen's winning dog fight strategy was simple and twofold: shoot down the planes that would cause the enemy the greatest loss, which Richthofen put into practice by targeting mostly two-seater planes; and never follow the enemy too close to the ground in range of soldiers in the trenches. The second rule was one he later broke, with fatal consequences.

The End of the Red Baron

Before the Allies managed to shoot down their nemesis, Richthofen felt premonitions of his fate. He was shot with a glancing blow to the head during a July 1917 dog fight with a British two-seater. Richthofen blacked out, but recovered just in time to bring the plane to a safe landing. During his hospitalization from that wound and after his return to combat duty, he suffered bouts of depression and became convinced that his number was almost up.

Sure enough, on April 21, 1918, one day after recording his eightieth kill, Richthofen got into a dog fight near the front lines. Seeing the chilling sight of the Red Baron's bright red triplane on his tail, the frightened pilot dove toward the ground. Against his own teaching, Richthofen followed the plane, giving Canadian pilot Roy Brown a chance to maneuver the German into his gun sights. At the same moment, Australian foot soldiers in the trenches turned their rifles toward the sky and began shooting at Richthofen's plane.

No one is certain whose bullet was responsible for killing the dreaded Red Baron because souvenir hunters picked the crashed plane clean. To this day, Canadians claim the honor of downing the most feared pilot of that, or any other, war. But the Australians dispute the claim and have made a strong argument that it was one of their sharpshooters who felled the Red Baron.

World War II: The Planes That Won the War

When the key antagonists in World War I faced off again in World War II, the airplane had matured into a formidable weapon of war.

And what a weapon those new airplanes were! The United States relied primarily on two types—the bombers and the fighter planes. The bombers were massive and majestic, able to carry more bombing power in a single flight than was dropped from World War I planes in months of flying. And the fighter planes were deadly killers, with enough strength and stamina to get back home, even if they were often shot full of holes and carrying a few pounds of enemy antiaircraft shrapnel.

The "Flying Fortress": The B-17 Bomber

The greatest air legends of the war grew out of the B-17 bomber, dubbed by Boeing the "Flying Fortress" but known by the men who flew and fixed it as "The Queen of the Sky." And the best known B-17 of them all was the *Memphis Belle*, a plane that its pilot, Capt. Robert K. Morgan, named after his sweetheart back home, Margaret Polk.

The Memphis Belle *and its crew, headed by Capt. Robert K. Morgan, were the first B-17 and crew to make it through 25 combat missions without losing a life. The* Belle *now rests on display in Memphis.*

Apparently, Margaret Polk was good luck for Morgan and his crew. *Memphis Belle* was the first B-17 to complete its quota of 25 combat missions in Europe without a single crewman being killed. Hoping to capitalize on that good luck, the Army Air Corps (as the Air Force was then called) sent Morgan and his very fortunate crew on a publicity tour to talk to civilians and soldiers and to arouse public enthusiasm for U.S. involvement in the war. We have mostly forgotten it now, but before the war most Americans, including flying hero Charles A. Lindbergh (see Chapter 5, "Lindbergh, Earhart, and the Rise of the Airlines") and industrialist Henry Ford, opposed the U.S. involvement. So, in terms of building the United States' resolve to continue fighting the war, Morgan's mission as a booster might have been even a more important one than his bombing tour over Germany.

Plane Talk

Margaret Polk was only one of the hundreds of hometown sweethearts who were remembered with airborne namesakes during the war. Pilots routinely named their planes, often after their wives or girlfriends, and adorned them with colorful—and sometimes risqué—"nose art." The practice has fallen out of favor with the more sensitive modern Air Force, which prefers brutish nicknames to romantic—and potentially sexist—ones.

From raucous to racy, "nose art" adorned the noses of most World War II aircraft. The themes comforted pilots, who missed home and loved ones.

Morgan and his men also became matinee idols, thanks to a documentary called *The Memphis Belle* by Hollywood director William Wyler. Wyler later made his name as a wartime filmmaker by directing the acclaimed *The Best Years of Our Lives,* and the Oscar®-winning documentary *The Fighting Lady.*

Plane Talk

When Boeing delivered a stripped-down B-17 to the Air Force in 1941, the price tag was a rock-bottom $252,000, not including the engines. By the time the government loaded the "Flying Fortress" with all optional equipment—luxuries like guns and propellers and so on—the sticker price, even in 1941 dollars, was a bit more shocking: about $350,000 (or in 1999 dollars, about $3.4 million). Boeing delivered 6,981 of the planes before the production line shut down.

But even after flying 25 European missions and getting all his men back safely, the war wasn't over for Morgan. A stroke of fate sent him back into battle in a different kind of airplane and in a whole different kind of war.

The B-29 "Superfortress" Bomber

During a tour through a Wichita, Kansas, factory, Morgan was given a peek at a secret new airplane that military officers hoped would reverse the nasty beating the Japanese were giving the Allies in the Pacific. The plane was the B-29 "Superfortress," and Morgan instantly fell in love with the big, blunt-nosed behemoth.

Like the B-17, the "Superfortress" was made by Boeing. It was a monstrous four-engine, 140-foot bomber that could fly almost across the United States and back on a single load of fuel. It carried 20,000 pounds of bombs, about the same as the B-17, but the "Superfortress" could fly over 5,800 miles at 220 miles per hour, while the older B-17 could only manage 3,800 miles at 150 miles per hour. In other words, the B-29 was made for missions across the Pacific to Japan, while the B-17 was best suited for the closely fought European war.

On Course

Morgan and the *Memphis Belle* were the subject of a 1990 movie, also called *The Memphis Belle*. It was a modest success by Hollywood's yardstick, but a blockbuster for World War II veterans and flying buffs. Matthew Modine played the part of Robert Morgan, but the film's true star was the fabulous bomber, a stand-in for the real *Memphis Belle*. Check it out if only to see the accurately recreated plane.

The B-29 "Superfortress" was the "Big Iron" that helped mop up the war in the Pacific. Like the B-17, it was made by Boeing, which would thrive after the war as an airliner manufacturer.

The military brass now gave Major Morgan his own command, and in the months between October 1944, and April 1945, Morgan flew his airplane, *Dauntless Dotty*, on another 25 bombing missions, including the deadly firebombing of Tokyo. In April, having survived 50 combat missions in two theaters of war, Morgan finally left the service.

The *Memphis Belle* survived the war and now is on permanent display on Memphis's Mud Island. But *Dauntless Dotty* didn't fare as well. Lt. William Kelly was flying *Dotty* home to the United States when he and the crew landed on Kwajalein Island for a bite to eat before starting the long trip to the mainland. When he took off, though, something catastrophic happened that no one has fully figured out. *Dotty* crashed into the Pacific, killing ten of the thirteen crewmen on board.

After flying 25 missions in the B-17 Memphis Belle, *Robert Morgan asked for another tour of duty, this time in the war in the Pacific against Japan. Morgan piloted* Dauntless Dotty, *a B-29, and again completed 25 missions before the war ended.*

Plane Talk

With the help of the B-17, the war in Europe ended May 8, 1945. But the Pacific war against Japan took months longer to win. When victory against Japan finally came, it was shortly after President Harry S Truman ordered atomic bombs dropped on the Japanese cities of Hiroshima and Nagasaki. In both cases, it was B-29 "Superfortresses" that delivered America's secret weapon. Col. Paul W. Tibbets dropped the first atomic bomb on August 6, 1945, from a B-29 called *Enola Gay* that was based on Tinian Island. Three days later, another B-29, *Bockscar*, piloted by Maj. Charles W. Sweeney, dropped the second atomic bomb on Nagasaki. The war ended on September 2, 1945.

The B-29 "Superfortress" called Enola Gay *dropped America's atomic secret weapon on the city of Hiroshima. A second atom bomb, dropped on the city of Nagasaki, helped convince the Japanese to surrender. The B-29 was pivotal in winning the war in the Pacific.*

Wild Mustangs: The P-51 Fighter Plane and Chuck Yeager

There may never have been an airplane more dashing and deadly than the P-51 Mustang, and the same can be said of a young pilot named Chuck Yeager. A natural-born pilot with eagle-sharp eyesight, Yeager also possessed a cool head in the most dire emergencies.

The sleek, growly P-51 Mustang was among the most beloved airplanes of World War II. It continues to thrive today in the form of restored "war birds" and air race planes.

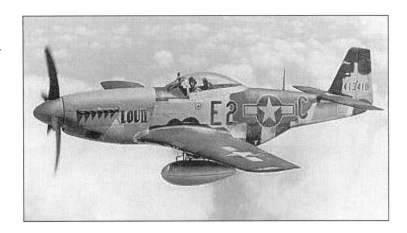

Born Charles Elwood Yeager in Myra, West Virginia, Yeager grew up a few miles down the Mud River in Hamlin. In the West Virginia hills, young Chuck developed the unmistakable accent that has been imitated by thousands of American pilots who came to idolize everything about Yeager.

Though he went on to fly virtually every military airplane that the Air Force flew, Brigadier General Chuck Yeager began his flying career as the pilot of a P-51 Mustang. Yeager and the P-51 Mustang rose to fame together. His 357th Fighter Group was among the first units to fly the new fighter, a sleek silver streak with a deep-throated growl.

Yeager began his military flying career in the days when American pilots still followed their propellers into dog fights, well before jets became common for U.S. pilots. Yeager shot down his first enemy airplane in March 1944, and the next day was shot down himself behind enemy lines. The French Resistance smuggled Yeager to Spain, a neutral country, and finally back to his unit.

By the war's end, Yeager shot down 13 enemy airplanes, including one German jet fighter that could outspeed the Mustang but not outmaneuver it. And of Yeager's 13 kills, 5 came in a single day!

Plane Talk

Several models of P-51 Mustangs were built during the war, and with 14,200 of them rolling off assembly lines, the fighter served the U.S. military into the Korean War and beyond. The fastest Mustangs could fly at speeds of 487 miles per hour with a range of 755 miles. The fighter's main mission was to guard clusters of bombers from attack by enemy aircraft while en route to their targets. There wasn't a more welcome sight for a nervous formation of bombers than the distinctive arrow-sleek Mustangs flying high and alert for danger.

The X-1

After the war, Yeager turned in his P-51 wings for a test pilot's helmet. He began working on secret airplane projects that were meant to give the United States a head start on the Russians. One of the races between the two rival nations was to fly faster than the speed of sound. A number of pilots had already flown faster than the speed of sound, but had done it in steep attack dives that often ended in disaster. Researchers worked to develop an engine powerful enough to overcome the dense compression of air molecules, called the "pressure wave," that built up ahead of a fast-traveling plane. Yeager, working as test pilot of the X-1 rocket plane, nicknamed *Glamorous Glennis* after his wife, finally broke the sound barrier in level flight in 1947—and survived to tell the tale. Researchers had found the right engine, and in Chuck Yeager, they had the right pilot.

On Course

Chuck Yeager's fame grew larger than ever after Tom Wolfe's 1979 book, *The Right Stuff,* was published. Yeager and a small band of California desert test pilots might have been the best flyers ever, and this book turns the spotlight on them and the first astronauts, the men of the Mercury missions. An excellent read!

Chuck Yeager retired from the Air Force, but he is still the most visible and respected symbol of a time when daring men risked their lives to push the boundaries of flight. Yeager continues to embody what author Tom Wolfe called *The Right Stuff.*

The P-51 Lives On

Though the jet age has left the P-51 far behind, it has not been long since the Mustang was actually part of a country's flying inventory. As recently as the 1980s, the tiny island nation of Dominica, wedged between the French protectorates of Martinique and Guadeloupe, flew Mustangs to protect its volcanic forests from invasion.

The Mustang has an even more prominent showcase in the Reno Air Races. The P-51 has become the airplane of choice for this fastest of motor sports events.

Every September, the fastest propeller-driven airplanes in the world gather at Reno/ Stead Airport in Reno, Nevada, to push their planes to speeds well over 500 miles per hour. Modified versions of P-51s and other World War II vintage airplanes with names like *Rare Bear, Strega,* and *Huntress* are flown by some of the best and most courageous pilots in the world. And it takes a heaping helping of fearlessness to fly around tight pylon turns at speeds over 400 miles per hour—with your wingtip just a few feet from the plane beside you, no less!

Plane Talk

One of the most spectacular crashes ever occurred at the Reno Air Races in 1979 and involved a highly souped-up P-51 Mustang called *Red Baron*. The Mustang, which featured two propellers that rotated in opposite directions, was being flown by pilot Steve Hinton. Hinton lost control. *Red Baron* struck the ground so violently that those who saw it knew they had witnessed the death of a great pilot. But when rescuers got to the wreckage, which seemed to be scattered over acres of the "Valley of Speed," they found Hinton still alive. It took years for Hinton to fully recover, but he eventually returned to the cockpit, having survived one of the worst crashes ever.

But when the excitement is over, regardless of who wins the race trophy, what pilots and nonpilots alike take away from the Reno Air Races is respect for the great airplanes of World War II, and reverence for the bravery of the daring pilots who flew them in defense of America.

The Least You Need to Know

➤ Aviation got its first serious test during World War I, and it passed with "flying" colors.

➤ "Eddie" Rickenbacker became a national celebrity for his flying feats.

➤ The Red Baron shot down more enemy planes than any other pilot.

➤ American pilots fell in love with the first great bomber, the B-17 "Flying Fortress."

➤ The second great bomber, the B-29 "Superfortress," delivered the war-ending blow to Japan.

➤ Flying legend Chuck Yeager began his storied career flying a P-51 Mustang, perhaps the most loved fighter plane of the Second World War.

Chapter 5

Lindbergh, Earhart, and the Rise of the Airlines

In This Chapter

➤ "Lucky" Charles Lindbergh makes history

➤ The search for Amelia Earhart

➤ The airline industry benefits from the popular heroes

In 1927, the cheering crowds in New York and across the nation were celebrating more than Charles Lindbergh's history-making solo trans-Atlantic flight. They were celebrating the conquest of a fearsome natural obstacle. And while they cheered the hurdling of an ocean, they were carrying the scenario to a separate conclusion: If a man could cross a vast ocean in a matter of hours, why not turn westward and leap across a familiar continent?

Ten years after Lindbergh's flight, when Amelia Earhart dared to circle the earth, millions of Americans again sat with their ears close to their radios, caught up in the excitement of the new era. While we sat listening, still another thought dawned in the national consciousness: Flying is open to everyone. Even the news of Amelia Earhart's mysterious disappearance didn't dampen America's newfound enthusiasm for flying.

So Lindbergh and Earhart have a place in history not only for their record-setting endurance flights, but for helping to turn America into a nation of flyers.

Charles Lindbergh, the Reluctant Hero

For most of us, even those of us born long after he achieved his greatest fame, Charles Lindbergh still is among history's most celebrated and revered personalities. But Lindbergh's impact on flying goes far beyond his most famous exploit—the 1927 flight that won him the Orteig prize and world fame. He was a pioneering air mail pilot, a crusader for political causes, and the man perhaps most responsible for helping to create an industry that has grown into one of the largest in the world: passenger airlines.

Turbulence

Sure, Charles Lindbergh was the first to fly nonstop from New York to Paris, a feat that earned him the $25,000 Orteig prize. But his flight was technically the *second* one to cross the Atlantic Ocean nonstop. The first flight, eight years earlier in 1919, was made by John Alcock and A.W. Brown, who took off from Newfoundland and landed in Ireland. It was Alcock's and Brown's bad luck that no one was paying prize money for that route.

Lucky Lindy

Charles Augustus Lindbergh was born into a Minnesota family that already had its share of public acclaim. His father, Charles A. Lindbergh Sr., was a longtime U.S. congressman, and his mother, born Evangeline Land Lodge, was a popular schoolteacher in his hometown of Little Falls.

Lindy attended the University of Wisconsin with an eye toward becoming an engineer. He was a poor student who didn't have much interest in books, preferring instead to get his hands dirty. He even tried his hand at farming. By the time Lindbergh was in his sophomore year, it had become perfectly clear to him and to his professors that he wasn't cut out to be an academic. To the relief of the university administrators, Lindbergh dropped out and began his flying career.

Plane Talk

In order to scrape up the money he needed to buy his first airplane, Lindbergh signed with a traveling troupe of daredevil pilots—called "barnstormers"—as a parachute jumper and wing walker. The job required Lindbergh to leap out of airplanes wearing primitive parachutes, which at the time had a disturbing tendency not to open. Even when they did open, the wearer could still fall fast enough to break a leg on landing.

Lindbergh the Daredevil

Lindbergh began his flying career billed as "Daredevil Lindbergh." He became an expert parachutist who thrilled crowds with death-defying stunts. What's more, as a wing walker, Lindbergh climbed out of the cockpit while the plane was in the air, and clambered around on the wings. He sometimes hung from the lower wing with nothing between him and the ground but a firm grip. To make the job even more dangerous, wing walkers usually refused to wear a parachute because of its bulk and weight. The fact that Lindbergh simply survived his barnstorming stint was enough to justify the nickname "Lucky Lindy"!

It wasn't long after Charles Lindbergh began his air mail career that he began to dream of greater things. It was during a routine flight that Lindy first realized he could write aviation history.

By the Book

The **Jenny** was a Curtiss JN-4 biplane. In the 1920s when the Jenny was the favorite airplane of barnstormers, airplanes had none of the radios or navigation equipment of modern airplanes. Pilots were forced to navigate by deductive, or "dead" (pronounced *dead*) reckoning using predicted wind information combined with estimated flying speed and flying time. In theory, that basic information was sufficient to navigate by, but in practice, pilots carried road maps.

Turbulence

When Lindbergh was an air mail pilot, flying letters and parcels around the United States was the most dangerous job anyone could have. Out of the first 40 pilots hired by the U.S. Post Office to fly the new air mail, 31 were killed in crashes.

Eventually, Lindbergh decided to come down off the wing and learn to fly. Still, the "Lone Eagle," as Lindbergh was later dubbed, began flying more like a "Lone Dodo," and nearly crashed his first plane. He had been able to pay for only eight hours of training with an instructor on board, and he had not yet "soloed" by flying alone for the first time. After eight hours in the air, Lindbergh ran out of money and couldn't afford any more lessons. What's more, his flight instructor was starting to have second thoughts about whether flying was such a safe way to make a living!

But that didn't ground Lindbergh. With the remaining few dollars from his air circus earnings, he bought one of thousands of World War I surplus planes, fondly known as *Jennys*. Still many hours short of earning his pilot's license, Lindbergh slapped down $500 for a Jenny, and promptly prepared for his first solo flight, whether he was ready or not.

On his first attempt, Lindbergh's airplane rolled across a field and struggled a few feet into the air. Lindbergh thought better of the takeoff and touched down again in what was partly a landing and partly a crash. But his plane wasn't damaged, and Lindbergh swung it around for another attempt. That was when a kind-hearted pilot who had watched the first takeoff offered Lindbergh a few tips, and with the words of that anonymous pilot ringing in his ears, Lindbergh took off into one of the most celebrated flying careers in history.

The "Flying Fool"

Lindbergh worked for a time as an air mail pilot, one of the most dangerous jobs anyone could have then. But for adventurous "Slim" Lindbergh, even the dangers of air mail flying weren't enough to satisfy his restlessness. During mail flights, his thoughts began to wander to new challenges, including the $25,000 Orteig prize that restaurateur Raymond Orteig had put up as a bounty for the first person to fly between New York and Paris. When Orteig offered the cash in 1919, he put a five-year deadline on the challenge. By 1924, no pilot had succeeded. Orteig gave pilots another five years to win the prize.

In 1926, Lindbergh paid Ryan Airlines Corporation to build him a plane capable of crossing the Atlantic. They created *The Spirit of St. Louis*, which was so stripped down that it was little more than a flying gas tank. Lindbergh decided that the safest place to position all that gas was close to the engine in front, so the tank was rigged directly in front of Lindbergh's lightweight wicker seat, meaning he could only see forward by swerving the plane and looking out the side windows.

Lindbergh, center beneath propeller, inspects The Spirit of St. Louis, *the plane that would carry him across the Atlantic in 33½ hours and propel him to unprecedented fame.*

Plane Talk

Lindbergh's famous timidity and camera shyness came to him naturally. His parents were of stoic, Midwestern stock and reluctant to show their emotions. Lindbergh's father once endured a stomach operation without anesthesia, and his mother, Evangeline, sent little Charlie off to sleep each night with a handshake.

Flying Into History

After a number of other pilots had died or been injured in unsuccessful attempts to win the prize, Lindbergh was finally ready to try his own luck. On May 20, 1927, after a cross-country shakedown flight from San Diego to New York with one stop in St. Louis, Lindbergh was ready to make his bid for a page in the history books. Too nervous to sleep for the previous 24 hours, he embarked upon his 3,600-mile, 33½-hour battle with fatigue, rough air, dangerous ice accumulations on his wings, and the nearly impossible task of accurately navigating with nothing but a compass, a clock, snippets of a map, and a gut sense of how the wind was blowing. Still, when he crossed the Irish coast 27 hours into the flight, he was only three miles off his intended course!

Plane Talk

Either Lindbergh had a nearly superhuman ability to judge wind direction or he was extraordinarily lucky. During the flight, he climbed and descended a number of times, effectively junking wind forecasts because wind shifts directions at different altitudes. The fact that "Lucky Lindy" was able to hit a navigational bull's eye under such conditions probably can be chalked up to good luck as well as a bit of skill.

At about 10 P.M. Paris time, more than 33 hours after he left Long Island's Roosevelt Field, Lindbergh circled the Eiffel Tower and headed toward Le Bourget airport and history. Radio broadcasts had been tracking the aviator's record-setting flight, and his progress was followed across the British Isles and rural France. By the time he circled for a landing at Le Bourget, some 200,000 wildly cheering Parisians had gathered, presaging what was to become Lindbergh's legacy—worldwide fame that he would never shed, no matter how profound his personal tragedies nor how offensive his views.

After his landing in Paris, "Slim" Lindbergh was ferried back to the United States in oceanliner luxury. He received medals and honors from a laundry list of nations, and then set about popularizing the budding airline industry.

Plane Talk

Lindbergh became adept at putting his fame to use for a good cause. For example, in the mid-1930s, after meeting Massachusetts rocket pioneer Robert H. Goddard, he persuaded the Guggenheim family to fund Goddard's groundbreaking research. Later, after the Japanese bombing of Pearl Harbor, Lindbergh threw himself into the government's war effort by making recruiting tours, teaching pilots how to squeeze more performance out of their planes, and flying in combat himself.

After his record-setting flight, Lindbergh traveled the world lecturing on the future of flying, which belonged to passenger airlines. He was hired as a consultant to both TWA—which immediately christened itself "The Lindbergh Line"—and Pan American Airways to scout out airline flight routes. But his greatest contribution was in the publicity he brought to civil aviation and the airlines.

Amelia Earhart Flies Into Immortality

At about the same time that Lindbergh was emerging as a media favorite, another figure was beginning to appear on the aviation scene. Amelia Earhart, a tough-minded former nurse with a nose for newsreel cameras and an instinct for publicity, was drawing the attention of flyers and celebrity-hounds alike. With a combination of

scripted events and legitimate flying moxie, Amelia Earhart emerged as a media darling with a reputation for daring flying.

In fact, Amelia was only a modestly skilled pilot. Though such a statement is akin to blasphemy to her fans, pilots of her day and since have acknowledged that, for all her courage and never-say-no enthusiasm, "Millie" Earhart was often over her head in the cockpit. Time and again she crashed airplanes or used faulty in-flight judgment, and just as often a forgiving, hero-making press painted the proto-feminist as "Lady Lindbergh" anyway due in no small part to her striking physical resemblance to Charles Lindbergh.

But outside the cockpit, Earhart was a true hero for reasons that went beyond the long-distance or high-altitude records she set. She was an outspoken advocate for women, social causes, and aviation. It's not too far a stretch to say that, along with Lindbergh (whom she knew well), Earhart helped propel the airline industry to a level of acceptance—even romance—it might have otherwise taken years longer to achieve.

Turbulence

Lindbergh's fame was accompanied by tragedy. On March 1, 1932, his infant son Charles Jr. was kidnapped from the New Jersey home where Charles lived with his wife, Anne Morrow Lindbergh. The baby's body was found a short time later, and police in 1934 charged a German-born carpenter with the crime. The suspect, Bruno Richard Hauptmann, was executed in 1936.

"Lady Lindy"

Amelia Earhart was born on July 24, 1897, in Atchison, Kansas, which still regards her roots there as one of its greatest points of pride. She grew up in solid middle-class surroundings and had her mind set on a career in medicine. Like flying, practicing medicine was regarded as a man's domain, but Earhart seemed willing, if not eager, to press on into arenas that were hostile to women. Her career goals were sidetracked in 1921 when she learned to fly from an eccentric woman pilot named Anita Snook, and then bought her first plane with money from her father.

Within a year, she had set a record by reaching 14,000 feet during a flight, and was already planning to capitalize on the publicity that woman flyers of her day could attract. In 1928, she became the first woman to fly the Atlantic. Her promoters dubbed her the "commander" of the flight despite the fact that the plane was actually piloted and navigated by two men. Amelia was no more than a passenger.

Amelia, her pride pricked by her passive role in the 1928 flight, crossed the Atlantic again in 1932, this time solo. Especially after the second Atlantic crossing, Earhart didn't discourage comparisons between herself and the laconic Lindbergh. In fact, her short-bobbed hair and her boyish aviator's garb made the comparisons to Lindbergh even more apt.

Plane Talk

Though Amelia wanted to be the first woman to do it, the globe had already been circumnavigated by air three times, first in 1924 by U.S. Army pilots and twice by colorful, one-eyed, mostly deaf Wiley Post in a Lockheed Vega he called *Winnie Mae*.

Taking the Long Way

One great challenge remained for all flyers, men and women: flying around the world at its greatest distance—the equator. In 1937, backed, and some say prodded, by her publicity-savvy publisher husband George Putnam, Earhart took off on a journey westward from Oakland, California. Putnam was already prepared to cash in on his wife's flight. His plans included a lucrative lecture circuit after her return, book and magazine deals, and hundreds of "First Day Covers" on board her flight to be sold to avid stamp collectors later. But this attempt ended in a crash when Amelia botched a takeoff from Honolulu on the second leg of the journey. The flight began again later that year, this time heading eastward from Miami.

On board for her world-circling flight was navigator Fred Noonan. Noonan was a former sailor and one-time navigation instructor for Pan American Airways, an airline that flew long international routes every day, including some of the very same hops that Earhart would fly. Few could outnavigate Fred Noonan, but few could outdrink him, either. His reputation as a drunk nearly cost him the job as Amelia's navigator and has been invoked frequently in the conjecture over what led to their disappearance.

Plane Talk

When Amelia and Noonan made their around-the-world flying attempt, they flew a Lockheed Electra 10-E equipped with radios that were primitive by today's standards. In 1997, 60 years after Earhart's doomed flight, pilot Linda Finch successfully retraced the flight, this time equipped with modern navigation equipment and larger fuel tanks.

Amelia Earhart had conquered the Atlantic Ocean, but one challenge remained for woman pilots—circling the globe. She captured the imagination of the world with her daring, then sparked decades of speculation when she vanished.

First Sign of Trouble

The world flight was heavily reported but mostly uneventful until Earhart arrived in Lae, Papua New Guinea. Pictures show an exhausted Amelia; Noonan might have slid back into the bottle. Whatever the facts, and they are maddeningly sketchy, Earhart and Noonan took off from Lae for a flight into a historical void. After more than 20 hours of flying toward a refueling stop on tiny Howland Island, Earhart and Noonan turned from celebrities into a decades-long *cause célèbre*. Amid spotty radio reception and a navigation-obscuring overcast, Earhart and Noonan disappeared without a trace. A search began that was so large and so drawn out as to take on a life of its own in the minds of Earhart mystery buffs. Many accused President Roosevelt and some of his advisors of using the search as a fig leaf for spying on the Japanese on behalf of China, a U.S. ally.

Fred Noonan was one of the world's finest navigators, but he was also a hard drinker with a taste for risk. Could he have been to blame for the death of Amelia Earhart?

Theories and Conspiracies

What happened on that final flight? Following are the theories—ranging from most probable to highly unlikely—behind the disappearance of Amelia Earhart and her navigator, Fred Noonan. Which one do you believe—or could there be still another explanation?

➤ **Earhart and Noonan ran out of gas and ideas.** After nearly 20 hours of flying, Earhart simply couldn't find Howland Island, which would have been a speck of land in a trackless ocean. She was forced to ditch the plane into the sea, and was killed or drowned in the crash or managed to scramble into a life raft before dying of exposure.

➤ **Earhart and Noonan were in no condition to continue flying.** There's no doubt that Earhart was exhausted after she and Noonan had flown 22,000 miles around the globe to reach Lae. At every stop they had been hounded by reporters, fascinated gawkers, and clumsy customs procedures. On top of all that, Earhart might have been pregnant at the time; another theory goes that she may have been suffering from premature menopause. On top of those mutually exclusive possibilities is that Noonan may have been drinking again, and may have been in no condition to navigate a plane to a pinpoint target in a vast ocean.

On Course

Hollywood has also been caught up in the crusading life and mysterious disappearance of Amelia Earhart. Two television films about Earhart have been made, one released in 1976 starring Susan Clark called *Amelia Earhart* and another in 1994, starring Diane Keaton, called *Amelia Earhart: The Final Flight*. Both give excellent insights into Earhart's life and mysterious death.

➤ **Earhart was on a spy mission.** President Franklin D. Roosevelt badly wanted to know what the Japanese were up to in the South Pacific as the Land of the Rising Sun became increasingly hostile to American ally China. The theory goes that he recruited Earhart to photograph Japanese ship movements, perhaps causing her to stray off course and get lost. Conspiracists say the unbelievably long "search mission" provided cover for more military spying.

➤ **Earhart became a propaganda tool.** Captured by the Japanese during a surveillance mission, Earhart was brought to the Japanese mainland and forced to broadcast to American forces during World War II under the name "Tokyo Rose."

➤ **Earhart died of disease.** Forced down on the island of Saipan, then controlled by the Japanese, Earhart died of dysentery and Noonan was beheaded. A different slant on that theory goes that Earhart survived the crash and the Japanese authorities, married a native, and lived happily in anonymity.

➤ **Earhart's navigator missed Howland Island and drifted to Nikumaroro Island, 425 miles southeast.** There, after ditching on a reef, the ill-fated pair succumbed to thirst and tropical heat.

➤ **The Roosevelt administration hid Earhart and Noonan on Britain's Hull Island.** A lost-at-sea story was concocted to cover a spy mission. Both aviators died in hiding.

➤ **She lived out her life in Saipan.** One disappearance theory holds that Earhart and Noonan purposely flew into Japanese-controlled territory around the islands of Micronesia in an attempt to spy on Japanese activity around Truk Island. The Japanese captured them and held them captive on Saipan, where both later died.

➤ **She lived out her life in New Jersey.** This theory is one of the most outlandish, as Earhart was a very well-known celebrity who would be recognized instantly wherever she went.

Theories continue to swirl around Amelia Earhart more than 60 years after her disappearance. What, or who, was really to blame?

The Airlines Reap the Benefits

From Lindbergh's flight in 1927 through the 1930s, when Earhart set record after record amid thick newspaper, radio, and newsreel coverage, the American public grew fond of the idea of traveling adventurously by airline. Airlines began to spring up and prosper, thanks in part to companies that operated cheaply and efficiently, but also because of the passenger-pampering luxury some of them offered.

As manufacturers like Boeing and Ford began to sense the birth of a new industry, airplanes metamorphosed into lumbering, ear-splitting luxury suites with wings. Food rivaling that offered in the finest restaurants was served to nattily dressed travelers who reclined in thick-cushioned comfort. They departed from exotic locations in the

South Pacific and the Spanish Main of South America in flying ships that bore names like *The Bermuda Clipper* and the *Clipper Evening Star*. Passengers sipped wine or, in the case of Western Airlines, champagne, while attractive stewardesses prepared cozy sleeping compartments for the fatiguing flights. Modern jet travel, even in the first-class compartment, can't hold a candle to the luxury offered in the golden age of the airlines.

The Boeing 314 helped Pan American Airways launch its legendary Clipper Service. Here, the Dixie Clipper *rides heavily and steadily through the water.*

One of the favorites of passengers, pilots, and airline executives alike was the Douglas DC-3, which made its inaugural flight in 1935. Before then, flying long distances was an experience that tested the mettle—and the patience—of even the most hardy traveler.

Passengers loved the DC-3's roominess and speed, which for the first time made flying comfortable. Pilots found the plane stable and easy to fly, or as pilots say, "honest." Most importantly for the growing industry, airline executives appreciated the DC-3's reliability and low operating cost. DC-3s were strong and reliable, meaning they cost less to repair. And their low cost meant that tickets were affordable, attracting more passengers. To this day, the 65-year-old "Grande Dame of the Skies" is working just as hard as she did in her heyday.

As airlines began to really rake in the profits, Boeing was the one that became most synonymous with air travel. Though Boeing didn't build the first commercial jet, its four-engine 707 is remembered as the airliner that connected America's east and west coasts, and helped coin the word "nonstop." For the first time, passengers could, without fear, board a plane in New York and step off in San Francisco or London a few hours later.

If there was one airplane that can claim credit for winning the devotion of the flying public, it was the DC-3, which served as everything from a war bird to charter plane. The "Grand Old Gal" is still in service today.

Plane Talk

The DC-3 has been part of some of history's most massive undertakings, including "flying the hump" over the Himalayas mountain range from India to China, carrying provisions to evade a Japanese blockade. Later, in 1948, the DC-3 blockade runner went to work again, supplying West Berlin with food and provisions for an entire year. To this day, the very sight of a DC-3 can bring a grateful tear to the eye of many a Berliner.

Such aviation feats would have been hard to imagine without Charles Lindbergh and Amelia Earhart. Though they never worked together, their influence on the American public was as strong as if they had coordinated their promotion of aviation.

Because the flying exploits of Lindbergh and Earhart took them around the world, American travelers for the first time began to think of the distant continents as places that could be reached by air, and not only by the slow-moving ocean vessels.

And thanks to radio, their flights, and particularly Earhart's, were adventures that Americans could follow in their living rooms. For the first time, water-cooler talk in steno pools and factory floors around the country centered on American aviators breaking flying records in faraway places.

Plane Talk

The genius and influence of Charles Lindbergh remains with us even today. When we board a Boeing 747, we are getting into an airplane that Lindbergh helped conceive in the late 1950s. He wanted to create the finest airliner of all time, and the massive 747 has lived up to that high standard. It's fitting that it was designed in part by one of the greatest voices for the airline industry.

The Least You Need to Know

➤ Charles Lindbergh worked hard to learn to fly and applied his skill to winning the lucrative Orteig prize.

➤ Amelia Earhart was a better women's advocate than pilot, and her disappearance might well have resulted from poor flying judgment.

➤ The Douglas DC-3 ushered in the airline industry.

➤ The airlines owed much of their success to the exploits of Lindbergh and Earhart, who fired the imaginations of a nation of would-be adventurers.

Chapter 6

Cessna, Piper, and the Emergence of Sport Flying

In This Chapter

➤ Sport flying: safer than ever before

➤ Aviation's popularity: "taking off"

➤ Plane makers Cessna and Piper make flying affordable and safe

➤ Manufacturers Beechcraft and Mooney add flash and speed

➤ The Oshkosh experience

Sport flying is booming. Airplane makers are speeding up their assembly lines, more people are getting their pilot certificates, and pilots are flying more hours now than they have in years. The figures make it pretty clear that the upsurge in flying activity is only going to accelerate. And for those of us who love nothing more than a busy airfield, that's good news.

Sport flying owes its popularity to two innovators who saw flying not as a daredevil sport but as a recreational pastime: Clyde Cessna and Bill Piper. Thanks to the companies they built and their vision for sport aviation, flying continues to become safer and more affordable.

By the Book

Pilots measure their flying experience in **hours,** which they record in a specially designed log book that can be found at any airport pilot shop or by shopping on the Web. A flight hour is recorded by a clocklike cockpit instrument called a Hobbs meter, which begins ticking when the engine starts running and stops when the engine stops.

Sport Flying: Safer Than Ever

Sport flying, that part of noncommercial, nonmilitary aviation that we do just for fun, is becoming safer every day. Gone is the era when flying an airplane was so risky that insurance companies wouldn't even write a policy for a pilot. Improvements to navigation equipment and safety-conscious plane building continue to make flying one of the safest ways you can choose to get from point A to point B. Flying has become so safe, in fact, that some say the statistics favor flying over driving or boating. As far as *sport* aviation goes, I won't go quite *that* far, but it may be true that airline flying is the safest means of transportation ever devised.

To demonstrate the improvement in flight safety, let's look at the numbers. Excluding airline statistics, military flying, and helicopters—in other words, looking only at fixed-wing general aviation—1997 (the latest year for which I have complete statistics) was the safest year ever. In 1997, there were 1,858 general aviation accidents, of which only 356 involved a fatality. That number might appear high, but it looks a whole lot better when you realize that general aviation pilots flew more than 25 million *hours* of cockpit time. It appears that better pilot training and superior technology is only going to improve on 1997's record.

The 1997 figures also look very encouraging when you compare them to 1982, when 3,233 general aviation accidents occurred in the course of flying more than 29.6 million flight hours. That year, 591 of those flying accidents were fatal.

Ask a pilot if flying is safe, and he'll probably say something glib like, "The most dangerous part of any flight is the drive to the airport." The fact is that flying has its share of danger, just as driving does. If you run out of gas when you're driving, safety is as close as the side of the road, whereas a pilot who is a mile or more above the ground must perform some very skilled flying if he's going to land safely. By the same token, when you're flying you're not in danger of a drunk driver crossing the median and colliding with you.

Yes, there's a certain amount of risk in flying. But if you decide that you have an irresistible passion for it, you can feel good about the fact that it's getting safer to do it all the time.

The Planes That Clyde Built

Clyde Cessna rates as one of the most eccentric airplane builders to ever turn a wrench. Cessna, who turned to aviation at the age of 31, trudged around his shop in threadbare old clothes and a shapeless fedora that made him look more like a panhandling drifter than the creator of the modern spirit of general aviation. In a plane he built himself in 1913, he would fly around on his errands. Whether it was going to the store or going to church on Sunday, Clyde Cessna did it by air.

He was absent-minded, too. In June 1917, he opened a flight school that quickly enrolled five students at a price of $400. But Cessna was so preoccupied with building his planes that he forgot to show up to teach the lessons, and all five students quit in a rage and sued Cessna for their money back.

Cessna, a gangly former car salesman, revolutionized the design and construction of airplanes by hiding the strength-giving parts inside his airplanes' wings, imbuing them with a graceful appearance. Where other designers had placed supporting struts and braces on the outside of the airplane, he created structural parts that would provide strength from the inside, reducing the number of exterior supporting struts and wires from a dozen to just two. But graceful though Clyde's planes were, they became known as bullishly strong, amazingly light, and quick to forgive the ham-handed pilot.

On Course

In terms of fatalities, general aviation has the advantage over recreational boating. In 1997, more people died in noncommercial boating accidents than in general aviation accidents. So why does it seem that flying is so dangerous? Airplane crashes grab more headlines than boating accidents, and generally have more witnesses. Once the media rushes to a plane crash, particularly one involving a celebrity like John F. Kennedy Jr., the coverage can capture our attention for days.

The Self-Taught Pilot

Cessna was a self-taught pilot who, like the Wright brothers, had to learn the basics of piloting the hard way, often crashing until he figured out how to land safely. He first flew in 1911, and soon was thrilling audiences around Wichita with his air-circus hijinks.

But the long time Clyde had taken to learn how to fly meant more than a few cracked-up homemade planes. If there was one thing Cessna longed for, it was an airplane that was strong and durable and could withstand the early struggles of beginner pilots.

In fact, if Clyde Cessna had been a better pilot and had not subjected his planes to so much abuse, Cessna airplanes might not have become the most popular airplanes ever made.

From the time he built his beloved *Silver Wings* airplane in 1913, Cessna gradually developed larger and more sophisticated designs that were known for their sturdy construction.

Flight schools beat a path to Wichita after World War II to buy up scores of the all-but-indestructible little planes that Clyde made. Airplanes with pedestrian names like Model 120 and Model 140 transformed post-war America into a nation of pilots. It seemed that everybody in the country either was a pilot or had a friend who was.

The Cessna 140 was a deluxe two-seat airplane with a cruise speed of over 100 m.p.h. The first 140s were delivered in 1946, but the spunky little plane is still in huge demand by pilots who often go to compulsive efforts to restore them to their original charm.

(Photo courtesy of Cessna Aircraft Co.)

The two-seat 120s and 140s were great training planes. But a need developed for slightly larger planes with more seating capacity; after learning how to fly, pilots wanted to take the whole family along. The graceful Cessna 170, sort of a flying station wagon, filled that need perfectly when it was introduced in 1947, and as the years passed, the company built models that became larger, faster, and more refined. Perhaps the culmination of these efforts is the high-powered Caravan, a single-engine workhorse that is simultaneously so brawny and graceful that some pilots swear it can carry anything that will fit inside.

The Cessna 170 deserves the title of the most graciously designed of all the models to fly out of Clyde Cessna's Wichita airplane factory. Its elegant lines and attentive interior touches make it a classic that is still popular today.

(Photo courtesy of Cessna Aircraft Co.)

To say the least, the Cessna company has thrived. Not only is Cessna the unchallenged champion in terms of the number of small, mostly single-engine airplanes that have rolled off its assembly lines—assembly lines that have been owned by Textron since 1992—but the company has also become one of the most prolific producers of small-business jets.

The Beloved Cessna

What is it about Cessna airplanes that makes them so beloved? I suppose part of the answer lies in how simply Cessna airplanes are designed. Pull up the *cowling* on a Cessna 152 trainer, for example, and you'll see an engine as uncomplicated as any engine larger than a riding lawnmower's. But that little engine puts out enough horsepower to carry the plane a few hundred miles at a hop or a few dozen times around the airfield (which is how most student pilots learn to fly).

By the Book

Airplane engines are inherently "dirty" from an aerodynamic point of view, meaning that the air has a lot of nooks and crannies to swirl in, which robs the airplane of speed. Designers shield the engines in **cowlings** of smooth metal that give airplanes a sleeker look and better performance.

Turbulence

Clyde Cessna undeniably changed the character of general aviation by manufacturing planes that were safer than any made before. But in a cruel irony, Cessna watched a close friend die horribly in an air racing accident in 1933 flying a plane Cessna himself had designed. Cessna lost his love for flying on that day, though not his love for building airplanes, and from then on did all he could to avoid getting into an airplane.

If the exterior is simple and functional, the interior of most small Cessna airplanes is positively Spartan. Seats are thin-cushioned and, except for sliding closer or farther away from the instrument panel, nonadjustable. The air vents are no more than big hollow tubes that suck outdoor air into the cockpit. In short, most of the smaller Cessnas are made for short flights or pilots who don't mind a little punishment. Only when you get into the larger, more expensive models do you start to enjoy real comfort.

The Cessna's instruments are simple, with few distractions to divert a pilot's attention. The planes are highly responsive to a pilot's control, and are more forgiving than a parish priest. That doesn't mean pilots don't have to be skilled to fly them safely; it does mean they are inherently stable and prone to giving pilots second chances. From their sturdy landing gear capable of shrugging off a student pilot's bouncy landing to a wing design that goes easy on pilots who fly too slow, the Cessna is a big-hearted plane in a small, plain-Jane package.

The Cessna 172 and its nearly identical smaller siblings—the 150 and 152—are the most popular training airplanes in the world. They have become favorites for their forgiving flying characteristics and for their low operating cost.

(Photo courtesy of Cessna Aircraft Co.)

Perhaps my favorite feature of most of the Cessnas is the front window that you can open during flight. Granted, the roar of the 100-plus mile-per-hour wind brings any cockpit small talk to a halt, but under the punishing sun of the southwestern United States, where I did most of my student flying, cooling in the breeze beat shooting the breeze any day.

Bill Piper Puts Pilots on Top

While Clyde Cessna and the Kansas company he created were becoming synonymous, Bill Piper was keeping pace. Piper, a former oil man from Pennsylvania, unwittingly backed a tiny local airplane company when his business partner pledged a few hundred dollars on his behalf. When the company collapsed as the Great Depression deepened, Piper bought the company for $761 in the bankruptcy auction and found himself in the airplane business. And he didn't even know how to fly!

Piper, who was scarcely ever called anything but "Mr. Piper," knew how to get all 100 pennies worth out of a dollar, which goes a long way toward explaining his success in a business that bankrupted dozens of others. He never owned more than one car at a time, and if his family took it on a long trip, he preferred to walk to town and back to his home near the Lock Haven, Pennsylvania, airport rather than pay for another vehicle.

He was also unflappable. When a spark ignited some rags in 1937, Piper's entire factory burned to the ground. Bill shrugged it off, saying, "At least we'll get some publicity out of it."

Plane Talk

Piper helped popularize the notion of piloting small airplanes as glamorous. In Hollywood, movie stars of the 1930s and 1940s were learning to fly, many of them buying Cubs to skim over the Sunset Strip and the luxurious beaches of Southern California. The Piper company couldn't have paid for that kind of publicity, and sales began to skyrocket.

From Oil Man to Air Man

Piper began manufacturing the Piper Cub, a low-price, simple airplane so light and easy to fly that even Piper himself became a pilot—at the age of 60. From an abandoned silk factory in Lock Haven, Piper's company grew into a maker of inexpensive airplanes—they cost only $1,325, and didn't increase in price for many years—that stood apart from Cessnas, and the most obvious distinction was where Piper chose to place the wings.

By the Book

All of Cessna's small airplanes follow a **high-wing** design scheme in which the body of the plane hangs below the wing. In the **low-wing** design of many Pipers and small airplanes, the body of the plane rests atop the wings, which serve as a step into the cockpit.

You Take the High Wing, and I'll Take the Low Wing ...

Aside from the Cub and its cousins, the Pacer and Tri-Pacer, Pipers became known for their *low-wing* design, which some pilots prefer to the *high-wing* design of most of Cessna's small models. There is a distinct difference in the flying characteristics of the two planes that becomes starkly noticeable particularly during landing. For the most part, the preference for the low-wing scheme doesn't go beyond cosmetics. Still, some pilots like sitting on top of the wing instead of dangling below it.

The location of the wing can be important to a pilot. For example, some pilots, often young ones who are just beginning their careers as professionals, take jobs flying along gas and oil pipelines in remote stretches of desert or forest looking for telltale signs of leaks. To do the job really well, they need to be able to look straight downward, which is where high wings make the job a lot easier. Other pilots count animals, something that helps fish and wildlife officials regulate populations. Wildlife pilots often fly very low while passengers count animals like moose, antelopes, even schools of fish and pods of whales, for hours on end. That job is a lot easier if the airplane wing isn't blocking the view.

My preference is for high-wing Cessnas, and I have a particular fondness for the classic lines and easy-going flying characteristics of the Cessna 170. For one thing, I find high-wing Cessnas easier to get into and out of. Piper's low wing sometimes makes for tricky footing when stepping on the wing—always the right wing—to reach the door, and an awkward step down into the cockpit. High-wing Cessnas can be entered from both sides of the cockpit—and exited from both sides, too, in case of emergency—and are as comfortable to get into as a two-door sedan.

What's more, I like the visibility Cessna's high wing gives me, not only during cruise flight, but when approaching the airport. In a low-wing Piper, and any low-wing airplane for that matter, the wings block my view of the airport during some phases of the landing approach, which I find a nuisance.

When "Hogs" Fly

No description of general aviation airplanes would be complete without including two other makes of airplane, each with their own rabidly loyal following: Beechcraft and Mooney. Both Beechcrafts and Mooneys are as strong as army tanks and blessed with enough power to outpace most other single-engine competitors. Owners of Beechcrafts and Mooneys both congregate in their own tight-knit clubs, and they identify with their airplanes with as much enthusiasm as Harley-Davidson owners do with their "hogs." In fact, scores of Mooney owners make a yearly pilgrimage to the Mooney factory in Kerrville, Texas, where they eat, drink, and tell flying stories, most of which center on their beloved airplanes.

Mooneys are a famously well-designed family of planes that manage to squeeze more speed out of each horsepower than virtually any other mass-produced plane. The credit goes to the company's designers, who obsess over every detail in trying to make their planes' skin smoother or finding a more aerodynamic way to hide a piece of equipment. Mooneys are so sleek, in fact, that they don't seem to want to come back to earth once they're aloft. Pilots have found them hard to slow down for landing, so designers have installed *spoilers* on the wings.

The Mooney M20 is among the most popular models the company has produced. M20s are plentiful in the used-airplane market, and, with a cruise speed of almost 200 m.p.h. from a modest, 200 horsepower engine, are one of the best performers among the inexpensive small planes.

By the Book

Spoilers are panels or plates that manufacturers install on the top surface of an airplane's wings to "spoil" the lift and allow a pilot to descend for landing or to slow down quickly in flight. (We'll go into lift and the other forces of flight in Chapter 8, "How Airplanes Fly, Part 2: The Aerodynamics of Flight.") If you've watched an airliner's wings during a descent and landing, you may have noticed metal plates located about half-way between the front and back edges of the wing rising into the airflow. Those are the spoilers, and when they move, they indicate that the pilot is trying to steepen his descent or slow down.

In the years since the M20 was first manufactured in the mid-1950s, Mooney has unveiled model after model of faster, sleeker airplanes, each with the Mooney signature vertical stabilizer that juts forward slightly as though eager to go even faster.

Beechcraft's signature model is the high-performance, single-engine Bonanza. Bonanzas are a bit more barrel-chested than Mooneys, but they're just about as fast and they provide passengers and pilots alike with plenty of room to spread out. (Mooneys are notorious for their tight, uncomfortable cabin, although it is that narrow waist that helps the planes fly so fast. It's your choice: speed or luxury?) Beechcrafts are put together so sturdily that closing the cabin door sounds like closing a bank vault.

The Bonanza has been manufactured with two different styles of tail. In one design, the tail retains the familiar combination of horizontal and vertical surfaces, which pilots call, appropriately, the horizontal and vertical stabilizers. (We'll talk about what these surfaces do in the next chapter.) But Beechcraft turned that familiar model on its ear in 1945 when it first flew a V-tail model. Like its name implies, the V-tail Bonanza has a tail design that eliminates the traditional horizontal and vertical stabilizers and replaces them with a V-shaped pair of surfaces called "ruddervators."

Beechcraft designers were criticized for the unconventional design, but the company was convinced the idea would catch on with the flying public, and it did. The V-tail Bonanza is one of the most strikingly beautiful planes you'll ever see, and thanks to a recent "patch" that cured some structural weakness the design suffered from, it is just as safe and fun to fly as any other airplane in the sky.

If price is no object, the best single-engine airplane, to my taste, at least, is the robust, speedy, and reliable Cessna 210 Centurion. I've already explained my preference for the high wings and the easy access to Cessnas, and add to those factors the 310 horsepower engine and a hefty list of extras and luxuries, and you have a fine airplane. Passengers like the large Cessnas for their generous leg room and, it bears repeating, an excellent view.

It's possible to pay over $200,000 for a mint-condition used Centurion—Cessna doesn't make new Centurions right now—but some well-maintained 210s are also being sold for as little as $50,000.

Oshkosh: The Sport Pilot's Rite of Passage

And you thought Oshkosh was only a label on your toddler's overalls! Actually, Oshkosh, a small town in Wisconsin, is to aviation what Indianapolis is to car racing. Every summer, beginning in the last week of July, this town of about 60,000 is overrun by more than 700,000 swarming aviation fanatics from all over the world. Visitors look at giant jets, secretive ultra-modern military planes, and small, racy propeller planes of all descriptions. But mostly, they are there to be a part of an aviation event that every pilot feels drawn to attend at least once.

So why have few people heard of Oshkosh, while the Indianapolis 500 is a national institution? For one thing, the Indy 500 was first held in 1909, while the Oshkosh festival marked only its 47th anniversary in 1999. For another, as long as more people drive cars than fly planes, auto racing will continue to receive more television coverage than events such as Oshkosh and the Reno Air Races (see Chapter 4, "Great Flyers of the World Wars").

But to the sport pilot and aviation buff, Oshkosh, a six-day event that the sponsoring Experimental Aircraft Association has dubbed AirVenture Oshkosh, is a kind of rite of passage. Once you've been there, you've always got a story to tell on a rainy day at the airport when you and your flying friends are hanging around the airport and doing a little bit of *hangar flying*.

The thousands of airplanes that fly into Oshkosh each summer turn the town's Wittman Regional Airport into one of the busiest in the nation. The Federal Aviation Administration staffs a temporary control tower that, for a few days, handles as many arrivals and departures as some of the world's busiest airports while ground workers lead hundreds of airplanes to parking areas that surround the airport. Cessnas, Pipers, and Beechcraft make up the majority of planes at Oshkosh, though there are dozens of

> **By the Book**
>
> **Hangars** are the buildings that house airplanes, sort of a garage for flyers. The word, like so many flying terms, is French, and it was used to describe a covered shed or stable. **Hangar flying** is what pilots call the good-humored story-telling that can, over time, elevate small events to mythic tales.

other great airplane lines represented, from the Grumman Tiger (the beloved model that endured terrible abuse from me as I was learning to fly) to the sleek-waisted Mooneys that look fast even when they're parked on the airport ramp.

Each year, pilots of Cessnas, Pipers, Mooneys, Beechcraft, and the hundreds of other models and variations of planes that can be found at America's airports find one common meeting point: Oshkosh.

The Least You Need to Know

➤ Sport flying is not only increasing in popularity, it's also getting safer.

➤ Cessnas and Pipers are the most popular, and least expensive, airplanes in America.

➤ Beechcrafts and Mooneys are not as affordable as Pipers and Cessnas, but they're popular airplanes with wildly loyal fans.

➤ The Oshkosh festival is a pilgrimage every small-plane pilot should make at least once.

Part 2

The Thrill of Flight

When asked what makes an airplane fly, I'm often tempted to answer, "magic." To me, the forces of aerodynamics are that marvelous and awe-inspiring. But as awe-inspiring as these physical forces are, they are easily understood, and can be applied to every invention of aviation.

Part 2 introduces you not only to airplanes, gliders, helicopters, and hot-air balloons, but to the aerodynamic forces that enable them to fly. You'll even get a look at some of the oddities of aviation, including a jet that behaves like a helicopter.

Chapter 7

How Airplanes Fly, Part 1: The Parts of a Plane

In This Chapter

➤ Identify the basic parts of an airplane

➤ The powerplant

➤ The fuselage

➤ The wings

➤ The empennage

➤ The landing gear

We've already seen that airplanes are far from the only kind of aircraft available to the recreational aviator. But there's something about the fixed-wing engine-driven airplane that makes it the most popular form of flying among pilots in the United States. (Gliding is also gaining in popularity. We'll look at the differences between flying airplanes and gliders in Chapter 9, "Soaring on Silent Wings: Gliding.")

The attraction that airplanes hold for many of us is rooted in nostalgia. The image of the dashing barnstormers of the 1920s and 1930s is deeply ingrained in our culture. The silk scarf and the swagger of those daring pilots have become part of an archetype that is purely American in origin; we see the barnstormers who pioneered the skies as direct descendents of the pioneers who tamed the Great Plains and the Rocky Mountains.

Maybe it's simpler than that, though. Maybe some of us love flying airplanes because they allow us to master an element that is foreign to us, though good pilots eventually learn that mastery of flight only comes with acknowledging its potential dangers and backing down when they are overmatched.

Airplanes give us the ability to break the two-dimensional restraints that bind us to the ground and enable us to view the earth from a lofty perspective where the fumes of traffic and the constant reminders of responsibility grow less important with distance, and where the elemental demands of the sky and the airplane occupy all our attention.

With that bit of hangar philosophy, let's begin to examine the delightful details of how an airplane flies. In this chapter we'll take a look at how the airplane is put together, and in the next chapter we'll examine the forces that keep it in the sky.

Putting Names to the Pieces

Airplanes are made up of thousands of parts, from the simplest assemblies of sheet aluminum and rivets to the most complex system of gyroscopes or radio navigation receivers. No two airplanes are exactly alike, of course, but they all have certain very basic features in common:

➤ The powerplant

➤ The fuselage

➤ The wings

➤ The tail, or empennage

➤ The landing gear

Let's examine these common components and the role they play in producing flight.

The Powerplant

The propeller, engine, and cowling together comprise the airplane's powerplant.

The Engine

Powerplants can consist of a number of different types of engines with varying capabilities of power, durability, and capability to perform at high altitude.

Reciprocating engines, the type of engine you have in your car, are familiar to most of us, and the engines in airplanes are not a lot different from those in cars. In many ways, airplane engines are simpler than car engines. Many of them use carburetors, which in automobiles have been replaced by fuel injection systems. One major difference between the two engines is that airplane engines are typically air-cooled, because radiators, water pumps, and the rest of the mechanical components that go along with the water-cooled engine of a car are too heavy for an airplane to carry.

Plane Talk

Airplane engines are equipped with a few safety features that car engines don't have. The most important are the magnetos that generate their own electricity once the engine is running. That means if the battery runs down in flight, the engine will continue to run, though some of the electrical equipment in the cockpit, like radios and lights, could stop working. In fact, airplane engines are equipped with *two* magnetos. Better safe than sorry.

An airplane with just one engine is called, quite logically, a single-engine airplane, while those with two or more engines are called twin-engine or multiengine airplanes. In a single-engine airplane, the cockpit and cabin that house the pilot and passengers rests behind the engine. In a twin-engine airplane the engines generally are mounted on each wing about a third of the distance outward from the cabin.

Twin-engine airplanes can fly at higher speeds than a plane with just one engine, assuming the engines are of comparable power. However, because drag increases with speed, a principle we'll explore in greater detail in the next chapter, twice as many horsepower doesn't translate into twice as much speed.

Also, twin-engine airplanes offer a backup engine in case one fails. That's reassuring to some pilots, but it must be said that flying some small twin-engine airplanes with only one operating engine is very demanding, and more than one pilot has crashed because he wasn't up to the task.

Turbulence

A common misconception is that twin-engine airplanes are necessarily more powerful than single-engine ones. Simply counting engines isn't enough to judge engine power. The Cessna Caravan cargo plane has only one engine, while a Piper Seminole has two engines. But the Caravan's single engine is capable of churning out 675 horsepower, while the Seminole engines combined can manage only 360 horsepower. Sometimes, one really beefy engine is a better choice than two lightweight ones.

Even some jetliners, such as the twin-engine Boeing 737, are notoriously difficult to handle in the event of the failure of one of its engines. Because of the difficult one-engine handling characteristics of some twin-engine planes, simply having two engines sometimes adds to the complications that can arise from the failure of one engine.

The Propeller

Powerplants can feature propellers with a host of characteristics. They can range from the simplest carved wood-and-lacquer prop that drives some older, smaller airplanes to the massive, four-bladed metal-and-composite propellers able to shed ice and to automatically adjust their *pitch* during flight. These "constant speed" propellers turn faster or slower during different segments of flight, almost like an airborne version of an automobile transmission.

The small airplanes that most private pilots use for flying lessons are equipped with the simpler fixed-pitch propellers. Their shortcomings in not being able to adjust to different speeds during flight—fastest rotation during takeoff and slowest rotation during cruise—is more than made up for in simplicity.

When a student pilot is learning how to control and maneuver an airplane, simplicity in a prop becomes a virtue. A fixed-pitch eliminates one thing the pilot must think about. Later, when he is more experienced, the pilot can more easily transition to a more complicated airplane, including one with an efficient constant-speed propeller.

The Cowling

The "cowling" is an important part of the powerplant, even though it doesn't produce any horsepower at all. The cowling is the curved metal covering over the engine. It's not there just to give the airplane a stylish flair. Its most important function is to smooth the surface around the engine.

As we'll see in greater detail shortly, air flows better over a smooth surface than a rough one. Without some kind of covering to smooth the way, the surface of an engine diverts air into any number of crevices and hiding places. Because it hides the rough edges, the cowling, which is usually made of lightweight sheet aluminum or molded Fiberglas, actually enables airplanes to fly faster—not to mention make a fashion statement!

The Plane Has a Body

That portion of the airplane that houses pilot and passenger is called the "fuselage" (pronounced *FYOO-suh-lazh*). The fuselage contains the cockpit, the passenger cabin, and the baggage compartment in most small airplanes. The fuselage also shelters the airplane's sensitive instruments.

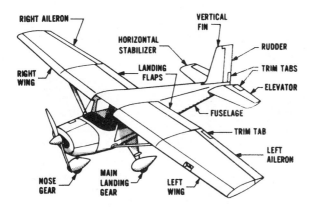

Knowing how the parts of a plane fit together is a key part of flying.

(FAA Flight Training Handbook)

The fuselage also anchors the rest of the airplane's structure: wings, tail, and landing gear. In single-engine planes, the fuselage anchors the engine with the help of a "firewall." Don't let the name worry you; the firewall acts more as a barrier for airflow and noise than for fire, which is an extremely rare occurrence in flying. But in the offhand chance that a fire does occur, the stainless steel firewall is there to protect you and your passengers.

In the front part of the fuselage is the cockpit—the area reserved in large planes for pilots and in small planes for a single pilot and perhaps a passenger.

The cockpit features a control panel of instruments and dials that help the pilot keep on top of navigation, communications, the condition of the engine or engines, and a host of other flight details.

On Course

If you live in a small town served by a small airline, you might be able to sit in the cockpit during an airline flight. When I lived in Prescott, Arizona, and flew to Phoenix on Cochise Airlines, I was in the habit of asking the pilot if he minded me joining him in the cockpit. Because the airplanes were small and required only one pilot, the co-pilot seat was not needed for a crew member, so I invariably got the best seat in the house.

The control panel includes a cluster of flight instruments directly in front of the pilot. We'll discuss most of the important instruments on the control panel in Part 3, "In the Cockpit." But in brief, the flight instruments include the attitude indicator, the directional gyro, the altimeter, the vertical speed indicator, the turn coordinator, and the airspeed indicator. The panel also features the dials and readouts of navigation radios, as well as communications radios.

Finally, the control panel includes a set of engine instruments that range from such basic readings as engine temperature and oil pressure to the more detailed readouts describing the conditions deep inside a jet engine—for example, the temperature of the gas as it leaves the exhaust nozzle.

The cockpit also houses the "steering wheel" that the pilot uses to control the attitude of the airplane. (Except don't call it a steering wheel—it sounds too much like what you'd find on bus, and airline pilots are touchy about being compared to bus drivers.) The big black wheel is called the "control column," and it is connected to surfaces in the wing and in the tail. As you might have seen in movies, the control column is pushed and pulled to help control whether the airplane's nose points up or down, and it can be turned left or right to bank the wings in one direction or another.

By the Book

When describing an airplane surface, such as a wing or a propeller, or any surface exposed to the outside airflow, we describe the forward edge as the **leading edge** and the rear edge as the **trailing edge.** The leading edge slices through the air when the airplane is in motion. The trailing edge is the last portion of that surface the air moves over. For aerodynamic reasons, the leading edge is more blunt in shape than the trailing edge, which tends to have a narrow, pointy shape.

Putting Wings on It

In low-wing airplanes—airplanes whose wings are beneath the cockpit rather than above it—the bottom of the fuselage provides the wings' anchor points. Of course, in high-wing airplanes, the anchors are in the fuselage ceiling. Through this section run the cables and electric wires that connect to the wing control surfaces and lights.

On the *trailing edge* of each wing are two control surfaces—the ailerons and flaps. The ailerons (pronounced *AIL-ur-rahnz,* which is French for "little wings") are movable surfaces attached near the outboard tip of the wing's trailing edge. They are controlled from the cockpit and help turn the plane. Also attached to the wing's trailing edge are flaps, hinged panels that are similar to ailerons but larger and attached closer in toward the fuselage. The flaps help control an airplane's speed.

The Ailerons

The ailerons move in opposite directions from each other when the pilot turns the control column. For example, if a pilot wants to bank toward the right, he would turn the control column to the right. The aileron on the right wing would rise slightly, causing the wind to strike it with a downward force. (We'll get into the aerodynamics of the turn in the next chapter.)

At the same time, the aileron on the left wing would dip slightly, causing an upward reaction. Together, the dipping of one wing and the raising of the other create a bank, and therefore a turn.

The Flaps

Flaps are familiar to anyone who has flown in a jetliner and watched the wings closely during the approach to landing. There was a point at which the trailing edge of the wing seemed almost to come apart, as enormous slabs of metal moved backward and downward in a curve until the wing seemed to have nearly doubled its size. Those flaps, called Fowler flaps, are the most complex of all the varieties available to designers. Small airplanes use simpler hinged flaps that are much lighter than Fowler flaps. Remember, small airplanes can't afford too much in the way of complex systems because of the weight restriction.

Simply put, flaps help an airplane fly slower. That's why you see them used mostly during landing, when a pilot wants to slow the plane as much as possible. The slower the plane is flying when it touches down for landing, the less the brakes have to work to bring it to a stop, allowing the plane to land on a shorter runway and to touch down at a slower, safer speed.

The Empen–What?

Another major structural component of the airplane is the "empennage" (pronounced *EM-puh-nazh*). The word empennage comes from the French word for putting feathers on the end of an arrow. The empennage is largely responsible for stabilizing the plane in flight.

The primary surfaces making up the empennage of most planes are a horizontal stabilizer and a vertical stabilizer.

The Horizontal Stabilizer

The horizontal stabilizer resembles two miniature wings attached to the back end of the airplane. On the trailing edge of the horizontal stabilizers are hinged surfaces called "elevators," which the pilot controls by pushing the control column forward and backward in the cockpit.

The Vertical Stabilizer

The vertical stabilizer helps keep the airplane from slipping through the air in a sort of sideways slouch. Think of what happens when your car door is slightly ajar while you're driving down the highway. When you try to open it in order to pull it closed, you notice how difficult it is to open. As you already understand instinctively, the pressure of the blowing air against the surface of the door tends to keep it streamlined in a closed position. When you push it out into the air stream, the air pressure resists.

The same principle is at work on the vertical stabilizer. When some force pushes the airplane into a slight sideways angle to the wind, whether that force comes from an errant gust of wind or an intentional input by the pilot, the vertical stabilizer tends to push the tail back into line. The airplane is most "comfortable," meaning its opposing forces are most in equilibrium, when the tail is exactly in line with the center of the propeller.

On Course

By a show of hands, how many believe the horizontal stabilizers produce upward lift just like the wings do? If you raised your hand, you'd be wrong. In fact, the horizontal stabilizers create a force that is *downward* in most flight conditions. We'll examine why in the next chapter when we talk about the effects of weight on the way an airplane flies.

Plane Talk

The empennage seems to have more than its fair share of surprises. First we learn that the horizontal stabilizer creates lift toward the ground instead of toward the sky. Now, we'll see that the vertical stabilizer is attached to the airplane askew, and it's done on purpose. During flight, and especially during a climb to a higher altitude, the airplane tends to turn toward the left. This is due to a complex combination of factors mostly connected to the torque produced by the engine and the peculiar aerodynamics of a propeller. (For more detail on torque, see Chapter 8, "How Airplanes Fly, Part 2: The Aerodynamics of Flight.") One thing that engineers do to try to offset an airplane's left-turning tendency is to attach the rudder to the vertical stabilizer at an angle that produces a permanent right-turning effect. If you stand behind a small airplane on the airport ramp, you can see the very small offset angle.

The Rudder

Attached to the trailing edge of the vertical stabilizer is the rudder, a hinged surface that is controlled by the pilot using two foot pedals on the floor of the cockpit. These pedals are located roughly in the same position as the brake and accelerator pedals in a car, but are larger and sturdier.

Rudders play a large but mostly unnoticed role in making a flight comfortable. It is the sideways, fishtail motion of a plane that creates airsickness in passengers. A heavy-footed pilot who misuses the rudders can make passengers feel sick faster than a case of ptomaine poisoning. By the same token, a pilot with deft touch on the rudders can tame even the most unruly and turbulent atmosphere.

We're Rolling Now

The last major component that makes up an airplane is the landing gear. Landing gear generally comes in two types: tricycle configuration or the more traditional conventional pattern.

On Course

Rudder pedals also serve as brake pedals on an airplane. When a pilot presses on the lower portion of the pedals, she controls the rudder surface. When she moves her feet up toward the top of the pedals, she is pressing the brakes. Brake pressure is used to slow the airplane after landing, but in most small- and medium-size airplanes, braking with one foot at a time also is how pilots steer on the ground.

Tricycle Gear

Tricycle gear is so named because its wheel configuration resembles that of a child's tricycle—that is, it has one lead wheel near the plane's nose and two main wheels behind it under the wings. Tricycle gear has become the most popular configuration in most planes rolling off of modern assembly lines because they make landing easier. The technical reason is that the airplane's "center of gravity," the point at which the plane would balance like a seesaw if placed on a fulcrum, rests between the main gear and the nose gear in a tricycle-gear airplane.

In practical terms, it means that tricycle-gear airplanes are more stable during landing, and any swerving caused by wind or poor control technique would tend to stabilize when the pilot steps on the brakes.

Tricycle gear also makes for better forward visibility when the airplane is taxiing on the ground, having a more level attitude than the conventional type.

Plane Talk

Airplanes are equipped with other types of landing gear besides wheels. For example, some airplanes can be transformed from a land plane to a seaplane simply by removing the nose wheel or tail wheel and attaching floats in place of the main gear. For flying into snow- and ice-covered terrain, pilots can attach skis to the gear. Even tires are versatile: Normal narrow tires are good for landing on paved runways and fat "balloon" tires are ideal for landing on grass.

Conventional Gear

As its name suggests, conventional gear is the older style that was a tradition in aviation until the past few decades. In addition to the main wheels under the wings, this configuration features a third wheel under the airplane's tail. The tail-down attitude caused by conventional gear makes the nose stick up high enough to obscure the pilot's view while she's taxiing. It also demands extra skill from a pilot during landing, especially in a crosswind.

In a conventional-gear airplane, the center of gravity is located behind the main landing gear, a less stable setup than in the tricycle-gear airplane. The result is an airplane that (as old-timers joke) the pilot has to keep flying "until it's parked and the wheel chocks are in place."

Because conventional gear reminds a lot of pilots of the "good old days," conventional-gear airplanes are still popular. Some pilots won't even consider buying anything other than a "tail dragger," even if they are somewhat more demanding to fly.

Retractable Gear

As we'll learn in the next chapter, anything that protrudes from an airplane into the air stream can slow it down. To make airplanes fly faster, engineers sometimes equip them with retractable gear that can be mechanically pulled up after takeoff. With the wheels tucked away, the airplane's exterior is smoother, and when you're talking about aerodynamics, smoother means faster.

But not every airplane has retractable gear. The main reason is that the hydraulics and motors that help pull up the gear are heavy and complicated. Heavy airplanes can carry less cargo, and complicated airplanes cost more to manufacture, maintain, and insure. So, smaller airplanes and those that put a premium on carrying cargo are usually equipped with fixed landing gear.

And there you have it: the major parts of a plane that enable it to fly. In the next chapter, we'll see how these parts work together with the pivot points and the four opposing forces on a plane to produce the magic of flight.

The Least You Need to Know

➤ The powerplant, including engine, propeller, and cowling, provides the thrust that makes flying possible.

➤ The fuselage holds the pilot and passengers, and serves as an anchor for the other airplane components.

➤ The wings anchor the flaps and the ailerons, as well as support the weight of the plane in flight.

➤ The empennage includes the horizontal and vertical stabilizers, as well as the elevators and rudder.

➤ The landing gear, whether modern tricycle style or the older tail-wheel type, gets the plane rolling.

How Airplanes Fly, Part 2: The Aerodynamics of Flight

In This Chapter

➤ Pitch, roll, and yaw

➤ Lift: the key to flying an airplane

➤ Drag: an unavoidable cost of flying

➤ Thrust: the driving force in airplanes

➤ The turn: one maneuver, many forces

In the last chapter we discussed the components that make up the airplane. In this chapter, we'll learn how those components work together to enable an airplane to fly.

Pivot Points: Pitch, Roll, and Yaw

When the pilot controls the ailerons, flaps, elevators, and rudder surfaces, he brings the three axes of motion into play.

Imagine a small toy airplane. If you imagine a wooden dowel or a metal wire running the length of the airplane from the tip of the propeller to the tip of the tail (the point where the vertical and horizontal stabilizers meet), you're visualizing the "longitudinal axis." Rotation around the longitudinal axis is accomplished by using the ailerons, and is called "roll." The pilot controls roll by turning the control column, or "steering wheel," left and right.

Now imagine a wire running from one wingtip to the other. This is roughly the position of the "lateral axis." The airplane pivots around this axis as a result of moving the elevators, and such pivoting is called "pitch." The pilot controls pitch by pushing the control column in and out.

Finally, imagine the place where the longitudinal and lateral axes meet. If you were to run a wire vertically through that point, that would represent the "vertical axis," which the pilot controls using the rudder. Movement around the vertical axis is called "yaw." The pilot controls yaw by using the foot pedals.

When an airplane is in flight, its movements take place around its longitudinal, lateral, and vertical axes.

(FAA Flight Training Handbook)

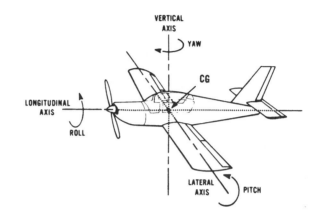

To sum up:

➤ The aileron control surfaces located on the wings, and moved by turning the control column left and right, cause roll around the longitudinal axis.

➤ The elevator control surfaces located on the horizontal stabilizers, and moved by pushing the control column in and out, cause pitch around the lateral axis.

➤ The rudder control surfaces located on the vertical stabilizers, and moved using the foot pedals, cause yaw around the vertical axis.

The three airplane axes meet at a single point called the "center of gravity," which is also the point where airplane designers consider the aerodynamic forces of flight to be concentrated. The center of gravity is a significant factor in such areas as calculating the stability and the maneuverability of an airplane, though that is a factor we generally leave to the engineers.

The Four Forces

Four opposing forces act on a plane during flight: lift, weight, thrust, and drag. When an airplane is flying straight and level, lift works upward and is opposed by weight, which acts toward the earth. Thrust is the propelling force that gives an airplane the speed required to stay aloft, and it is opposed by drag, the force which tends to slow down an airplane. Let's examine each of these forces a little more closely.

Lift: The Gift of Newton and Bernoulli

Lift is the force that makes flight possible for any aircraft that relies on an *airfoil,* including airplanes, gliders, and helicopters. (You'll learn in Chapter 11, "Up, Up, and Away: Hot-Air Balloons," that balloon and blimp flights are made possible by buoyancy.) Simply put, lift is the force that pushes an airplane upward.

Lift is not produced by a single force or property. Instead, it is a combination of two forces that work together. We'll look at one component of lift that can be characterized by a law of physics first written down by Newton, and another, more subtle form that was the brainchild of a lesser-known physicist named Daniel Bernoulli.

By the Book

An **airfoil** is a surface that generates an aerodynamic force because of its shape. A wing is an airfoil, as is a horizontal and vertical stabilizer, and even the propeller.

For Every Action ...

Sir Isaac Newton, the eighteenth-century philosopher, mathematician, physicist, and man for all seasons, put down in writing one of the laws of motion that explains the first element of lift. To paraphrase, Newton wrote that every action causes a reaction of equal force and in an opposite direction.

To understand what this means in terms of airplane flight, think of a wing as a simple flat metal plate. If we place that flat plate in a steady stream of moving air, such as in a wind tunnel, and position the plate so that it is perfectly streamlined in the wind, the air above and

Turbulence

This discussion of lift and other aerodynamic forces is going to stop short of the extreme detail that pilots and engineers like to indulge in. Those who crave the mathematical minutiae can find plenty of excellent resources in Appendix C, "Recommended Reading."

below the plate will flow past at the same speed and no lift will be created. But if we tilt the plate upward in the air stream, some of the air will strike the bottom of the plate and deflect downward. In Newton's words, the plate has "acted" on the air stream by changing its direction. The "reaction" is a force pushing in the opposite direction, upward. Voilà—lift.

Pressure

As I hinted earlier, there's a little more to it than that. A Swiss mathematician named Daniel Bernoulli was working on complex formulas that explained changing pressure caused by flowing masses of water when he derived a formula, now called the Bernoulli equation, that explains lift. Here's what Bernoulli discovered, and what gave birth to a million aerodynamic equations: When a fluid accelerates past an obstruction, like the surface of a wing, its pressure decreases. To be precise, a special case of Bernoulli's equation says that [pressure + ($\frac{Density}{2}$ × (velocity)^2)] equals a constant value—at least in an open, continuous flow of fluid. In other words, increased velocity results in decreased pressure.

On Course

Because the Bernoulli equation is such a crucial part of understanding the lift force that affects airplanes and other objects in flight, you might think Daniel Bernoulli had a direct interest in aviation when he derived his famous equation. Actually, he was working on a mathematical process related to water flow when his equation occurred to him. He died in 1782, one year before the Montgolfier brothers invented a balloon for the first human flight.

Actually, the principle can be explained pretty simply. Wings are shaped with an upper surface that is curved, or "cambered" (to use the aviation term), and a lower surface that is much less curved. When an airplane is in flight, some air is going over the top, curved surface, and some is going under the bottom, flatter surface. Because the air moving over the top, curved part of the wing must move faster to cover more surface than the air moving under the bottom, flat part of the wing, the pressure of the air on top drops slightly.

That small pressure difference is the key to creating lift, because high school physics tells us that an area of high pressure tends to move toward an area of low pressure. In flight, that means the higher pressure below the wing tries to move toward the lower pressure above. Because the body of the wing is in the way, the high-pressure air takes the wing along with it, lifting it as it goes.

In brief, that's the concept that put magic in the smooth curve of an airplane's wing. Together with Newton's law of action and reaction, Bernoulli's equation provides the explanation of the physics of flight.

Lift Has Its Limits

Engineers have created a large variety of airfoil designs based on whether they want their planes to make use primarily of Newton's action-reaction lift or Bernoulli's low-pressure lift. The type of lift depends on the type of plane and the type of flying it will be expected to do.

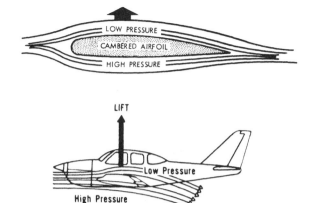

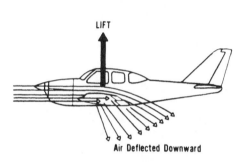

When Bernoulli joins forces with Newton, the result is lift.

(FAA *Flight Training Handbook)*

If you slice a wing from leading edge to trailing edge, you see its cross section. Some cross sections have a stout, thick shape. These generally produce a lot of Bernoulli-style lift thanks to the highly curved upper surface, and enable the plane to fly at relatively low speeds of 50 to 60 m.p.h. You find these wings on general aviation airplanes and any others that need to fly slowly.

Other wing cross sections are nearly as slender as the cross section of a knife blade. These wings produce very little lift on the basis of their shape, so they rely on high-powered engines, usually jets, that can produce lots of speed. You generally find knifelike wings on high-speed jet fighters and civilian planes like the Concorde, which create tremendous engine power, or thrust. These wings rely less on Bernoulli's low-pressure lift and more on Newton's action-reaction lift.

The Angle of Attack

Every wing has a limit to how slowly it can fly, and that limit is based on its *angle of attack*. Whenever a plane flies too slowly for the wing's angle of attack to produce lift, the wing "stalls," and the plane quickly starts descending.

109

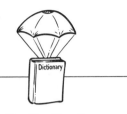

Sometimes you hear news reports about an airplane "stalling." Those reports usually don't have anything to do with the engine stalling as can happen sometimes to a car on a hot day. They usually are referring to a wing stall. If a wing stall happens at an altitude high enough for the pilot to recover, the only result is a shaken-up pilot. But if it happens at a low altitude, such as during an approach to landing, the plane often hits the ground before it can recover enough speed to keep flying. Those kinds of accidents make up most of the accidents on approach to landing. Flight instructors spend a lot of time drilling their students on maintaining safe speed during the approach to landing.

Carry That Weight

Weight, or acceleration caused by gravity, is the most familiar of the four forces of flight, because it's something we encounter each day. In straight and level flight, weight gradually decreases as fuel is burned during flight. Other than that, weight is a constant, at least whenever the airplane is flying straight and not climbing.

But during turning flight, the centrifugal force created during the turn adds to the weight of the plane. In very steep turns, the centrifugal force can double the apparent weight of an airplane. Of course, no mass has been added to the plane, but the centrifugal force caused by the turn makes everything feel heavier.

Manufacturers limit the maximum weight that a plane can weigh at takeoff because of the strength that must be built into the plane's structure to withstand the punishment of turbulence and harsh handling of controls by pilots.

What a Drag

Lift is a marvel, but it's not free. For every ounce of lift created by an airplane's wings and other control surfaces, we pay a price in drag, a force that works to slow the plane down. It is because of drag that we have to equip airplanes with engines to produce thrust (which we'll get to in a minute). There are two primary forms of drag: parasite drag and induced drag.

Parasite Drag

Parasite drag is easy to visualize: Think of the force you feel on your hand when you stick it out the car window at highway speed. The same force acts on the airplane as it flies. The structure of the airplane is sleek and aerodynamic, but it still creates a lot of wind resistance.

We call this component of parasite drag "flat-plate drag." To arrive at an airplane's flat-plate drag ratio, airplane designers look at all the surface area on an airplane and make some allowances for the drag-reducing qualities of its design. By arriving at a flat-plate drag ratio, designers are saying that the surface area of an airplane is equal to the drag of an imaginary flat plate of a certain size.

For example, a small, two-seat Cessna 152 has a flat-plate area of slightly over 6 square feet. That's pretty small considering how much total surface area the airplane has. But by comparison to other planes, the Cessna 152 is a "dirty," or drag-intensive, airplane. The Beechcraft Bonanza sports a flat-plate area of only 3.5 square feet, and the sleekest of all mass-produced general aviation airplanes, the Mooneys, have a flat-plate area of around 2.8 square feet.

Another component of parasite drag is the wind resistance caused by skin friction. If you examine the skin of an airplane at a microscopic level, you'll see a jagged surface with lots of nooks and cavities that are too small for us to feel, but more than large enough for air molecules to hide in. Like small eddies along a riverbank that hold water stationary while the stream nearby flows rapidly, the jagged irregularities on a plane's surface hold a thin layer of air perfectly still, even though the airplane might be moving at a very high speed. As you move a little farther from the plane, but still at a microscopic distance, the air moves a little faster, and at a few millimeters from the skin, the wind is moving at full speed. The viscosity of the air, or its resistance to flowing smoothly, is to blame. That viscosity adds to parasite drag.

Induced Drag

In addition to parasite drag, which is caused by the physical structure of the airplane, airplanes must also overcome "induced drag," which is an unavoidable byproduct of lift. A wing's lift doesn't actually produce lift that is directed straight up. In fact, the lift is directed slightly backward.

On Course

Some flight instructors dust part of the airplane's skin with talcum powder to demonstrate the fact that the jagged surface of the airplane's skin holds air still at a microscopic level. Because talc is so light, is should blow off the airplane at high speed. But because the powder is so fine that it settles into the microscopic nooks in the wing, it is sheltered from the main flow of air, just as air molecules are. At the end of the flight, no matter how fast the plane moved, the talc will still be where it was before the flight.

Lift is generated in a perpendicular direction to the "chord line," which is an imaginary straight line connecting the wing's leading edge to its trailing edge. In flight, the wing is inclined slightly upward in the front, meaning the chord line is inclined at an angle, too. The lift force, therefore, is tilted backward slightly.

To return to high school physics for a moment, a force that is acting at an angle can be mathematically divided into its vertical and horizontal components. Most of an airplane's lift is directed upward, but it has a backward component as well. That component is the induced drag.

The higher the airspeed, the lower the amount of induced drag. The higher speed increases the wing's Bernoulli-type lift. The pilot can decrease the angle of attack by pitching the nose slightly downward. When the angle of attack is decreased, the chord line doesn't tilt upward as much as it does at slow speed, and a flatter angle of attack—a negative angle of attack is possible even at very high speed—shortens the backward component of the total lift, or the induced drag.

By the Book

Thrust is force that must be generated to counteract drag. Some airplanes are equipped with piston engines that turn a propeller. Others are powered by jet engines, which heat large volumes of air by burning kerosene or some other fuel. The heated, expanded air accelerates out of the engine's exhaust, creating power to drive the airplane forward.

Some large planes, particularly jets, feature angle of attack meters that display the precise angle between the relative wind and the wing's chord line, but in smaller planes, pilots use airspeed as a rough measure of angle of attack—low speed means high angle of attack and a potential danger of reaching stall speed.

That's not to say that total drag decreases at high speed. Total drag is very high at low speed, when induced drag accounts for most of it, and decreases as speed increases. But at some speed, which is different for each type of wing, the increase in parasite drag overtakes the decrease in induced drag, and drag increases with speed.

Thrust: The Driving Force

Airplanes need *thrust* to provide the forward speed that the wings transform into lift.

Thrust is what we get when an engine takes in air and accelerates it. When the air gains velocity, it causes thrust. When thrust and drag are in balance, an airplane's speed stays constant. When thrust is greater than drag, speed increases, and when thrust is less than drag, the plane slows down.

A propeller generates a thrust force by taking a relatively large amount of air and accelerating it by a small amount. A jet engine takes a relatively small amount of air and accelerates it a lot. Either way, the result is thrust.

Plane Talk

Saving weight on an airplane is a constant consideration for airplane engineers. Even on large airplanes with very powerful engines, there is a limit to how much equipment can be carried. That's because each model of airplane has a maximum weight it can carry safely. In addition to the basic weight of the empty airplane, you have to add the weight of fuel and the weight of passengers and cargo. So any luxury equipment, such as air-conditioning units and on-board bathrooms, reduce the amount of fuel the plane can carry (and that means reduced flying time) as well as the passenger and cargo capacity. If you think it's no fun flying in a modern jetliner, with no leg room, it'll take some adjusting to get used to the Spartan conditions of a small airplane.

Jet-Powered Thrust

Jet engines, or to call them by their full name, turbojet engines, rely on the principle that high-pressure air shot out of one end of an engine creates a force in the opposite direction.

In a jet engine, normal atmospheric air is allowed in at one end of the engine, is compressed and mixed with fuel, and then ignited. The explosion causes the burning mixture of fuel and air to expand and shoot out of an exhaust pipe. Whichever direction the exhaust shoots out, a force is created in the opposite direction that can be harnessed to accelerate an airplane—or a speed boat or anything else that you attach the engine to, for that matter.

Since jets were first invented in the 1930s, they've grown to be a lot more powerful, a lot more reliable, and a lot quieter. They now produce so much power thrust that engineers are building larger airplanes that carry more than 500 people in luxurious comfort.

Making All the Moves

The forces of flight come alive when a pilot or flight student puts one hand on the control, the other hand on the engine throttle control, and presses her feet to the rudder pedals. Once the airplane is in flight, at a safe altitude for some practice flying and in an area mostly free of other airplanes, she can experiment with lift, weight, thrust, and drag.

Plane Talk

Almost every model of airplane is equipped with dual controls, meaning that each of the front seats has a set of rudder pedals and a control column within easy reach. This allows a flight instructor to fly along and easily reach the controls to demonstrate a maneuver. Airplane pilots generally sit in the left seat, which is the seat an airline captain sits in, and the right seat is either for flight instructors, co-pilots in large airplanes, or passengers in small planes. The presence of dual controls means nonpilots will sometimes have the flight controls within easy reach, but anyone who is not a pilot or student pilot should never touch the controls without the pilot's permission.

On Course

I often use the word "gently" when I refer to making a control movement. That's because pilots are rarely gentle enough in making control movements, or as I prefer to think of them, control *pressures*. Flying is an exercise in grace and subtlety. Abrupt or excessively large control movements make for rough, uncomfortable flights. And besides, they lack beauty. Gentle control movements hold part of the secret to beautiful flying.

In Control

One of the things a student pilot learns during a first flight is the function of the control column. The control column moves forward and backward as well as left and right. The control column is directly related to lift. Remember, when lift exceeds weight, the airplane climbs, and when lift is less than weight, the plane descends.

There are two ways for the pilot to increase lift: by pulling the control column gently backward or adding engine power by pushing the throttle control forward. In practice, a pilot would probably do a little of both, but we'll see what each does separately.

When the pilot pulls the control column backward, the elevator controls tilt slightly upward on the horizontal stabilizer. The relative wind strikes the up-tilted surface and produces a Newtonian reaction downward. When the tail is forced down, the nose is tilted upward. The wings also tilt up, increasing the angle of attack and creating lift.

Another way to add lift is to increase the thrust. When the pilot adds engine power by pushing the throttle forward, the airplane begins to accelerate.

When the relative wind speeds up, the pressure of the air flowing over the wings drops further, and Bernoulli's lift takes over. The airplane climbs.

Experienced pilots know that if they carefully coordinate the change in both pitch and power, the airplane flies more smoothly. If a pilot pitches the airplane up, for example, without adding power, it will take just a few seconds for the plane to slow down and begin to descend again. It would be like starting up a hill in your car without continually pressing the accelerator; pretty soon you wouldn't go any higher, and the steeper the hill, the faster you would lose speed.

Turn, Turn, Turn

Another thing a pilot learns early on is how to turn. Turning an airplane seems simple—you just bank the airplane while staying at the same altitude. But in truth, every turn requires a smooth coordination of the elevators, the ailerons, and the rudder.

To begin a turn, a pilot first looks for *traffic,* other airplanes, in the direction she is going to turn.

Once the pilot is sure there are no planes in the direction she's going to turn, she makes a gentle bank to the right by moving the aileron controls. The movement of the control column is almost identical to the turning of a steering wheel in making a right turn in a car.

When the control column is turned toward the right, the aileron on the right wing deflects upward; at the same time the aileron on the left wing deflects downward. That's because the ailerons are rigged to always move in opposite directions to each other.

The relative wind strikes the turned-up aileron on the right wing, pushing the wing slowly downward. By the same token, the rushing

By the Book

The word that pilots use to refer to other airplanes flying nearby is **traffic.** Before any maneuver, in fact at all times during flight, pilots should be scanning for traffic. Airplanes in the sky are often hard to see, particularly on bright, hazy days. So it's important to beware of air traffic during flight maneuvers, as well as at all other times.

Turbulence

If you think flying is a very physical activity, think again. Most airplanes are designed to save the pilot from having to do much work. A "trim" control relieves any pressure the pilot might have to hold onto the control column for any length of time, and at most the pilot might move the controls a few inches in any direction. The most physical exercise during a long flight comes in reaching back for the sandwich in your flight bag.

On Course

It sometimes takes a keen eye to see the subtle movements of the ailerons, especially in a jetliner that's flying very fast. That's because the speed of the relative wind flowing across the wings is so fast that the ailerons only need to move a millimeter or so to take effect. The slower the airplane flies, the more noticeable the movement will be, because slower air is less effective. Larger deflections are needed to control the airplane's bank angle.

over the left wing creates even more lift than usual because the down-turned aileron gives the wing an exaggerated curve. (You'll recall that the curved upper surface of the wing is what gives it lift, and greater curve means greater lift.)

Now the rudders come into the picture. When the ailerons are being used, each wing experiences different amounts of drag. The wing that is swinging upward has more lift, but with extra lift comes extra drag.

While the left wing is rising and feeling more drag, the right wing is dropping. Because it's losing lift, it is also feeling less drag. So even though the pilot wants to turn right, she's noticing the drag of the left wing is pulling the nose slightly to the left.

The solution is a small foot pressure on the right rudder pedal. Even a small amount of rudder pressure will move the rudder surface enough to keep the nose turning right, counteracting the left-turning tendency created by the differences in aileron drag. Of course, the same principles apply to left turns, which require a slight pressure on the left rudder pedal.

The elevator controls must also be used during a turn—even if the pilot doesn't want to climb or descend. Imagine the bank angle has been established at, say, 30 degrees. Because lift acts directly perpendicular to the wings, the lift force is acting at a 30-degree angle from straight up.

But weight always acts straight down. Let's say the airplane weighs 2,500 pounds. No matter what the bank angle, the weight remains constant. But when the wings bank and the lift force is deflected, the lift is no longer opposite to the direction of weight. Now, with the lift pointed sideways, the weight exceeds lift. Unless the pilot does something, the plane will start a slow descent.

In order to restore the lost lift, the pilot pulls back gently on the control column, increasing the wings' angle of attack and restoring lift.

And, finally, because the pilot is creating extra lift, she's also creating more drag. That means she has to increase the throttle to provide the extra thrust to balance the increased drag.

Here we have one of the simplest of maneuvers, the basic turn. But it involves all the flight controls the pilot has at her disposal. The ailerons are deflected, the rudder is pressed, the elevators come into play, and the throttle balances the increase in drag.

With practice, the turn, like most of the maneuvers of flight, becomes second nature.

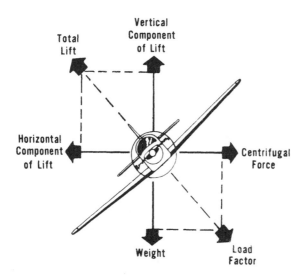

Total
Lift

Vertical
Component
of Lift

Horizontal
Component
of Lift

Centrifugal
Force

Weight

Load
Factor

A turning airplane creates centrifugal force that makes the airplane behave as if it has gained weight.

(FAA *Flight Training Handbook*)

The Least You Need to Know

➤ Lift combines simple "action-reaction" force with the gentle but effective force of low-pressure air.

➤ Drag takes a stern toll on an airplane, and engineers work hard to reduce it.

➤ Thrust, which opposes drag, is caused when an engine accelerates air using a propeller or a jet engine.

➤ The airplane's control surfaces are used together to create the basic maneuvers of flight.

Chapter 9

Soaring on Silent Wings: Gliding

In This Chapter

➤ When it comes to gliders, thin is in

➤ The "big quiet": the one advantage gliders have over powered planes

➤ The aerodynamics of glider flight

➤ The enormous power source of the engineless glider

➤ Becoming a glider pilot

For some, the beginning of summer is not signaled by the first pitch of a baseball team or by the beginning of school vacation. No, for those who love gliders and glider flying, summer truly begins the day they see the first glider circling overhead in the gentle grip of a sun-powered upward rush of air.

In most regions of the United States, glider flying is a sport that must be enjoyed during the few warm months when the sun's warmth and steady but benign winds provide the energy gliders require in order to spend hours at a time in silent, birdlike flight.

The Glider and the Plane

Perhaps the best way to start looking into the world of gliding is by comparing the glider to the airplane.

When you look at a glider resting beside a conventional powered airplane, one of the first things you notice is how long and skinny the wings are. Compared to those of a glider, the broad wings of an airplane look like a pair of barn doors.

The glider also sits very low to the ground. In fact, it sits so low that you might not be certain it has any landing gear at all. But if you bend down, you can see the curve of the rubber tire peeping out of a little cave where it mostly hides out of the airstream. That's your first sign that glider designers are obsessed with reducing air resistance. They never stop fussing about drag and how to reduce it.

Max Karst flies his ASW-15B over the mountain-tops of the Cascade Range east of Seattle.

(Vince Miller)

Plane Talk

Sleek modern gliders are a far cry from the pioneering gliders that Otto Lilienthal and the Wright brothers built in the very early days of flight. (See Chapters 1 and 2 for more on these great aviation innovators.) Early experimental gliders were largely responsible for perfecting the shape of wings and the engineering techniques used to make aircraft strong and durable. That meant they were often unsophisticated and bulky. Lilienthal didn't survive the experimental phase of his research into flight, but the Wright brothers picked up his baton and refined his gliders into the first airplanes. All fixed-wing aviators trace their legacy to Lilienthal and his gliders.

You also notice how the glider is tipped over onto one side. It rests on one wingtip or the other because there's only the one tire under the cockpit. There's nothing like the conventional airplane's two main landing gear plus a nose wheel to stabilize it on the ground.

What's more, you see that the body and skin of the glider are amazingly "clean"— that is, there are no parts of it that jut into the air. The skin, which is usually made of Fiberglas or some other very light material, is buffed and polished until it gleams. The light weight of the Fiberglas is a testament to the glider designers' aversion to excess weight, which is almost as pathological as their fear of drag.

That careful attention to reducing drag and weight is due to the final difference between the glider and the conventional airplane: The glider has no engine. How is it possible, you ask, for a plane to fly without an engine? Read on!

Thin Is In

Because gliders don't carry their own source of power, they are designed to waste as little energy as possible. One of the glider design's hallmarks is its long, skinny wings, which have a far higher *aspect ratio* than the wings of most powered airplanes. This special shape helps reduce induced drag, the kind of drag that is created as a by-product of lift. (For a review of the forces of flight, including lift and drag, turn back to Chapters 7, "How Airplanes Fly, Part 1: The Parts of a Plane," and 8, "How Airplaines Fly, Part 2: The Aerodynamics of Flight.")

Nice Pair of Wingtips

Ask an aerodynamicist what the most efficient wing is, and she'd say "One that has no wing-tips." Of course, every wing has to have a tip of some sort, since every wing has to end somewhere. So what does this curious statement mean? Let's find out.

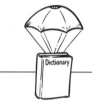

By the Book

Aspect ratio is an aerodynamics formula that measures how skinny or squat a wing is. It divides the wing's span by its front-to-back chord. That comparison means that a narrow wing, like a glider's, will have a higher aspect ratio than the wing of a powered airplane.

As we saw in Chapter 8, the curved, or "cambered," upper surface of the wing creates an area of low pressure, or pressure that is at least lower than the air traveling along the bottom side of the wing. Physics tells us that the relatively high-pressure air under the wing has a natural tendency to migrate toward the area of low pressure above. For the most part, the wing's structure gets in the way, but there's one place on every wing where the high-pressure air below can see its way clear to the low-pressure air above: the wingtip.

*Vince Miller follows Max
Karst down a ridge of the
Cascade foothills near
Seattle.*

(Vince Miller)

Because the high-pressure air has an escape route at the wing tip, the air below the wing takes on a slightly "spanwise flow," as designers would call it. In other words, instead of flowing straight from the leading edge toward the trailing edge, the high-pressure air under the wing shuffles slightly toward the wingtip. And the *closer* to the wingtip the air moves, the more *rapidly* it moves.

At the very tip of the wing, the high-pressure air swirls upward, creating a little tornado of twisting air called a "vortex." This vortex creates a force that pulls backward on the wing in the form of drag. To reduce this drag, aerodynamicists discovered that if air has less distance to travel over from the wing's leading edge to its trailing edge, the spanwise flow can be reduced. So they shaped the wing as thin as possible, while lengthening them to keep the same total area.

With the spanwise flow reduced, the power of the wingtip vortex is weakened, and a weak vortex means less drag.

Plane Talk

Aircraft designers are smart folks. They figure, if the wingtip vortex is always going to be there anyway, why not make it do a little work? They answered that question by turning the very end of the wing upward to create a "winglet." A winglet looks like someone has bent a couple of feet of both wingtips straight up and down. This shape helps squeeze a little bit of upward lift from the wingtip vortex.

Wheels Can Be a Drag

Of the different types of drag, parasite drag (see Chapter 8) takes the most massive toll on fixed-wing flyers. A glider's lack of power makes it even more important to reduce parasite drag as much as possible.

In a conventional small airplane, one of the biggest culprits in producing parasite drag is the landing gear. Landing gear is needed only twice during flight, during take-off and landing, but it sticks out in the wind for the duration of the flight anyway. And planes that are designed to retract the gear during flight pay a penalty in the extra weight and complexity of all the hydraulics and motors that make the gear move up and down.

A glider can afford neither of these luxuries, so glider designers usually equip their craft with only a single wheel, right below the cockpit. They shelter the wheel as much as possible inside the smooth, aerodynamically clean fuselage. The small curve of the wheel that peeps out of its well has a lot smaller effect on parasite drag than the three wheels and wheel struts that are typical on conventional airplanes. And it certainly weighs less than a lot of hydraulics and motors.

Nevertheless, in some high-performance gliders, the wheel is retractable, just like the gear on high-performance airplanes and jetliners. The single wheel can be pulled up into the body of the glider during flight with a simple lightweight mechanism to cut down even further on parasite drag; the wheel can be lowered just before landing.

Taking Off

Glider pilots can orchestrate their takeoffs in a couple of ways. The most common method is the tow plane, a conventional powered airplane that uses a rope to drag a

By the Book

Glider pilots typically prefer to fly from their own airports, which they call glider ports, or **sailports.** The reason is that by FAA regulation, gliders have the right of way over powered aircraft in approaching the airport—after all, an unpowered glider only has one chance to get the landing right. Gliders can easily disrupt the flow of airplanes in and out of many airports; glider-only airports are less intrusive.

glider a couple of thousand feet above the ground before the glider releases the rope. The glider's flight begins as the tow plane returns to the airport.

At some glider airports, or *sailports,* a car is used to do the same thing. A driver races the car down the runway with the glider in tow. The glider lifts off behind the accelerating car, and when it's high enough, the pilot pulls a knob to release the tow rope. The glider flies away, and the car returns to its start point to tow the next glider.

At some glider airports a stationary winch is used to tug the glider into the sky. A rope is unspooled from the winch and attached to the glider. On a signal from the pilot, the winch is engaged, and the motorized spool reels in the rope with enough speed that the glider is able to develop enough lift to take off. At the right altitude, the pilot pulls a release knob inside the cockpit to disconnect from the rope.

However the pilot chooses to manage it, the idea is the same: to get the glider high into the sky, where it can find enough energy in the atmosphere to keep it flying.

Contestants prepare their sailplanes for a day of competition in a National Sports Class Contest sponsored by the Seattle Glider Council. The contest was held at the Ephrata, Washington, airport.

(Vince Miller)

The Glider's "Engine"

Glider designers may have dispensed with the engine, but that doesn't mean gliders fly without power. True, gliders don't carry their own powerplant with them, like an airplane. Still, they do use energy to get aloft, and they use energy to stay aloft as long as possible. It's just that the power comes from somewhere else—the atmosphere. Gliders are designed with so much lift and so little drag that they are perfectly suited to absorb energy from the atmosphere in the form of heat and wind.

Thermal Power

As we'll see in Chapter 17, "Talking About the Weather," the sun is the driving power behind virtually every force in the atmosphere. One of the forces powered by the sun is the daily cycle of thermals. Each day, the sun's heat warms the air near the ground, decreasing its density and causing it to lift in giant globules of hot air called "thermals." Once a thermal breaks free from the ground, it bubbles upwards at a rate of thousands of feet per minute.

Thermals form most readily on southward-facing slopes and in light winds. Glider pilots know what kind of terrain is most likely to spawn thermals and are sensitive to the telltale signs of them. When a pilot flies into one, she'll feel a gentle—or a not-so-gentle—"kick in the pants," a mild shudder followed by a slight sensation of heaviness.

On Course

You might have a tabletop thermal generator up in the attic or in your kids' rooms—the lava lamp. Lava lamps work on the same principle as thermals, from the heating of a fluid, to the rising current, to the eventual cooling and sinking. Just as the light bulb in a lava lamp powers the lamp's fluid currents, the sun powers the earth's thermal activity.

The shudder is the first jolt of upward-moving air striking the bottom of the fuselage and wings. A particularly high-powered thermal can give the glider a solid jolt, which is followed right away by upward acceleration. The acceleration makes the pilot begin to feel slightly heavier.

Sometimes a pilot will feel one wing rise slightly more than the other, a sure signal of which direction to turn in order to stay within the rising packet of air. As soon as she feels the thump of the thermal, the pilot banks steeply into a turn, and continues to circle as long as the lift continues. Once a thermal peters out, the pilot comes out of the turn and starts seeking another thermal.

Plane Talk

Despite the seeming contradiction, a small family of gliders do carry their own engines. Motor gliders are particularly popular in Europe, but have a loyal following around the world. A small, lightweight engine allows these gliders to stay in the air longer than they might otherwise be able to. Others even have engines with enough power to take off and climb to altitude, before the engine is turned off and the pilot glides to earth.

By the Book

Range currents are the winds that are deflected upward by the slopes of mountain. But their lift comes at a price. In addition to lifting the air and deflecting the wind skyward, mountain ranges can create powerful and complex eddies of wind that glider pilots learn to recognize and avoid.

Clouds are reliable signposts for lifting air. Thick, fluffy clouds called cumulus (see Chapter 17 for more on reading the clouds) are created by upward-moving columns of air. An observant glider pilot looks for straight-line cloud streets of cumulus clouds that betray the presence of vertical shafts of air. A well-developed cloud street can keep a pilot flying until the sun goes down.

Flying the Range

Even where there is too little solar energy to produce powerful thermals, there's another atmospheric engine that can be harnessed to power a glider: wind.

When wind blows against slopes of hills or a range of mountains, it is deflected upward. Glider pilots long ago learned exactly where the best lift is in this upward rush of air. *Range currents* supply some of the most reliable lift a glider pilot could hope for, and experienced pilots can use a combination of cloud streets and range lift to make long cross-country flights that last hours and cover hundreds of miles—all without a drop of gasoline!

Landing the Glider

Glider pilots approach the airport for landing at about 1,000 feet above the ground, at a 45-degree angle to the runway they have decided to land on or that other gliders are using. The runway in use will generally be the one that points into the wind, giving planes that are landing and taking off the advantage of a headwind.

By the time he has approached within ¼ mile or so of the runway, the glider pilot turns to parallel the runway, but flies downwind, that is on the "downwind" traffic pattern leg. The downwind is entered at roughly 600 to 700 feet above the ground.

With the runway still parallel to him, say to his left, the pilot flies downwind until the point on the runway where he intends to land is slightly behind him. That's when he begins a 90-degree turn toward the runway (to the left). Once the turn is complete, altitude should be about 500 feet from the ground, and the landing point should be ahead of the pilot and to his left.

On Course

Like cacti and old prospectors, glider pilots thrive in the heat. One of the hotbeds of gliding is the Mojave Desert, where I got my first taste of the sport. Pearblossom is one of the sun-baked towns where thousands of glider pilots ride summertime thermals for hours at a time. In the morning, as the sun starts baking the desert, the drone of tow planes begins, and it doesn't end until nearly sundown. Throughout the day, the sky is thick with gliders.

When he approaches the imaginary extended line of the runway, the pilot begins a 90-degree turn onto the final approach leg. Once the turn onto final approach is complete, the glider should be at an altitude of 200 to 300 feet and descending exactly in line with the center of the runway.

As he descends, the pilot uses a combination of elevator control and spoilers to help him remain pointed directly at his intended landing spot. If he appears to be falling short of his aim point, he closes the spoiler and uses the best airspeed to add distance to his glide. If he's gliding too long, he will use spoilers and perhaps a maneuver called a slip that increases drag by flying the glider slightly sideways to the wind.

When he's about 10 feet off the ground, the pilot uses the elevator controls to raise the nose to a level attitude in preparation for landing. The plane will glide a short distance beyond the aim point the pilot used during his approach, which the pilot has already accounted for in selecting his approach.

By the time the gentle level-off maneuver, or flare, is complete, the glider will be a couple of feet off the ground, and the pilot will use the spoilers to help bring the glider gently to the ground in a smooth landing.

Gliding Conditions

A glider is at home almost any place where the sun shines and the wind blows, but some regions offer better gliding conditions than others. Desert regions heat quickly with the morning sun and quickly generate high-energy thermals that give gliders a powerful boost.

A prominent mountain ridge in the presence of a steady wind becomes an updraft generator of unequaled power. Combine the desert climate with the topology of the desert Southwest, and you have all the best ingredients for good gliding.

Of course, gliding is popular in every region of the country and around the world, even in many northern latitudes. In the absence of supercharged thermals and ridge currents, glider pilots learn to make the best of the wind and sunshine they have.

In the Cockpit

Glider cockpits are far less complex than those of conventional airplanes. The pilot uses a stick rather than a control column, and the instrument panel is dominated by a big red knob that disconnects the tow rope when the glider has reached the proper height.

The instrument panel generally includes an airspeed indicator, an altimeter, a g-meter (to register the number of gs a pilot reaches during aerobatics, a subject we discuss in detail in Chapter 16, "Cloud Dancing: Air Shows and Aerobatics"), and a variometer, a sensitive altimeter that quickly tells the pilot how many feet per minute she is climbing or descending. The variometer is important to a glider pilot, because it can be used in thermal flying to refine a flight path and take the very best advantage of the rising air.

A glider cockpit also features a spoiler control. With the lift of a lever, the pilot can raise narrow panels on the wings' upper surfaces, and sometimes on both the upper and lower surfaces, that disrupt the smooth flow of air over the wing and destroy lift. At the same time, the spoilers add a dash of drag.

When would the pilot want to destroy lift and increase drag? When landing. The spoilers can add a critical element of control for approaching the airport and maneuvering to a landing. That's because gliders are naturally sleek and difficult to slow down. Without spoilers, a little extra speed or altitude can turn a safe landing into a crackup.

There's one other instrument in the cockpit of a glider—a slip indicator. The slip indicator is a simply constructed instrument; it consists of a curved tube of fluid-filled glass with a ball resting in the bottom of the tube at the low part of the curve. The ball simply rolls to one side of the glass tube or the other, indicating whether a turn is "coordinated," meaning the tail follows directly behind the nose. In an uncoordinated turn, the tail either swings wide around the turn or slides inward to the inside of the turn. Either way, the sideways movement through the air adds drag, something that glider pilots try to avoid.

Turbulence

If the glider pilot begins to climb too early before the tow plane has lifted off the runway, the upward tug on the tow rope can send the tow plane out of control. Once aloft, the tow rope can become too slack and can foul the glider's controls. On rare occasions, the tow plane itself can be forced to release the tow rope, leaving the glider pilot with a dangling rope to get rid of before landing.

Gliders generally have simpler instrument panels than powered aircraft, and they often operate where elaborate communications equipment is not required. But for their simplicity, gliders demand an extra level of knowledge that powered pilots often take for granted.

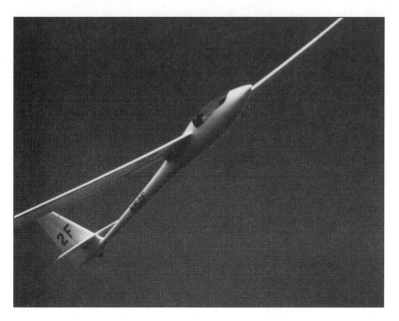

E.C. Welch completes his task with a "contest finish" (low and fast) over the Ephrata, Washington, airport.

(Vince Miller)

Turbulence

Gliders have no engines, but don't imagine that makes them unsafe. Glider pilots typically go flying only in good weather, which eliminates one of the most common causes of crashes—namely, bad weather. What's more, gliders are easily controlled and able to land at low speeds, taking most of the risk out of an emergency landing.

Glider pilots must develop a sixth sense about the behavior of wind, almost to the point of "seeing" the erratic curls and twists of the invisible air currents near mountains and beneath clouds.

What's more, glider pilots must be very good at planning their approach to the airport and at "sticking" the landing, or doing it right the first time. Though off-airport landings happen sometimes and are generally done safely, glider pilots develop very precise skills that enable them to reach the landing strip every time.

How Much Will It Cost?

One of the virtues of gliding is its low cost compared to other forms of flying. For example, a training program involving 20 air tows could cost as little as $650. And gliders are relatively inexpensive to buy, compared to an airplane. A glider in good condition can range in price from as little as $3,000 to $30,000 or more. Even at the top end of the price range, gliders can be purchased for a fraction of the cost of a powered airplane, not to mention a sport helicopter. Most pilots buy a trailer to help transport the glider, though that's not always necessary if you like to store it at your home airport. Still, when you combine the low cost of a glider with the low cost of an air tow, $20 or less per tow, gliding adds up to one of the least expensive forms of aviation.

For Nonpilots: Getting Started

For the beginning pilot who wants to make gliding his first entry into aviation, the same prerequisites apply as for powered airplanes. (See Chapter 13, "Getting Off the Ground: Becoming an Airplane Pilot," for a complete discussion of getting started in sport flying.)

Plane Talk

Many glider pilots like to fly alone, with no chatty passengers to spoil the solitude and quiet. Gliders, especially the high-performance ones, contain only one seat, but training gliders are always equipped with two, one for the instructor and one for the student.

The differences come in the amount of flight time a glider student spends in the air and what he practices. Here's a list of the possible options the FAA offers before qualifying someone for a private pilot certificate in gliders.

➤ Seventy solo glider flights, including 20 flights during which 360-degree turns are made.

➤ Seven hours of solo flight in gliders, including 35 glider flights launched by ground tow or 20 glider flights launched by air tows.

➤ Forty hours of flight time in gliders and single-engine airplanes, including 10 solo glider flights during which 360-degree turns are made.

Pilots who already have a private pilot certificate and at least 40 hours of time as pilot in command of an airplane (PIC) need only make a minimum of 10 solo flights in a glider to qualify to add a glider rating. Of course, they'll require some flight time with an instructor and some ground school to learn the ins and outs of gliding and how it differs from powered flying, but the regulations don't specify how much of each is necessary.

A private pilot must pass a practical test with an FAA-approved examiner before receiving his glider rating, but he won't have to take a written exam. (See Chapter 13 for a full discussion of the FAA testing process.)

For Power Pilots: Making the Transition

A power pilot's experience with controlling an airplane will help speed the learning process and trim time and money off the training costs for becoming a glider pilot. But a power pilot still has to pass FAA exams to become a certified glider pilot.

But note that for a pilot who already has a "power ticket," as glider pilots call a power-pilot certificate, making the transition from flying powered planes to flying gliders is more than simply learning how to control a different model of airplane. Glider flying is an entirely different kind of aviation, requiring a keen sensitivity to the atmosphere and the subtle signs of lift and wind, not to mention the grit of character that lets pilots set off for hours of flying with nothing but their wits to rely on.

The Least You Need to Know

➤ Gliders bear a resemblance to powered planes, but thin wings and trim bodies set them apart.

➤ Part of the appeal of gliders is the "big quiet" that comes from flying without an engine.

➤ Gliders fly by the power of sun and wind.

➤ Glider instrument panels feature the barest essentials, including the tow-rope release knob.

➤ Gliding is far less expensive to learn and to buy into than powered flying.

How Do Helicopters Fly?

Helicopter pilots and fanciers get plenty of ribbing from airplane folk. Airplane pilots like to say that, to be technically correct, helicopters don't actually "fly": They beat the air into submission. Others joke that helicopters don't use aerodynamics to fly: It's just that they're so ugly they repel the ground.

What's behind the light-hearted rivalry between *fixed-wing* and *rotary-wing* pilots? In a word, jealousy. The envy is on both sides. Airplanes fly faster than helicopters, they fly more smoothly, and they can dazzle spectators with wild feats of aerobatics. On the other hand, helicopters possess versatility that airplanes don't. They are able to take off and land almost vertically. That means they can safely make their way into small clearings and building tops that airplane pilots can only dream of. A helicopter pilot on a leisurely flight up the beautiful Pacific coast of California, for example, can land on a deserted stretch of beach for a picnic lunch.

And, contrary to the common myth, helicopters don't "fall out of the sky" if they lose engine power. They glide downward quite safely using a technique called autorotation, which we'll discuss later in this chapter.

By the Book

Heavier-than-air craft, which doesn't include balloons and airships, fall into one of two categories—fixed-wing and rotary-wing. **Fixed-wing** craft are those aircraft that get their lift from wings that don't move, while the lift-producing surfaces of **rotary-wing** craft spin around. Airplanes and gliders have fixed wings, while helicopters have rotary wings.

Igor Sikorsky's Wild Ride

Remember Leonardo da Vinci's first helicopter, which we discussed in Chapter 1, "The Earliest Aviators"? Well, it wasn't a very workable design, but it was one of the first sophisticated approaches to flying by using a rotating *airfoil*.

The idea was knocked around for a few hundred years until the twentieth century, when a gifted engineer named Igor Sikorsky cobbled together the first practical prototype of a modern helicopter.

Sikorsky was born in Kiev, in what is now Ukraine, in 1889. As a youngster, he read Jules Verne's air adventures and learned of Leonardo da Vinci's speculations on flight. Sikorsky was energized by news of the Wrights' flight in the United States and mesmerized by the dirigibles that Count Ferdinand von Zeppelin was building in Germany. His early enthusiasm for flying turned Sikorsky toward a career in aviation, where he excelled.

In his later years, Igor Sikorsky could look back at three major advances in aviation that he helped pioneer: multiengine airplanes, seagoing Clipper airplanes, and helicopters.

After graduating from engineering college in St. Petersburg, Sikorsky tinkered with his helicopter designs. He built his first one, a flop, in 1909, at about the time pilots in Europe were first managing to duplicate the Wright brothers' controlled flight in a fixed-wing craft. Sikorsky built another helicopter in 1910, which actually managed to get off the ground, but only after he found a featherweight pilot brave—or foolhardy— enough to get into it.

Frankly, neither Sikorsky nor anyone else at the time knew enough about rotary-wing aerodynamics or engine design to provide a ghost of a chance of building a workable commercial helicopter.

Sikorsky put aside his helicopter work for a while and turned toward fixed-wing projects. In 1913, while working for a Russian railroad company, he built the world's first multiengine airplane, which featured a revolutionary enclosed cabin that enabled passengers to fly in comfort. It also featured an outdoor balcony equipped with a search light that allowed passengers to sightsee in daylight or at night. Sikorsky's plane even included the world's first airplane restroom!

By the Book

Any surface that is designed with a shape that helps it create a lifting force is called an **airfoil.** As we saw in detail in Chapters 7 and 8, rudders, elevators, ailerons, and propellers are airfoils, as are an airplane's wings and a helicopter's blades. In a helicopter, the airfoil usually has a rounded upper surface and a rounded lower surface. The leading edge of the airfoil, the one that cuts through the air first, is rounded, and the trailing edge tapers to a relatively sharp point.

Plane Talk

As a youngster, little Igor experimented with a toy that resembled a rubber-band– powered helicopter. The Wright brothers, too, were entranced by a toy helicopter their father gave them as a present. Is it merely a coincidence that the inventors of the first fixed-wing powered airplane and the father of the helicopter were inspired by rotary-wing dreams? Perhaps the answer to the helicopter's allure lies in its ability to move vertically, backward, fast, slow, even come to a full "stop" in the air. It's the realization of man's age-old dream to completely conquer flight.

By the Book

Helicopters receive their primary lifting force from one or more **rotors,** which are made up of long blades shaped so they will produce aerodynamic lift when rotated. That might sound simple, but crafting a rotor that not only produces lift but also is capable of increasing or decreasing its lift depending on pilot control, or is able to tilt toward the front, back, and sides for maneuverability, was perhaps the greatest engineering feat in aviation until the invention of the moon rockets.

Years later, Sikorsky turned his mind to bridging the ocean barrier between continents. From his New York factory not far from the same Roosevelt Field where Charles Lindbergh later departed for his historic Atlantic crossing (see Chapter 5, "Lindbergh, Earhart, and the Rise of the Airlines," for the full rundown on Lindbergh's flight), Sikorsky worked on designs for the "flying boats" that would later gain fame as the Pan American Clippers.

The success of the Clipper aircraft enabled Sikorsky to return, once and for all, to serious work on the helicopters that had fascinated him since his youth in Russia.

In 1931, Sikorsky patented the familiar pattern of one *main rotor* and one *tail rotor*. In 1939, his first prototype succeeded in flying for the first time. Over the next few years and following a number of crashes and continued refinement, Sikorsky designed the S-4, which became the first helicopter to be mass-produced.

Taming the Wild Rotor

The more you learn about rotary-wing aerodynamics and construction, the more you come to one conclusion: It's an absolute miracle that helicopters ever manage to get off the ground.

It may not have been a thing of beauty, but the VS-300 could boast the first practical helicopter design. Note the distinctive fedora hat worn by test pilot Igor Sikorsky.

As with so many pioneering aircraft, helicopters took off in popularity thanks to the military. The armed forces first put helicopters like the Sikorsky HNS-1 to work on rescue missions, and later added weapons and high-technology devices.

If that's true, then Igor Sikorsky was a miracle worker. In creating the first workable helicopters, Sikorsky had to do two things. He had to master the enormous complexity of a functional and durable rotor system. And he had to come to grips with aerodynamics even more complex than those that confronted the designers and pilots of fixed-wing airplanes.

Let's take a look at the fundamentals of what makes a helicopter fly, and how its distinctive combination of main rotor and tail rotor give it such versatility.

Plane Talk

When flying an aircraft as complex as a helicopter—which some people joke is no more than a thousand parts flying in close formation—early pilots wanted all the luck they could get. In the 1940s, some Marine pilots who flew Igor Sikorsky's earliest helicopters took it into their heads that the old genius's fedora might have some particular good luck attached to it. The fedora took on a superstitious aura, and Marine pilots found excuses to visit the inventor in hopes of doffing his hat for a few seconds, hoping for invincibility. After old Igor died in 1972, the hat was lost until a grandson happened upon it in an attic. The famed fedora is preserved in Sikorsky's office, which is now a museum.

On Course

Sikorsky's career was helped along thanks to another Russian, Sergei Rachmaninoff. After the young Sikorsky immigrated to United States, the famous conductor, composer, and pianist financed the aeronautical engineer's first successful airplane model, the Sikorsky 29A. One of the first uses Sikorsky found for his new 29A was to transport two of Rachmaninoff's pianos to New York for a performance.

Turbulence

There are plenty of rules and regulations that govern where a helicopter pilot can fly. Local laws and federal aviation regulations governing landing and operating an aircraft are dizzyingly complex. It takes a well-trained and fully informed pilot to sort them out. Make sure any pilot you fly with is up to date on regulations before landing anywhere except an approved airport.

The Dynamics of Helicopter Flight

If you were to slice through a rotor blade, you'd see a shape that looks like an elongated tear drop. The blade has a blunt leading edge, bulges out in the middle, and comes to a relatively sharp trailing edge. Put it all together, and you have an airfoil.

In an airplane, the fixed wings are the main airfoils that produce the bulk of the lift that helps the craft get off the ground. The propeller pulls the plane forward and creates a wind over the wings, which, in turn, generates lift.

Helicopters take away the "middle man." Instead of using the propeller to pull the plane rapidly through the air, helicopter engineers enlarged the propeller, turned it so it rotates horizontally, and spun it fast enough to generate all the lift itself. And instead of calling it a propeller, helicopter designers call it a rotor.

Imagine you're sitting in the cockpit of a helicopter and the rotor is starting to spin. You'll see the rotor blades swing around from your right side, past the front, then to the left. If you were looking down on the helicopter from above, the rotor blades would be sweeping counterclockwise. Remember that little fact. It'll be important in a few minutes when we talk about the purpose of the tail rotor.

As the engine turns, the rotor begins to spin faster, becoming a blur of color. When the rotor is turning really fast, it almost seems to take on the appearance of a disc, a solid object that measures the same diameter as the rotor blades when they are standing still.

In fact, that's what helicopter pilots and engineers call it—a rotor disc. And when they talk about the aerodynamic forces at work on the helicopter, they're mostly talking about what's happening in the main rotor disc.

Spinning Into Flight

Imagine the rotors are made of simple flat plates of metal. That's not the case, of course, because as we've seen, the rotor blades have a special airfoil shape. But to understand what forces are starting to take effect in the rotor disc as the blades spin faster and the helicopter prepares for flight, it helps to imagine the rotor blades as flat.

When the helicopter is on the ground and the pilot doesn't want it to take off yet, he positions the *collective pitch control* so that the blades are perfectly horizontal. It's as if you flattened the blades of a room fan so that the fan created no breeze.

Now let's say the rotors are spinning at full speed. Of course, like our room fan with the flattened blades, the rotor blades won't be creating much of a breeze. Imagine placing that fan on a slippery block of ice. It's easy to visualize that with flattened blades, even on the most slippery surface, the fan won't move.

By the Book

The **collective pitch control** is a lever located on the left side of the pilot's seat. It resembles a parking brake hand lever, but is more beefed up. Moving it up and down changes the amount of twist, or "pitch," of the rotor blades.

Now imagine you can somehow cause the spinning fan blades to regain their twist a few degrees. Immediately, the fan will begin producing a breeze. Not only that, on the slippery ice it will gradually begin to slide in the opposite direction that the breeze is blowing. The action of the fan blades regaining their twist is a room-fan version of collective pitch control, and the fan beginning to slide is the helicopter beginning to rise.

The force we've been talking about is lift, the simple reaction that happens, for example, when the wind blows a barn door shut. To paraphrase Sir Isaac Newton, every action produces a reaction, and in the case of a helicopter, the action of deflecting air downward produces a reaction, which is to drive the rotor blade upward, and the helicopter along with it.

When you calculate the weight of the air that is being deflected by a helicopter's spinning rotors at full speed, and you apply some aerodynamics formulas filled with Greek letters and plenty of algebra, you discover that a rotor produces more than enough force to enable the helicopter to fly.

Putting a Whole New Twist on It

Now that the rotor is turning at full speed, it's creating a force called torque. Torque is the measure of how much a force acting on an object causes it to rotate. At least that's its scientific definition. In practice, it means that when the rotor turns counterclockwise, the rest of the helicopter will tend to rotate clockwise.

By the Book

The **throttle** in a helicopter performs the same function that it does in a car or motorcycle. It connects to the engine and controls the amount of fuel being burned and the power output of the engine. In fact, a helicopter throttle is located on the collective pitch control and is a rotating handgrip exactly like those used on motorcycles.

Turbulence

There's a natural rivalry between airplane pilots and designers and helicopter pilots and designers. One of the ways this rivalry manifests itself is in terminology. You'll notice plenty of examples where helicopter pilots use different names for objects similar to those in an airplane. Helicopter pilots even fly from a different side of their craft than airplane pilots do: Helicopter pilots fly from the right side, airplane pilots from the left.

To counteract the torque effect, helicopter engineers created the antitorque rotor. That's the small rotor spinning in the tail of the helicopter, and it's controlled in the cockpit by two floor pedals called, logically enough, antitorque pedals. (Helicopter pilots are a literal bunch.)

If the antitorque rotor was not operating, here's what would happen. The pilot would use the *throttle* to spin the rotors at the proper number of revolutions per minute, or rpms, for flight. With his left hand, he would pull up on the collective pitch control, which would increase the pitch of the blades, as we've just seen. The lift created by the rotor disc would slowly lift the helicopter off the ground. And then all hell would break loose.

Because the rotor is spinning in a counterclockwise direction, as viewed from the top, a helicopter without an antitorque rotor would begin spinning in the opposite direction as soon as it broke free of friction on the ground. (It would spin in the opposite direction because of old Ike Newton, remember, who said every reaction is opposite of every action. Since the rotor is spinning in one direction, the body of the helicopter would spin in the other.) The antitorque rotor, which spins about six times faster than the main rotor because its smaller size means it must work harder for the same effect, is used to stop that spinning.

The helicopter designer, in effect, took a smaller version of the main rotor, tipped it on its left side, and mounted it on the tail, which has a tendency to swing in a clockwise direction. The blades are angled in such a way that when the antitorque rotor is spinning, its force tends to push the tail in a counterclockwise direction, which counteracts the main rotor's torque.

In essence, then, the antitorque pedals perform the same role for the tail rotor as the collective pitch control performs for the main rotor. They alter the angle of the blades to adjust for changes in main-rotor torque when the pilot changes power.

Because the natural torque effect on the helicopter is in a clockwise, or "right-turn," direction, when a pilot presses down on the right antitorque pedal, the tail rotor blades flatten to produce less force. That lets the natural torque effect take over and rotate the helicopter to the right. On the other hand, when the pilot applies left-foot pressure, the tail-rotor blades go to a higher pitch, causing the helicopter to rotate toward the left.

Going Places

So far, we've seen how the helicopter lifts off the ground by increasing the pitch, and thereby the lift, of the main rotor. We've also seen how the antitorque rotor prevents the helicopter from spinning in circles. Now, we'll look at how the helicopter moves forward, backward, and side to side.

To begin, visualize the main rotor disc as a solid object. The lift it creates can be thought of as a force arrow sticking out of the disc and pointing exactly perpendicular to it, or in the example we've been looking at so far, straight upward.

Turbulence

Whatever you do, don't call the antitorque pedals "rudder pedals." Helicopter folk may be the greatest folk on earth, but they don't take kindly to fixed-wing terminology. In fact, helicopters don't have rudders in the same sense that airplanes do. If you want to remain on good terms with your helicopter-flying friends, refer to the foot pedals by their proper name.

If the pilot could tilt that disc a few degrees forward, backward, left, or right, that arrow—or "lift vector," to give it its impressively technical-sounding name—would then tilt with it. Whichever direction that lift vector points is where the helicopter's going to go. Helicopter pilots control the direction of the lift vector using the *cyclic pitch control*.

When the pilot moves the cyclic pitch control, a whole lot of complex things begin to happen in the hub of the main rotor, where all the mechanisms that control the rotor are located. The simple thing to say would be that the cyclic pitch control tilts the rotor one way or another, which in turn deflects the lift vector and changes the path of the helicopter. But that would gloss over a universe of complicated machinery that people like Igor Sikorsky spent decades of energy to perfect.

So let's take a few paragraphs to understand the complex inner workings of the swash plate assembly (the cluster of mechanical components and links located near the rotor hub), which transfers the pilot's control movements in the cockpit into pitch changes in the spinning rotor disc.

Plane Talk

Of course, no technology pioneer, including Sikorsky, succeeds independently of others. There is always a trail of innovation that can be traced back for decades, centuries, even millennia. In the case of helicopters, the Chinese deserve credit for the first written description of a rotary wing. Their version involved rotor blades made of wood carved from the inner part of a jujube tree and straps of ox leather to set the whole thing in motion. Other inventors conceived of the various components that eventually came together in the modern helicopter, and it only awaited energetic and clever thinkers to put the pieces together into a flyable helicopter.

By the Book

The **cyclic pitch control** is a metal stick that projects from the helicopter floor between the pilot's knees. With her right hand, the pilot moves the stick front to back to control the forward or backward speed, and left and right to move sideways.

The Swash Plate Assembly

To visualize the swash plate assembly, let's construct an analogy of it from familiar objects. We'll start with two hockey pucks, laid flat and stacked one on the other. While you're at it, imagine there's a layer of tiny ball bearings between the two hockey pucks so the top one can spin easily while the lower one remains stationary.

Now imagine standing four pencils on end and placing the stacked hockey puck and ball bearing unit on top of them. One pencil is toward the nose of the imaginary helicopter, another toward the tail, and the others are on the left and right sides. (Sure, right about now the whole thing comes tumbling down. But cut us some slack and imagine the whole assembly is being held firmly upright and nothing's falling apart.)

Next, place another four pencils on the upper puck. In a helicopter, those pencils represent the "pitch links" that control the pitch of the individual rotors, either increasing or flattening their pitch.

Finally, drill a hole through the hockey pucks to allow a main rotor shaft to pass through. In a helicopter, the bottom of the shaft would be attached to the engine and transmission and the top would serve as an anchor for the pivoting rotor blades. The main rotor would be linked to the upper swash plate, or top puck in our imaginary model, so when you spin the main rotor shaft, the upper swash plate rotates at the same speed, while the lower one remains stationary, like the body of the helicopter.

In its barest terms, the hockey-puck-and-pencil model you've imagined represents the swash plate assembly, and it contains the essence of the cyclic pitch control system. (Of course, the technically minded can research the system in far more detail in books listed in Appendix C, "Recommended Reading," and on Web sites listed in Appendix D, "World Wide Web Resources.")

Going Forward

Here's what happens in flight when a pilot wants to control the forward track of his helicopter, for example.

To move forward, the pilot would move the cyclic pitch control stick forward, causing the front pencil to drop down and the rear pencil to lift up. That would tip the hockey pucks, or in the real helicopter, the swash plates, forward. The upper swash plate, rotating on its bed of ball bearings, would also tilt forward, pushing its rear pencil up and pulling its front pencil down. In the example of forward flight, the left and right pencils would neither rise nor fall. They would only come into play if the pilot were moving the cyclic pitch control stick left or right.

To say it another way, when one of the rotor blades began to swing toward the rear of the helicopter, its "pitch link" that we've been representing with rotating pencils resting on the top puck would be pushed upward. That would cause the angle of the blade to increase, give the blade more lift, and cause it to rise. At the same time, the pitch link on the blade that was swinging toward the front would respond to the downward tilt in the swash plate, flattening the pitch of the blade. The blade would lose lift as a result and drop downward slightly.

On Course

Torque is created only when the helicopter's engine is delivering power to the rotor. Reducing power reduces torque. So if a tail rotor or the tail-rotor controls fail during flight, the pilot will cut power to the engine to stop the tendency for the helicopter to rotate toward the right. Without power, the pilot will have to begin planning a forced landing, which we'll discuss shortly.

On Course

MD Helicopters of Mesa, Arizona, has a unique alternative to the traditional tail rotor. It devised a system called NOTAR, for "no tail rotor," which uses a jet of air to produce the thrust normally created by the spinning blades of the rotor. And because the tail rotor is responsible for much of the noise a helicopter makes, NOTAR helicopters are much quieter.

Put it all together, and you have a rotor disc that tilts forward and a lift vector pointing in the same direction. The result is a helicopter moving forward.

The same principles apply to other directions as well. The helicopter's ability to move backward or to slide sideways is one of its key attractions, and it is made possible by the cyclic pitch control.

When the Fan Stops Turning

Perhaps the most pervasive myth about helicopters is that when they lose engine power, they're doomed to crash. In reality, a helicopter pilot has plenty of landing options open to him if the engine goes south—but he has to be on his toes.

Even without engine power, helicopters can glide to the ground using a principle called autorotation. But it's a maneuver that requires a lot of skill and a refined sense of timing, and pilots have to spend many hours practicing such landings.

When the engine is working correctly, it pulls air from above the main rotor and accelerates it downward using the angled blades of the rotor to generate lift. When the engine fails, though, the pilot must control the helicopter so that the direction of the wind through the rotor comes from below. That wind helps keep the rotor turning and producing enough lift to allow the helicopter to glide.

As the pilot nears the ground for an autorotation landing, he doesn't have any engine power, so he has to make his one landing attempt count. Just before the helicopter reaches the ground, the pilot uses the cyclic pitch control to tilt the rotor toward the tail. That motion allows the rotor to generate extra lift for a few moments and slows the downward speed. The pilot must have accurate timing. If he's done it right, that extra lift comes just in time to set the helicopter down safely. Good pilots make it look easy, but an autorotation landing can frazzle a student pilot's nerves.

Helicopters like this CH-46E Sea Knight use two main rotors rather than one, eliminating the need for an antitorque rotor and increasing the amount of weight it can carry.

(U.S. Marine Corps photo)

Plane Talk

Actor Harrison Ford learned firsthand how risky autorotation landings can be. In summer 1999, he and a flight instructor were practicing the maneuver at a small airport northwest of Los Angeles when something went wrong. The helicopter, a Bell 206 Jet Ranger, crash-landed in a dry riverbed and toppled over on its side. The actor and his instructor both walked away from the crash.

Amazing Future

Helicopter engineers are at work at labs and airports all over the country trying to refine and improve helicopters. One man, Ron Barrett, has invented a new electronic method of controlling the pitch of helicopter blades.

Barrett devised a combination of materials that contort when exposed to an electric field, a characteristic known as piezoelectric elasticity. He discovered that by applying small electric charges to a series of precise points along a helicopter's rotor blade, he could cause the blade to twist to control the lift it produces.

145

The Barrett blades could reduce the number of parts in a helicopter's hub dramatically. Already, in a test model, a hub using 94 parts was replaced by one needing just five. If the technology ever finds its way into commercial use, it could dramatically reduce the high cost of inspecting and maintaining helicopter hubs.

Another man, James Cycon of Sikorsky, found a new way to stack the blades of a helicopter. Instead of one main rotor and one tail rotor, Cycon simply stacked two blades rotating in opposite directions, thereby canceling each other's torque. The result was a flying doughnut of sorts. Both rotors are shrouded inside a covering that protects the blades, meaning that the unmanned craft, which Sikorsky called "Cypher," can fly into forested areas, for example, without being damaged by tree branches or other obstructions that could bring an ordinary helicopter crashing to the ground.

Plane Talk

Did you think automobiles were the only vehicles equipped with air bags? Maybe not for long. Engineers and researchers are experimenting with the notion of installing side and front air bags in military helicopters. Helicopters fly at reasonably slow speeds. Landings are even slower, often much slower, than automobile crash speeds. Side air bags make a lot of sense, too, because the spinning rotor has a bad habit of causing helicopters to tip over during a crash. What if an air bag accidentally went off in flight? No problem. The bags deflate so quickly after blowing up that pilots had no problem continuing to fly safely.

How Much Will It Cost?

There's a dang good reason that you don't see as many helicopters taking off and landing from your local airport on a sunny summer day as you do airplanes and gliders: Helicopters are too expensive for almost anyone to afford. In fact, pound for pound, helicopters are undoubtedly the most expensive form of aviation around—not counting Pentagon-funded military aviation, of course.

Even the smallest helicopter model now in widespread use, the two-seat Robinson R-22, will set you back almost $160,000 fresh off the factory floor. Its slightly larger cousin, the four-seat R-44, sells for more than $280,000. For true rotor-heads, nothing is going to get between them and the helicopters they love. But the "inexpensive" R-22 boasts a top safe speed of less than 100 miles per hour, far slower than any airplane being produced today.

Helicopter flying lessons aren't cheap either. The price of the Robinson R-22 plus an instructor for an hour runs $170 or more. Rental of a truly powerful helicopter, a Bell 206 Jet Ranger, costs $625 per hour, and that's *without* an instructor. In addition to the cost of the helicopter and instructor, the costs that we outline in Chapter 13, "Getting Off the Ground: Becoming an Airplane Pilot," apply to helicopter students as well.

Still, there's something to be said for an aircraft that's capable of landing almost anywhere it's legal and safe to land, from a deserted beach to a mountain meadow to a desert mesa. That's the capability that helicopter pilots love, not to mention the challenge of flying a craft that is among the most difficult in the sky to fly really well.

The Least You Need to Know

➤ Helicopters, dreamed of for centuries, became a reality after airplanes were invented, thanks to Igor Sikorsky.

➤ Helicopters are slower, more costly, and less comfortable than airplanes, but far more versatile.

➤ The rotor hub contains a complex mechanism that alters the lift produced by the main rotor.

➤ A helicopter's tail rotor works to counteract the powerful spinning force created by the main rotor.

➤ When a helicopter loses power, a pilot can safely glide to a landing thanks to the principle of autorotation.

Chapter 11

Up, Up, and Away: Hot-Air Balloons

In This Chapter

➤ Ballooning and a Greek philosopher

➤ From liftoff to landing

➤ Reading the wind

➤ The surging popularity of hot-air ballooning

➤ Helium balloons circle the globe

Balloonists became the first true aviators when the Montgolfier brothers invented the hot-air balloon in the eighteenth century. From the day the Montgolfiers staged their balloon demonstration for Louis XVI and Queen Marie Antoinette to the late nineteenth century, when people tried to motorize them with primitive gasoline engines, balloons were literally the only way to fly. (For a review of the role of balloons in the history of flight, turn to Chapter 1, "The Earliest Aviators.")

With the turn of the twentieth century and the Wright brothers' invention of the airplane, however, interest in balloons faded. Only recently has ballooning—and its close cousin, blimp flying—experienced a renaissance, thanks in part to advertisers, a history-making world-circling flight by a brave team of aeronauts in 1999, and a group of flyers in a field outside Albuquerque, New Mexico.

Ballooning: It's a Gas!

What makes a hot-air balloon fly? The answer couldn't be any simpler: Warm air rises. Period.

Of course, the details of how to generate the heat, harness the hot air, and control a balloon in flight make the sport of ballooning a far more complex matter. But the underlying principle is simple enough.

The Air That You Heat

If you weigh two equal-size parcels of air that are at different temperatures, the warmer one will weigh less. For example, if you fill one large trash bag with cool air from your basement, and fill another one with hot air from the attic, the one filled with attic air will weigh less. Of course, a trash bag only holds a couple of cubic feet of air weighing about a pound, so you'd need a pretty sensitive scale to measure the tiny difference!

But when you start talking about a bag of air holding from 70,000 to 100,000 cubic feet of air standing seven stories high or taller, and measuring more than 50 feet across, the difference in weight becomes considerably more measurable. And on this enormous scale, the buoyant effects of warm air are amplified exponentially.

Plane Talk

Everything about hot-air balloons is done on a massive scale. A balloon builder might use enough fabric to cover a fifth of an acre, and stitch it into the proper shape using some three miles of thread.

The air inside a hot-air balloon is heated by propane flames shooting from the nozzles of liquid propane gas tanks. The tanks range in capacity from 10 gallons to 20 gallons each. Burning between 30 and 40 gallons of propane per flight, the burners generate 10 million to 30 million British Thermal Units, or BTUs.

The flames generated by the propane burners keep the air inside the balloon's *envelope* much hotter than the surrounding air even on a warm summer day. The difference in temperature between the air inside the envelope and the air outside it becomes even more pronounced in the cool hours of the morning and evening, when balloon pilots prefer to fly because of generally calmer wind.

The Envelope, Please

The balloon's *envelope* is coated with a layer of polyurethane impregnated with chemicals like silicone or neoprene to fill in the natural pores in the cloth and hold in the hot air better. The air inside a balloon reaches temperatures of over 200°F—pretty hot, but not hot enough to ignite the envelope material. Often, designs, logos, or slogans are placed on the outside of the envelope using an appliqué technique that lets balloon owners and sponsors create words and designs large enough to fill a billboard. As we touch on later, the sport of ballooning is not exactly immune to the commercialization craze.

By the Book

A balloon's **envelope** is the bright, colorful, sometimes oddly shaped nylon or polyester fabric bag that contains the hot air that keeps the balloon aloft.

A Lesson from Archimedes

Now that we've heated the air inside the balloon's envelope using the burners, let's look at the physics behind what makes the balloon actually fly. The whole thing goes back to a Greek math whiz named Archimedes. According to legend, Archimedes stepped into a too-full bath and had a flash of insight that balloonists can relate to.

When Archimedes stepped into a tub that had been filled to the rim, he noticed he became lighter and lighter as more of his body went under the water. Not only did he seem to become lighter, but the water level rose and spilled over the edge of the tub as he sat down. In an inspired moment, Archimedes understood that the amount of weight he seemed to lose was equal to the weight of the water that spilled out of the tub.

The first thing Archimedes did was jubilantly holler, "Eureka!" ("I found it!") as he ran naked through the streets of Syracuse, Sicily. The next thing he did was write down what we know as Archimedes's principle: A body immersed in fluid loses weight equal to the weight of the amount of fluid it displaces. Because air is a fluid— or rather, a gas that *behaves* like a fluid—Archimedes' principle applies to balloons.

Let's say the envelope of a balloon holds three tons of air when fully inflated. Now, let's say that air has been heated by a few million BTUs of propane flames until it is good and warm and, as we've seen, a little lighter. Instead of weighing three tons, it now weighs only two and a half tons. It's still occupying the same volume as three tons of unheated air, though, so the balloon is about a half-ton, or 1,000 pounds, lighter than air. It's ready to fly!

Plane Talk

A hot-air balloon is lighter than air at ground level, but there's a limit to how high it can fly. As it ascends, the air in the atmosphere gets less dense, or "lighter," which is why mountain climbers have trouble breathing at high altitudes. At a few thousand feet off the ground, the weight of the air will be so low that it will be about the same as the hot air inside the balloon, and the balloon can't go any higher. While hot-air balloons have floated as high as about 37,000 feet, most balloon pilots prefer to fly near tree-top level, and no higher than about 1,000 to 3,000 feet above the ground, depending on conditions.

By the Book

The **gondola** is the basket that carries a balloon's pilot, passengers, and the few things needed during flight—including the champagne! The gondola also includes the framework that anchors the envelope and holds the propane tanks and burner nozzles. Baskets are usually made of woven rattan and willow sides attached to a plywood floor. Gondolas are short on amenities, but strong enough to survive lots of rough landings.

Liftoff!

Once a balloon crew, usually four to five people plus a pilot, arrive at the launch site, they begin a takeoff ritual that can take anywhere from a few minutes to a half-hour to complete.

First, the envelope is laid out on its side and connected to the *gondola*, which is also laid on its side. While a pair of crew members hold the mouth of the envelope open, the pilot begins to inflate the envelope using a cold-air fan. The cold-air fan opens the balloon's envelope enough to allow the pilot to walk into it to inspect the fabric of the envelope and the interior rigging and pulleys. The ropes that snake through the pulleys operate the fabric panels in the balloon's crown that can be opened to release hot air quickly, either for a rapid descent or to keep the balloon on the ground after landing.

The inspection complete, the pilot gives his assignment orders to the chase crew. Some will be needed to hold the gondola down as the balloon inflates and lightens. Others will have to grab hold of the crown rope that hangs outside the envelope from its top center. The chase crew is crucial to keeping the balloon steady as it bobs in a downwind direction while inflating.

As the balloon envelope gets closer to full inflation and liftoff, the pilot helps the passengers into the gondola and gives them a safety briefing before the crew lets the ropes loose.

But the takeoff isn't complete yet. As the balloon gets lighter and lighter, but not ready for actual takeoff, the pilot will order "hands off." He wants to get a feel for the balloon's buoyancy and test the effect the winds might have on it when it lifts off.

The pilot orders "hands off" once more, and continues to inflate the balloon to its full buoyancy. Once he is certain the winds are safe and the balloon has enough lift to clear any nearby trees, buildings, or hills, the pilot orders "hands off" one last time, and the ground crew lets go. The balloon is flying!

When the balloon lifts off, the ground crew's job is just beginning. They jump into cars, trucks, and vans and race downwind, maps and walkie-talkies in hand, to try to keep up with the balloon and arrive at the landing site before, or at least very shortly after, the pilot lands.

Blowin' in the Wind

Once in the air, the pilot controls the balloon's altitude by firing the burners to rise into the winds blowing in one direction or permitting the balloon to cool in order to descend into the winds blowing in another direction.

The wind is everything to a balloon pilot. It determines not only the distance a balloon will travel in the time it takes it to use all its propane fuel, but it also determines where the pilot should take off from. That's right—a balloon pilot doesn't necessarily start his flight planning by thinking about where he will land. Sometimes the planning process runs backward.

Turbulence

If you're even the slightest bit squeamish about heights, you may want to ease into hot-air ballooning before taking a full flight. Airplanes have a cabin structure that lends a sense of security and reduces the sense of vulnerability. To test your reaction to a balloon flight, take a tethered flight that ascends only a few dozen feet off the ground.

On Course

Joining a ground crew is a good first step to becoming a full-fledged balloon pilot. It puts you in contact with others who share your interest and gives you a close-up introduction to the sport, not to mention a chance to hitchhike a balloon flight on occasion. You might even find that the thrill of chasing your team's balloon and helping it land and recover safely is more fun than riding along.

153

The Plan

Let's say a hot-air balloon pilot wants to make a flight that lasts about an hour, and he wants to land in Uncle Herman's pasture. The planning process doesn't begin with the question of where to take off from. Instead, the pilot, using the best weather information available from government agencies and reports from other pilots, starts his planning by figuring out the winds at different altitudes and tracing backward. Based on the winds near the ground and the winds aloft, where would a balloon have to take off from to fly over Uncle Herman's spread one hour later?

Once the answer has been calculated carefully, the balloon pilot can lay out his maps and begin to calculate his takeoff point. That's where he and his crew drive their trucks, vans, and trailers and begin the task of launching the balloon.

Other times, a balloon pilot decides his course based on where he wants to take off from and how long he wants to stay aloft. Using maps and carefully studying wind information published by the weather service, the pilot plots the location where the balloon will probably come down. With an X marking the spot, he discusses driving routes with his ground crew, and a plan is laid out to get the envelope rolled up and get everything stowed in the chase truck.

But in most cases, pilots and chase crews simply enjoy the mystery of not knowing where a flight will take them. They find a convenient launch site, send up a small helium balloon to test the direction of the wind above the ground, and take off. Once in the air, the pilot begins planning his route and, later, identifying good landing sites. Meanwhile, on the ground, the chase crew does its level best to keep up.

Plane Talk

If you own property that has a prominent tree line on the upwind side of a broad pasture with no tall obstructions, you can expect to get a call by a pack of balloonists one day. The protection from wind offered by the trees and the open takeoff area are perfect for ballooning, and once local balloon pilots find such a place, they often impose on the owner to let them fly there. If you're one of the owners, make the best of it: Demand a free ride now and then, and don't forget the champagne payoff!

Even with all their modern technology and government safety regulations, balloons still carry an aura of leisure and romance.

(Allen Matheson, Photohome.com)

As Different as Anabatic and Katabatic

Balloon pilots soon get on intimate terms with the wind. Most of us think of gusts and breezes, if at all, as having an unpredictable, capricious nature, but to a balloon pilot, they follow some rules of thumb. Once you become a balloon pilot, understanding these wind patterns will become almost second nature:

➤ **Day, or anabatic, wind.** Don't sweat the Greek word. Anabatic simply means uphill, and anabatic winds are the wind currents that sometimes flow uphill when daytime sun heats a south-facing hillside or mountain slope that gets full sunshine. Because anabatic winds often flow in a different direction from higher-altitude winds, balloon pilots can use them to steer course, though with plenty of caution.

➤ **Night, or katabatic, wind.** Three guesses what this one means. That's right, katabatic winds are the downhill breezes that develop after sunset when the uphill anabatic winds lose energy. Katabatic winds can be deep and powerful, so pilots usually give those south-facing slopes a respectful margin.

By the Book

Ascending in a balloon is a matter of adding heat and buoyancy to the balloon by firing the propane burner, or by tapping into an anabatic wind. **Descending** is somewhat more passive, relying on gradual cooling of the air in the envelope or catching a ride on a descending wind. For a quick drop, the pilot can pull a cable in the gondola that vents hot air through the top of the envelope and guarantees that the balloon loses altitude quickly.

➤ **Ridge waves.** These can cause a bumpy ride, but they're usually not hazardous. As their name implies, ridge waves are winds that are flowing perpendicular to a series of ridges; they can rise and descend in waves that resemble the gradual upward and downward pattern of sea swells.

➤ **Valley wind.** This is a fun wind pattern for most balloon pilots because it can allow them to turn on a dime, or on what passes for a dime in ballooning circles. Wind flowing in the deepest part of a valley tends to parallel the valley's trough, and if the wind aloft is crossing the valley at a perpendicular angle, a descent into the valley wind can cause the balloon to turn sharply, a relatively spectacular maneuver in a sport where direction changes generally happen slowly.

There are other wind patterns, and the more experience a pilot has in *ascending* and *descending,* the more variations on the basic wind patterns he will add to his mental catalog.

Down Time

When a balloon pilot runs out of propane and hot air, it's time for a landing—no matter what lies below. That's why balloonists keep a little fuel in the propane tanks just in case. There's no feeling like being out of fuel and headed straight toward a Saguaro cactus or a radio transmitter antenna as you approach to land. If you have fuel left in the tanks, a few seconds of burn will slow the descent just enough to clear a dangerous obstacle. That's why pilots land with as much as 40 percent of their fuel still in the tank. It just doesn't make sense to push the limits of safety.

When the time and location are right for a landing, the pilot begins to let the air cool in the envelope. The balloon starts down, and with short blasts on the burner, the balloon enters a controlled descent of about 600 feet per minute, give or take 200 feet per minute. When the balloon is very close to landing, the pilot uses the burner to slow the descent rate to a gentle 100 feet per minute when it's time to touch down.

When selecting a landing spot, pilots have to keep two important questions in mind: Is there enough clear space downwind for the envelope to deflate, and can the chase crew get to the balloon from a nearby road without too much trouble? (We'll take a closer look at the chase crew later in this chapter.)

When considering whether there is enough downwind space for the envelope to deflate, the area required depends on the wind speed. If the wind is fairly calm, the balloon will descend nearly vertically and the gondola, will often remain upright after landing. In such a case, the landing should be planned for a clearing that provides at least 70 feet or so of clear space downwind so that the envelope can be conveniently laid out, deflated, and prepared to be packed away.

If the wind is blowing much faster than a couple of miles per hour, the pilot has to plan for a larger clearing in which to land. That's because the wind will drag the balloon over the ground for some distance after it lands. When it's windy, a balloon could take as much as 1,000 feet to come to a full stop with the deflated envelope laid out along the ground.

Rocky Landing

Most of the time, the landing of a hot-air balloon is pretty uneventful. But the rare exception makes for the stories that balloon pilots tell around the late-night campfires at balloon festivals.

When the winds are strong, balloons can be smacked around pretty badly during landing. The gondola can hit the ground hard, then be dragged for hundreds of feet before the hot air can be vented and the envelope comes to rest. Rocky terrain can toss passengers and pilots around like dolls.

Sometimes the winds pick up unexpectedly, and there aren't many options but to get the basket on the ground as quickly and as safely as possible. Depending on the geography, that could mean coming down in a pasture, where cow flops put a whole new twist on the definition of a landing hazard. Sometimes, the landing takes place in a cultivated field, flattening a swath of marketable crops in the process.

Turbulence

Almost any obstacle holds the potential for danger during a hot-air balloon landing. In the West and Southwest, cattle fences that are nearly invisible from the air suddenly look pretty threatening during the last part of a landing approach, especially if the fence is made of barbed wire. And power lines seem to be everywhere. Seasoned pilots learn to see these obstacles well in advance and make smart decisions ahead of time.

On Course

When you see a balloon landing in anything but a calm wind, you can bet the pilot has been planning his approach for 10 minutes or more. From hundreds of feet in the air, a pilot has to select a series of possible landing sites depending on how the wind might behave near the ground. Then, having memorized some alternatives and taking a mental note of power lines, fences, cattle herds, and other dangers, he begins a descent that could cover three miles or more.

157

Turbulence

Do you think having a parachute on your back would make ballooning a little safer? Think again. Most experts say that a parachute fall should begin at 2,000 feet above the ground. Balloons sometimes don't get much higher than a few dozen feet. Also, because of their large surface area and wind resistance, balloons don't fall very fast even at their worst.

Perhaps the most dangerous landings happen near cities or towns where balloons are forced down in a residential area. It seems a summer doesn't go by that the local headlines don't include some sort of ballooning mishap such as a landing on a residential street or in someone's swimming pool. In some cases, injuries can result, but they're usually no more severe than a few bumps and bruises.

The Thrill of the Chase

If you're not in the balloon's gondola during a flight, there's still a lot of fun you can have as a member of the chase crew.

Chase crews are an integral part of hot-air ballooning, and there are plenty of balloon fanatics who prefer the joy of the chase to the placid dreaminess that the pilot and passengers enjoy in flight. Those who stay with a balloon crew long enough and become good enough at their job sometimes earn a special nickname— "Ace-Chase."

Plane Talk

As a first-time balloon passenger, you'll have a ceremonial initiation to look forward to. After your first flight, you'll stand silently in front of your experienced ballooning friends while they solemnly read this poem:

> The winds have welcomed you with softness
> The sun has blessed you with warm hands
> You have flown so high and so well
> That God has joined you in your laughter
> And has set you gently back into the loving arms of Mother Earth.

Then they'll have you clasp your hands behind your back and lift a glass of champagne using only your mouth and your teeth. Once you drink down the champagne without spilling a drop and without using your hands, you're a member of the ballooning fraternity.

At the beginning of a flight, chase crew members help haul the heavy equipment out of a truck, lay out the envelope, and help attach it to the gondola. They lay out the ropes and lines that are used to control the balloon during inflation. They attach fuel tanks to the balloon and check the few modest *instruments* that the pilot uses to keep tabs on the flight.

Chase crew members help hold the envelope open while it begins to inflate, they help passengers and pilot get settled in for the flight, and they hang on to the balloon to provide human ballast as it grows buoyant enough to take off. With an order from the pilot, the crew members release their grip on the gondola, and the balloon is on its way.

Using a combination of road maps, their own notes from scouting trips, a two-way radio linkup with the pilot, and some tips and hints from local residents, the chase crews follow the balloon across the countryside in a caravan of trucks, vans, and cars.

By the Book

A balloon's **instruments** are very simple compared to an airplane's. Generally, a balloon pilot has only an altimeter to measure height above the ground, a vertical speed indicator to display the speed of climb or descent, and a pyrometer, which measures the temperature of the air inside the balloon's envelope.

While balloons usually cover the ground far more slowly than a car can travel, the balloon has the advantage of getting to its destination "as the crow flies." The chase crew, on the other hand, has to contend with traffic lights, dead-end roads, pasture gates, and unfriendly property owners who don't share a fondness for ballooning. There are even some balloon haters out there, who may have been spoiled to the joys of the sport when unskilled or inconsiderate crews trampled their crops, damaged their property, and generally made pests of themselves.

The very best chase crews can predict the future—that is, accurately judge where the balloon might be heading, and get there first. That gives the crew time to find convenient access roads or at least to get permission from a land owner before traipsing all over his property. Pilots can help chase crews immensely by planning—and executing—a landing within easy distance of a road or vacant field.

Once the landing is made and congratulations are passed around, it's time for the chase crew and the pilot to lay the envelope out carefully so that it can be stuffed into a bag and stored. The gondola is disassembled and hauled onto a truck. After most flights, the crew pops the cork for a champagne celebration, then heads off for a hearty breakfast to talk about the morning's adventure.

Plane Talk

From the striking beauty of the balloon to the memories of Jules Verne balloon adventure novels to the thrill of being so far off the ground and yet so safe and at ease, ballooning possesses an undeniably romantic quality. One unmarried woman I know once told me that she would instantly agree to marry any man who proposed to her in a balloon. Every year, hundreds of people become engaged in a hot-air balloon, and some even make headlines by being married in the gondola of a balloon.

By the Book

In a sport dominated by tradition, one of the most stunning, both for pilots and for spectators, is the **mass ascension.** As its name suggests, the mass ascension involves a large number of balloons inflating and lifting off together into the air. It's a remarkable sight, and an equally impressive sound as dozens of powerful propane burners ignite.

Champagne and Propane

The credit for ballooning's "takeoff" in recent years goes in part to a group of hardy aficionados who gave it a spark of life and a splash of color. In 1972, the first gathering of 13 balloons lifted off from Coronado Center shopping plaza in uptown Albuquerque. The pilots who made that *mass ascension* certainly had no inkling that what they were starting would become the Albuquerque International Balloon Fiesta, the greatest pilgrimage for hot-air balloonists around the world.

Now, nearly 30 years later, the Albuquerque event has turned into a nine-day extravaganza that rivals the largest air shows for powered airplanes in terms of size and impact among balloon pilots and fanciers. It has become a worldwide draw, attracting no less than one-fifth of all the balloons in the world.

Of course, where there's one festival, there's usually another. In the case of ballooning there are other major annual events that bring out hundreds of balloons and thousands of spectators.

In Indianola, Iowa, at the National Balloon Classic each summer, locals play host to a hundred balloons or more for a week. Every day, balloonists fire up their burners for two flights, one in the early morning and one in the early evening, when the winds are lightest and least treacherous. In the meantime, the festival resembles a county fair with performances by bands, road races, and a host of other activities to keep the family entertained.

Mass ascensions, in which a number of balloons launch at the same time, might be one of the most beautiful sights in aviation. Though the scene looks chaotic, pilots and crews are careful to stay safe.

(Allen Matheson, Photohome.com)

Plane Talk

One of the most spectacular events at any gathering of balloonists doesn't take place in the air at all, but on the ground. It's the "glow," and it begins in the late dusk or in the pitch black of night when dozens of balloonists light up the dark with the multicolored glow of burner flames inside the colorful craft. The key to getting the most light out of the propane flames is to adjust the burners to produce a flame that is not very efficient at producing heat, but is quite efficient at producing light. The night sky, lit up with a thousand colors amid the roar of butane burners, is an experience you'll never forget.

The popularity of annual days-long events like the Albuquerque International Balloon Fiesta and the National Balloon Classic is a sign of the increasing popularity of perhaps the most civilized of all forms of aviation. After all, where else does each flight come with a requirement to toast a successful landing with a tipple of champagne? Of course, balloon pilots are certified by the Federal Aviation Administration just like airplane pilots, so by law they can't take a nip of the bubbly until the flight is over.

But I still say balloon pilots know how to celebrate a successful flight better than any other flyer. As balloonists love to say, hot-air ballooning is "powered by propane and champagne."

Imagination and Technology

Imagination and technology converge in ballooning as in no other aviation sport. Thanks to computers and specialized software, there's almost no limit to the variety of designs of modern hot-air balloons.

Take the 1999 Albuquerque International Balloon Fiesta as an example. The balloons came in the shape of an enormous bald eagle, a huge, pink Energizer Bunny™, a Mountain Dew™ can, a La-Z-Boy™ recliner, and even a Harley-Davidson motorcycle. (Do you get a sense that this sport, like others, has become a trifle commercialized?)

The 1999 National Balloon Classic featured a giant Burger King Whopper™ and a sky-high mock-up of a bottle of Mrs. Butterworth's™ syrup.

There were also plenty of balloons without noticeable commercial connections, though these are often sponsored by a friendly local business looking for a little publicity. For example, there are giant eagles and parrots, a Canadian Mountie on his horse, a race car, and—my personal favorite—the almost life-size space shuttle.

Special shapes help promote ballooning by bringing commercial support to an expensive sport, making it easier for pilots and crews to attend more events. They provide a dazzling spectacle as they cross the countryside. And they help promote the sport by bringing millions of delighted spectators out to balloon events each year!

On Course

The combination of champagne and ballooning is a centuries-old French tradition. It probably originated from pilots wanting something nice to offer irate farmers and land owners if they were forced to land in the middle of a field or a backyard.

On Course

Some special balloon shapes take advantage of the hot-air balloon's natural shape. The three best examples I've seen are the design in the shape of a golf ball mounted on a tee, an ice-cream cone, and a giant lightbulb.

One of the most entertaining parts of ballooning, both for pilots and spectators, is the dazzling variety of balloon designs that resemble everything from bottles of pancake syrup to hamburgers like this one.

(Allen Matheson, Photohome.com)

What Will It Cost?

Ballooning is among the easiest and least expensive forms of aviation you can get hooked on. If you decide to join with a few friends or family members to share the costs, ballooning can be downright cheap—well, cheap compared to the cost of airplane flying.

If you want to test your reaction to going aloft in a hot-air balloon, you can probably find a local ballooning flight school that, for about $150 or less, will take you on a flight and let you experience the feeling firsthand.

On Course

The Balloon Federation of America, www.bfa.ycg.org, has a list of clubs and other contact information.

163

Turbulence

Balloon pilots are certified by the Federal Aviation Administration, just like airplane pilots. They train and study for hours in order to fly their craft in a way that is safe to passengers and to people and property on the ground. And because they are so good at what they do, they make it look easy. But never think you can be a safe balloon pilot, or a pilot of any aircraft, for that matter, without expert training and plenty of hard work.

Ballooning schools are not nearly as common as training centers for other forms of aviation, except in some of the traditional ballooning hot spots such as New Mexico and other Southwestern states. But some searching on the Internet or asking around your local airport will turn up some leads.

Once you're hooked on hot-air ballooning, you may start thinking about buying your own rig. Plan on paying between $15,000 and $35,000 for a new balloon, including envelope, gondola, instruments, burners, and fuel tanks. Insurance will add another $2,000 or so per year. Another cost savings over airplanes is in storage. For a balloon, you aren't compelled to rent a hangar at a local airport or pay storage fees—just put the gondola and the rolled-up envelope in your garage.

You'll need a private pilot certificate to fly a balloon. Lessons you'll need in order to earn your private pilot's certificate will add about $1,500 to your expenses provided you already have your own balloon and equipment. If you use the equipment provided by a flight school, the cost jumps to almost $2,500. Your instruction will involve almost 10 hours of flight training and another 10 hours of ground school. Most flight schools will include training materials in the price, but expect to add another $200 or more to pay an examiner's fee once it's time to take your final flight and ground exams. Yes, once again we see that aviation can be an expensive hobby.

Happy ballooning!

The Least You Need to Know

➤ Archimedes' principle—that a body immersed in fluid loses weight equal to the weight of the amount of fluid it displaces—explains the buoyancy of hot-air balloons.

➤ From takeoff to landing and recovery, ballooning is a team effort.

➤ A balloon pilot must have a thorough understanding of wind patterns.

➤ Turn to Albuquerque or the other annual balloon festivals for the closest look at the sport.

Chapter 12

Hybrids, Oddities, and Curiosities

In This Chapter

➤ Blimps: a closer look

➤ Gyroplanes: making a comeback to former glory

➤ The Harrier jump jet: helicopter or airplane?

➤ Rozier balloons: around the world in 19 days

In Part 2, "The Thrill of Flight," we've looked at the most common flying machines in which people take to the skies. But the dream of flight has not been realized only in the airplane, the helicopter, the glider, and the hot-air balloon. Other flying machines, though too impractical for general recreational use, enable people to accomplish incredible feats, whether it be flying around the world nonstop or just getting a really, really cool view of a football game.

Perhaps the best way to end this part of the book is to take a look at a few of these flying machines.

Giant Gasbags: Blimps and Airships

Thanks to companies like Goodyear and a growing number of its competitors, airships are the most recognizable of all the lighter-than-air craft. Blimps have become regular features at sporting events and special occasions all over the world for a couple of reasons.

First, with a maximum airspeed of about 35 miles per hour, blimps can virtually hover over a single location for hours at a time. Second, there's no more attention-grabbing billboard than a blimp trumpeting an advertising slogan.

Airships very nearly died out due to public panic after the Hindenburg disaster in 1937 killed 36 people in the air and on the ground. But engineers learned valuable lessons from the accident, most notably to use helium rather than hydrogen gas. Hydrogen gas is explosive, and piping it into a tinder-try wooden framework covered with fabric that burns faster than paper was tempting fate, to say the least.

Engineers found that blimps filled with explosion-proof helium instead of hydrogen produced almost as much lifting power. And they provided enough peace of mind that blimps have become an accepted part of the sports and advertising landscape.

Plane Talk

There is plenty of mythology over how blimps got their name. Some dictionary editors throw up their hands and say the origin of the word "blimp" is unknown. Others say the word is related to "limp," but because inflated blimps are far from limp, the idea seems far-fetched. The word actually derives from a British Navy officer's joke during World War I when airships were an important part of the military arsenal. The young officer, in a moment of whimsy, flicked his finger against the taught rubber skin of a giant airship and put a name to the sound he heard: "Blimp!"

Anatomy of a Blimp

Blimps function much like a series of connected gas balloons with engine-driven propellers to give the whole contraption a little forward speed. Blimps are equipped with controls that enable the pilots to pitch the craft up and down or to yaw it (turn it) left or right.

Inside the taught skin of a blimp are thousands of cubic feet of helium and one or more bags of air called ballonets. A cubic foot of helium, which is a volume slightly larger than that of a shoebox, can lift just over an ounce. That's not much, but helium's lifting power lies in large numbers. When you pump 170,000 cubic feet of helium into a blimp's envelope, you have an airship capable of lifting almost 11,000 pounds. Some airships hold enough helium to allow them to act as airborne cranes.

Here's how the ballonets and helium envelope work together to keep the blimp flying.

On the ground, high atmospheric pressure squeezes the helium so much that it occupies a smaller area, meaning the blimp's skin would wrinkle like a prune. After all, blimps don't have any internal frame. They're nothing more than fabric bags, keeping their shape only because of the pressure of the helium inside.

To prevent the blimp from wrinkling and losing its shape, large ballonets attached to the inside of the main helium bag are inflated with air, filling part of the vast interior space with air rather than helium. The air-filled pilot-controlled ballonets give the helium a smaller volume to fill while still filling up the familiar cigar shape.

As the blimp climbs to higher altitudes, the atmospheric pressure outside the blimp decreases. As a result, the helium inside the main envelope is able to expand while the ballonets are allowed to collapse so that helium can fill the entire envelope.

The Takeoff and the Landing

Though blimps are considered lighter-than-air aircraft, pilots can control their buoyancy and adjust their weight during a flight. During takeoff, some blimps are adjusted to "fly heavy," meaning they are not weightless, but rather the volume of helium is adjusted so the blimp settles naturally to the ground. For example, if a Goodyear blimp settled down on a bathroom scale in its takeoff configuration, it would weigh about 150 pounds. Because it weighs that much, it must actually take off almost like an airplane, though from a much shorter runway, making a short forward run before the pilot uses the elevator controls to pitch the nose upward so the thrust from the propellers gives the blimp an upward push.

Here's how a blimp gets off the ground. A ground crew, which can number as many as 15 people, grasps a railing near the base of the gondola. In unison, they press down hard on the rail, pushing the blimp down on its springy landing gear tire. The bouncy rebound, caused by springlike assemblies inside the gear mechanism, sends the blimp a few feet into the air, and while it's airborne for a few seconds, the pilots check to make sure it's balanced and ready to fly.

Then, for the actual takeoff, the crew does its bounce maneuver again while the pilot applies full throttle to the two propeller-equipped engines that pump out as much as 800 combined horsepower. With that, the blimp lumbers into the air for a flight that can last several hours.

Plane Talk

In the 1930s, the heyday of the rigid-frame dirigibles that were the forerunners of blimps, gondolas held more people than modern airships can, and carried them in cruise-ship luxury. Some of the old airships held passenger sleeping compartments, observation decks, dining rooms, chefs' kitchens, showers, and even libraries.

Just as with a hot-air balloon, landing a blimp is not an elegant procedure. The two-person flight crew points the giant gasbag downward toward the mooring area, where the ground crew waits. As the blimp is slightly lighter than air, the pilot must drive it downward with engine power. If both engines quit during this phase of the flight, it's interesting to note, the blimp wouldn't crash, but instead would slowly rise higher into the air.

As the blimp nears its mooring mast, a rigid pole rising high off the ground to anchor the blimp, several crew members grab a long rope that hangs permanently from the nose of the envelope. Meanwhile, other members of the crew reach up and grab the gondola hand rail and use their body weight to anchor the blimp while the pilots adjust the helium pressure to give the airship some weight.

Between flights, blimp crew members service the giant machine, which has a habit of swiveling around its mooring mast with the wind like an oversized weather vane. Even on the ground, blimps attract steady crowds of curious onlookers, so that blimp ground crews and pilots spend most of their work hours doing public relations, which for many operators of blimps, such as Goodyear, is precisely the point.

The Goodyear Mystique

The term "blimp" brings to mind just one word for most people: Goodyear. The giant gray Goodyear blimp with its "winged foot" logo emblazoned on the side has become perhaps the most recognized corporate symbol in America, and Goodyear has capitalized on the corporate good will that its decades of blimp flying have created.

Goodyear dominated the blimp scene for decades, but now a handful of competing blimp makers are pushing their way into the limelight. One of them is The Lightship Group. The company's blimps, or lightships, contain a powerful internal light that shines brightly enough to light up advertising logos even at night.

Another company, Global Skyship Industries, equips its blimps with a powerful lighted sign comprising hundreds of individual bulbs, similar to the Goodyear blimps. But Global Skyships can carry more people at a time than the Goodyear blimp, and in greater comfort—meaning it has an on-board restroom.

Goodyear provides its own pilot training, as do most of the blimp manufacturers. That's because there are no commercial schools open to the public where someone can learn to fly a blimp. It's something like an apprenticeship program in which grizzled veterans pass along their expertise to the next generation. And, of course, blimp pilots are certified by the Federal Aviation Administration.

Unless you're a dignitary, a cameraman or -woman, or can otherwise cajole an invitation, it's unlikely that you'll ever be able to climb aboard a blimp for an actual flight. Crew members may, however, let you look around the cabin and cockpit when the blimp is waiting between flights. If you *are* offered a ride in a blimp, don't pass it up. Like a first kiss, a blimp ride is a once-in-a-lifetime thrill.

An Odd Hybrid

The gyroplane might be the best aircraft you never heard of.

Gyroplanes, or "autogyros" as they are also known, are a strange-looking hybrid of helicopter and airplane, with both a propeller and a rotor. The propeller is usually mounted on the nose, although some new, lighter designs feature the propeller behind the pilot in a "pusher" configuration. The rotor is mounted on top of the gyroplane, just as a helicopter rotor's is, but it differs from a helicopter's in a couple of ways. First, the gyroplane's rotor is not engine-driven. Second, a gyroplane's rotor is tilted slightly backward (for reasons we'll discover shortly).

Gyroplanes are remarkable for how little distance they require for takeoff and landing. Some can even take off and land vertically like a helicopter, though that capability requires the use of some extra equipment that in effect creates a collective pitch control like that in a helicopter. Once they're in flight, gyroplanes can fly at speeds much slower than airplanes, thanks to their free-spinning rotor. Their slow speed means that they don't need long runways to land like airplanes do. So gyroplane pilots have more takeoff and landing options available to them than an airplane pilot does.

The Free-Spinning Rotor

The secret of the gyroplane's impressive maneuverability lies in its free-spinning rotor.

Once the propeller begins to move the gyroplane forward, its free-spinning rotor begins to turn. Remember the backward tilt of the rotor that I alluded to? That's so that it can use the wind caused by the craft's forward motion. It spins in the wind like a windmill. Also, the fact that the rotor is free-spinning means it doesn't create any torque.

Plane Talk

In the 1940s, Fairey Aviation produced a gyroplane called a Fairey Rotodyne that had a unique feature that enabled it to take off vertically like a helicopter. At the tip of each of the four rotor blades, the company installed tiny rocket engines that the pilot lit during takeoff and landing. The problem the design ran into, aside from a general consumer distrust of anything so odd, was the ear-splitting noise emitted by the tiny rockets. At 600 feet, the noise was nearly 100 decibels. The company eventually quieted the little rockets a bit, but by that time, prospective buyers had lost interest.

A gyroplane like the Groen Brothers H2X is a return to a bygone era of aviation. In decades past, manufacturers turned out gyroplanes almost as fast as they produced fixed-wing planes. Some even found their way into service as mail planes.

(Groen Brothers Aviation)

The spinning rotor blades, powered only by wind, act just like the rotors of a helicopter when it is in autorotation. Autorotation, remember, is what enables a helicopter to glide rather than fall if the engine fails. The upward-rising air rotates the propeller and reduces the speed of descent. But the gyroplane differs from an autorotating helicopter because the gyroplane has a working engine that continues to propel it forward. As long as a gyroplane has forward speed to turn its rotor, the rotor will continue to create lift.

Of course, because a gyroplane's rotor blades are in a perpetual state of autorotation, if the engine does fail, the pilot simply points the gyroplane toward the ground to keep up its speed—turning the gyroplane, in effect, into an autorotating helicopter—and looks for a safe place to make an "off-airport" landing.

So, with all this going for it, why did the gyroplane fade from the spotlight? Bad timing. The gyroplane evolved at a moment in history when it couldn't quite match up against two other developing technologies—the airplane and the helicopter. Gyroplanes couldn't fly as fast as the airplanes that were being developed in the early 1930s. They also couldn't fly very slowly, not to mention hover, like the helicopters that were showing early promise. In a stroke of bad luck, gyroplanes found themselves caught in a historical squeeze play.

The Next-Generation Gyroplane

Far from being a dead technology, gyroplanes are again being manufactured, and with new techniques that promise to make the newest designs far better and safer than those of decades past.

In the Arizona desert near Buckeye, employees of Groen Brothers Aviation are working to perfect a family of Hawk gyroplanes. These distinctive gyroplanes feature a rear-mounted pusher propeller that puts the engine and propeller behind the plane and keeps the forward view unobstructed.

The company has already made a number of successful flight tests with their prototypes, including demonstrating how the gyroplane can be used to spray crops with herbicides and pesticides, a job that is typically done by helicopters and airplanes.

On Course

You probably didn't know that even up until a few decades ago gyroplanes were so common that even the post office used them to carry mail between cities. American-made Pitcairn gyroplanes hauling loads of mail even took off from the roof of the Philadelphia Post Office.

Because gyroplanes are easier to fly than helicopters and because they can take off and land on shorter runways—even vertically in the case of the Groen Brothers model—gyroplanes could find their way into flying from surveillance jobs, such as wildlife census flights, to law enforcement and crop dusting.

Harrier Jump Jet: Airplane or Helicopter?

In addition to being one of the most curious of all military jets, the British Aerospace Harrier's military type designation, AV-8B, is also a pretty respectable pun for a jet that can "aviate" with more agility than any of its hangar mates.

The Harrier is the only military plane to succeed at fitting a complex system of "vectored thrust" nozzles on a military plane, and make it strong enough and reliable enough to fly in combat if need be.

In fact, the Harrier has seen plenty of combat since it was first rolled out for military duty in 1969. The Royal Air Force flew the jet during the Falklands War in 1982. And during the Gulf War, the United States Marines, whose version of the Harrier is built by McDonnell Douglas under a license from British Aerospace, flew the "jump jet" against Iranian targets.

The secret to the Harrier's vertical takeoff is the four rotatable exhaust nozzles from its jet engines. From the cockpit, the pilot can rotate the nozzles in virtually any direction, from pointing backward for ordinary forward acceleration, to pointing

downward for vertical acceleration. The nozzles work on the same principle as any jet engine: A reaction force is exerted in the opposite direction to the exhaust nozzle by the heating and expansion of the fuel inside the engine's combustion chamber.

The pilot-controlled nozzles give the Harrier amazing agility, not only for vertical takeoffs and landings, but also for in-flight "viffing." Viffing is a word that means "vectoring in forward flight," the technique of rotating the nozzle during flight to help evade an enemy.

For example, if a Harrier pilot is being pursued by an enemy fighter, the pilot can quickly swivel the nozzles from the rear, where they provide forward acceleration, to the front, where the thrust will quickly slow the plane down. In flight, the Harrier's rapid deceleration would cause any pursuer to go rocketing past it. With a deft control movement, the Harrier pilot could swivel the nozzles backward again for forward thrust, and suddenly go from being the hunted to being the hunter.

When a Harrier is on display at air shows, it's always a crowd favorite. The high wing has a distinctive landing gear arrangement that draws the attention of pilots accustomed to the tricycle arrangement—that is, accustomed to two sets of landing gear located about halfway down the fuselage and set on either side of the plane, plus a nose gear.

The Harrier has a distinctive setup of one nose gear and one main fuselage gear, both lined up on the center line of the airplane so that the Harrier looks like it's riding a bicycle. To keep it from tipping over, a single wheel drops down from beneath each wing. The location of the wing gear gives the Harrier important stability during landings, when it tends to tip from one side to the other pretty noticeably.

The Harrier isn't only an oddity. It's also a serious weapon. It can fly at speeds approaching Mach 1, which is over 700 m.p.h. at sea level. It can carry Sidewinder heat-seeking air-to-air missiles, air-to-ground Maverick missiles, and a six-barrel machine cannon, among other things.

The Harrier is fun to watch take off and land, but not if it's flying in your direction and you're the enemy!

Plane Talk

A Seattle man, John D.R. Leonard, took the Pepsi Challenge seriously when a company commercial advertised that consumers could redeem seven million "Pepsi points," at a cost of $700,000, for a Harrier jump jet. Leonard accumulated the points and arrived at Pepsi headquarters to exchange them for a fighter jet, but was told the commercial was a spoof, and there was no Harrier anywhere in the prize package. Leonard sued the company for breaking their promise, but a judge saw the humor in the ad, even if Leonard didn't, agreeing with Pepsi that the ad was fanciful. For his trouble, Pepsi sent Leonard packing with some free Pepsi points.

Floating Around the World

Balloonists began setting their sights on conquering vast distances almost from the time the sport was born. In the 1970s, 10 attempts to cross the Atlantic Ocean by balloon failed before the first success. That success, by Maxie Anderson, Ben Abruzzo, and Larry Newman, was called the Double Eagle II expedition, and it landed in France after taking off from Maine during the summer of 1978.

In the last few years, the race for the ultimate ballooning record, a nonstop around-the-world flight, heated up. These attempts, like others since the 1970s, used a different type of balloon from the recreational hot-air balloon. Because the around-the-world flights would take more than 10 days to complete, the fuel demands of a hot-air balloon with its propane burners was too great to allow it to make it even a fraction of the way.

The solution was a hybrid balloon design that crossed a hot-air balloon with a balloon filled with helium gas. The design, called a Rozier after the first man to fly in a balloon, solved the sticky heat-loss problems of long-duration flights.

How the Hybrid Works

The Rozier balloon uses a bag of explosion-proof helium gas in a large sealed bag that fills the widest part of the balloon (called the "crown"). Below that bag, air can be heated by a propane flame in exactly the same way as a recreational hot-air balloon.

But it isn't the hot air that does the work. In the case of a Rozier balloon, it is the helium that does the bulk of the lifting, while the heated air is used only to keep the

By the Book

To test **Charles's Law,** which states that when pressure stays constant, lower temperature will reduce the volume of a gas, stuff a helium party balloon in your kitchen freezer. Although the balloon is sealed, the cold temperature causes the vibrating molecules to slow down and cluster closer together, reducing the balloon's volume. Now take the shrunken balloon out of the fridge and notice how much buoyancy it has lost. Once it warms up to room temperature, the balloon will return to its original size and buoyancy, just like a Rozier balloon does in the sunshine.

helium warm and toasty at night, when lower temperatures would normally cause the helium balloon to shrink and lose buoyancy.

Remember the lesson Archimedes taught us? In the case of a helium gas balloon, the Archimedes principle means that the larger the helium balloon, the more air it displaces, and that means the more lifting force the helium will create. Well, cold night air causes a helium balloon to shrink, thanks to something scientists call *Charles's Law.* In practical terms, Charles's Law means nighttime temperatures send gas balloons on a beeline for the ground—something that makes a balloon pilot cringe.

In early 1999, at least four groups of balloon enthusiasts prepared separate attacks on the around-the-world record. One of them, the *Breitling Orbiter 3*, took off from Switzerland on March 1 and headed south into the high-altitude winds near the equator. Nineteen days later, the balloon and its two crew members, Bertrand Piccard and Brian Jones, crossed over Mauritania, North Africa, and the same line of longitude they had departed from in Switzerland. It was the first time a balloon had finished a nonstop flight around the globe without refueling. The last great ballooning feat had been conquered!

Plane Talk

In 1982, a California truck driver made news with a gas balloon flight of his own. Larry Walters of North Hollywood filled 45 weather balloons with helium, attached them to an aluminum lawn chair, and took off. Equipped with a pellet pistol, a parachute, a CB radio, and a large bottle of soda, Walters floated to 16,000 feet in the middle of busy airline routes. An airline pilot reported the floating lawn chair to air-traffic controllers, who alerted police. When Walters started to get numb from the cold and the thin air, he used the pellet gun to shoot some balloons and begin his descent. On landing, his contraption got tangled in power lines and caused a neighborhood-wide electrical blackout. The FAA fined Walters $4,000 for operating without the proper paperwork and for not staying in radio contact with air-traffic controllers. Don't try this at home, kids!

The Least You Need to Know

➤ Blimps are more than flying billboards—they're serious flying machines.

➤ Gyroplanes are no longer only for aviation historians—they're a growing part of flying.

➤ The Harrier jump jet takes off and lands like no other jet you've seen, but it's a real fighter, too.

➤ Helium balloons, including the *Breitling Orbiter 3*, have rewritten the sport's record book.

Part 3

In the Cockpit

"The aeroplane has unveiled for us the true face of the earth."
—Antoine de Saint-Exupéry, French aviator and writer

For most pilots, the urge to fly is closely tied to the urge to travel. Some pilots want to discover what there is to see at their destination. For others, the journey itself justifies the trip.

The art and science of navigation help pilots apply the simple tools of maps, compasses, and timepieces to the job of making their way from departure point to destination. Ancient ocean navigators were the first to understand the principles of navigation, and the rules haven't changed very much for modern navigators in the air.

As an added bonus, we'll look at the principles behind the kind of aerobatic flying that is on display every summer at air shows across the country. Understanding how "stunt pilots" control their airplanes to create thrilling air show maneuvers will only add to the fun.

Chapter 13

Getting Off the Ground: Becoming an Airplane Pilot

In This Chapter

➤ The costs of flying

➤ Pursuing your pilot certificate

➤ What to look for in your instructors

➤ So what about the plane?

So you want to become a pilot. You feel like flying is in your blood, getting that pilot certificate is the goal you've set for yourself, and you won't rest easy until you've done it. What do you need to do now?

What Does It Cost to Become a Sport Pilot?

Let's get one thing cleared up right away. You thought golf was an expensive hobby? I'm giving you fair warning: Flying is an expensive passion to quench, and it takes dedication and professionalism to do it safely. Because it requires months or years of study and practice to become a proficient pilot, think twice about starting if you don't think you'll have the time and money to see it through.

Here's a list of the things you'll need or want on your way to becoming a pilot:

➤ A medical certificate

➤ Flying tools, books, and equipment

➤ A program of instruction, including airplane rental, ground instruction, and flight instruction

➤ The accoutrements of flying, some necessary and some just to make you look good

➤ Study aids and video programs

➤ An FAA written test and an FAA flight test

As you can see, there's quite a bit you'll have to get on your way to earning your pilot certificate. (And that's just getting the certificate. The cost of renting or purchasing an airplane is still a distant consideration.) Let's take a look at each bulleted item in more detail.

By the Book

The first, and for most people, only, pilot certificate you'll study for is a **private pilot** certificate. (Don't call it a license; that marks you as an amateur. Only car drivers and poets possess a license. If you feel you really have to impress someone, you can call it your "private ticket.") From there, you can get a commercial pilot certificate, which is the minimum you'll need if you want to make some money in the flying game.

The Medical Certificate

The FAA (Federal Aviation Administration), the division of the Department of Transportation that oversees the nation's pilots, airways, and airplanes, insists that pilots be in reasonably good health so that we don't have too many airplanes falling out of the sky with critically ill pilots at the wheel. It's only fair to you, your passengers, and those on the ground that you are mentally and physically fit to fly.

Frankly, the medical exam for *private pilots* is not much of a barrier to hurdle. You'll find that if you're in decent health, have good eyesight (or just good glasses), and have healthy hearing or a good hearing aid, you won't have much trouble passing the exam.

You'll have to find a certified aviation medical examiner to administer your physical, and the cost can vary immensely, depending on your doctor. Check with your health insurer to see if your policy covers the exam. If you have to pay it out-of-pocket, expect to pay $60 or more. Call your local FAA office for a list of qualified medical examiners in your area, or ask a pilot friend which doctor he or she uses.

Plane Talk

The vision requirements for private pilots may surprise you. You don't need to have perfect 20/20 vision to become a private pilot, or even an airline pilot. The only requirement the Federal Aviation Administration makes is that your vision be "correctable" to the point where you can see well enough to be a safe pilot. That means your color vision must be good, you must have good depth perception, and you must be able to get glasses that make your eyesight at least 20/20.

There are three types of medical exam you can take: first-class, second-class, and third-class. Unless you intend to become a professional pilot, you need only a third-class medical. If you are contemplating a flying career, you should pay the extra money to receive the more stringent first- or second-class medical exam. The second-class exam qualifies you to fly commercially but not for the airlines; the first-class exam qualifies you to fly for the airlines. Getting one of these more comprehensive exams early on in your career will guarantee that, at least for the time being, you meet the more demanding health requirements necessary to become a cockpit pro. If you can't pass it, it's best to know now before you invest too much time and money.

By the way, your medical certificate doubles as your student pilot certificate, so take good care of it. You're required to carry it with you any time you fly, including on your first *solo* flight.

Tools of the Trade

When you take your first steps to becoming a pilot, there will be a few things you'll definitely need to have and a few things you'll probably want to have.

By the Book

Your **solo** is that first day your instructor steps out of the airplane, signs off on a couple of documents, then sends you "around the patch a few times" by yourself. That's the first time you're a real pilot, and your instructor and friends will probably help you celebrate by cutting the back out of your shirt and hanging it on the FBO (fixed-base operator) wall with your name on it. So wear an old shirt, and enjoy the day—you'll never forget the great feeling!

In the "must have" category are some things that, collectively, will probably cost a few hundred dollars:

➤ **Logbook.** Not only does your logbook record the strict details of your training flight to prove your experience to the FAA, it also serves as a repository for your memories of your flights. In addition to the simple recording of flight hours, I use my logbook to record the names of people I fly with, where we went, what we did and saw, what the weather was like, and an item or two that will remind me of the flight years later.

Student logbooks are relatively inexpensive, certainly less than $20. Larger, more durable, and more comprehensive professional logbooks can get a little pricey, so remember: You'll have plenty of supplies to buy; you might not want to go top-shelf for the simple things just yet.

➤ **Headphones.** Headphones are important, and your instructor will probably insist that you buy a set. The very best can cost hundreds of dollars, and they're worth it. Headphones allow crew members to speak to each other easily while they hush much of the engine noise. The top-line models feature noise-canceling circuits that are startlingly effective—but be prepared to pay a lot more money for them.

➤ **Charts, books, and flight-planning paraphernalia.** Your instructor will have a lot of suggestions on what you should buy. One thing you'll certainly need is an electronic *flight calculator.* These are specially programmed calculators that store many of the formulas of flight planning in a memory chip to make plotting courses and accounting for winds a snap, not to mention the dozens of other calculations required to plan a flight.

Flight calculators come in a variety of price ranges. Ask around for the model that has the best features for what you want to do. ASA and Jeppesen both put out quality models, but try them out in your airport's pilot's shop before buying.

Navigation charts, specialized flight clipboards to hold the charts on, specialized navigation protractors, and a handful of other necessities will probably cost under $100, depending on how thrifty you are and how hard you look for a bargain.

By the Book

Flight calculators are speedy, technologically advanced versions of the old-fashioned slide rules that pilots have used for generations to calculate everything from how many miles they can fly on the amount of fuel in the tanks to deducing how fast the wind is blowing and from which direction.

Plane Talk

The art of using the venerable old slide rules, which come in two forms called E6B and CR-2, is in danger of being lost on a fresh generation of flight calculator–poking pilots, but a flyer who is comfortable "spinning the wheel" of the CR-2 has a bond with the great pilots of the past. Even on the flight decks of the largest ultra-high tech jumbo jets, you're likely to find a veteran old captain with a CR-2 tucked away in his shirt pocket "just in case."

A Word About Sunglasses

One item you probably *should* spend a little bit of money on is sunglasses. Don't be tempted by the low-quality, high-fashion ones you can buy at the local shopping mall. Manufacturers like Vuarnet and RayBan put a lot of research into making sure that their lenses have no distortion and their tint doesn't alter the color of objects. They also design their glasses to work comfortably when worn with a headset.

Remember, this is *flying* we're talking about. You'll be facing directly into the sun a good deal of the time. You'll also be flying above the clouds, where the sunshine reflecting off snow-white cloud tops can be blinding. You'll have to be able to see clearly, no matter what. This is no time to skimp on quality.

Because you want good sunglasses, you should be ready to pay a fair price. RayBans, which set the standard for cockpit attitude with its sunglasses a

On Course

Here's a money-saving suggestion: Take a look at the pilots' bulletin board at your local airport. Many of your fellow pilots will post notices of items they are selling, and you can pick up some excellent bargains. Also, don't forget the Internet auction sites, which will probably have some of the merchandise you want at bargain-basement prices.

few years back, retail for $65 or more. Classic Aviators by Serengeti will run you more than $100, and Serengetis are probably worth even more than that for their durability and incredible ability to tame the sun. Of course, if you're like me and wear glasses, you'll have to have the lenses ground to your prescription strength, which adds still more cost.

There are plenty of other things you'll want to buy, from "My Other Car Is an Airplane" bumper stickers (don't) to a good flight bag to carry all the tools of the trade (do). You've been warned—this game can get expensive.

Turbulence

I repeat: Don't skimp on good vision aids in flying.

By the Book

An **FBO,** or fixed-base operator, is the airport business where you can rent an airplane, sign up for a flight-training course, find a flight or ground instructor, buy pilot supplies and aviation fuel, rest between flights, plan out your next flight, check on the weather, and even have a donut and coffee before that early morning takeoff. Most airports, even those in small towns, have an FBO, and large airports might have several.

Winning Your Wings: Instruction

Now it's time to talk about the most expensive part of your investment—the ground school, the flight instructor, and the airplane. Here, again, there are times to skimp and times to open up your pocket-book.

Ground School

Ground-school training is the time you spend in a classroom or in one-on-one academic instruction with your instructor. Ground-school training is just as important as flight time when it comes to molding a safe, mature pilot. For that reason, this is no time to pinch pennies.

If one-on-one ground school fits your budget, ask around for the very best ground-school instructor, then contact him or her and get together for a chat. Find out if your personalities match, yes, but most important, find out if he or she has the serious, focused approach you want in a ground instructor. You don't want a ground instructor who will spend his time—which means your money—telling you stories about his adventures in the air or whose lessons veer into irrelevancies.

Don't be afraid to interview your ground instructor, just as you shouldn't be shy about interviewing your flight instructor and the operator of the *FBO* where you rent your training plane. Ask to see his certificates, and ask for the names of previous or current students so you can interview them about the instructor.

This isn't like learning to drive, where your first teacher was your dad or one of the unlucky teachers who was stuck teaching driver's education in high school. In your flight training, it's your own money you're spending, and the stakes in terms of safety and cost are much higher. Take your time and choose a high-quality instructor.

The costs of one-on-one ground school instruction can add up. Expect to pay $30 per hour or more for as much as 20 hours of instruction.

The least expensive path through ground school is to join a small class of fellow student pilots. This approach has other advantages besides lower cost. For example, students can meet outside class to discuss lessons, something that could help you keep up your stamina and enthusiasm.

Ground-school courses are offered by most FBOs, and some community colleges offer them for the low price of a continuing education course.

During ground school, you'll learn the basic principles of flight, the aviation environment such as airspace, airport and radio communications, airplane mechanical systems and performance capabilities, weather theory, how to read and interpret weather charts, basic and radio navigation, flight physiology, and how to plan a flight and make sound decisions.

If these topics pique your curiosity and fire up your intellect, "Get thee to an airport!"

Flight Instructor

Choosing a competent, professional flight instructor is perhaps the most important thing you'll do as a pilot in training. You'll never forget your first flight instructor, and you'll want to remember him or her for all the right reasons. Too often, pilots use flight instructing as a stepping stone to other jobs, and that means their first priority is not how well their students are learning, but how many flight hours they've been able to get in a cockpit, where every tick of the clock adds to their resume and brings them closer to an airline job.

Again, spend time with a prospective instructor, maybe over a cheeseburger and fries at the airport coffee shop. What do you want in a flight instructor? You want him to put your training on the top of his priority list and to have an enthusiasm for flying that is contagious, that will rub off in the cockpit.

Here again, don't squeeze your nickels too hard. The higher price of a very good flight instructor is an investment in your enjoyment of flying for the rest of your life. For that reason, don't be afraid to keep looking if you have any reservations about a potential flight instructor. Your training is too important—and too expensive—to settle for second-best.

In most cases, your instructor's hourly fee, about $25 to $30 per hour, will be included in the total cost of your private pilot training course. If it's not, make sure you add the instructor costs to the cost of renting your training plane. You'll realistically need 20 to 30 flight hours of instructor time, and another 20 to 30 hours of flying alone, to get your certificate.

Turbulence

Beware shoddy maintenance. If your FBO cuts costs by trimming maintenance, find another FBO, even if you have to travel to another airport. Wander down the flight line where your FBO parks its trainers and see what kind of condition the planes are in. Are the tires heavily worn? Are streaks of oil leaking from the engine? Is the interior cared for, even if it's not immaculate? Use your gut sense, but also talk to mechanics and others on the field.

On Course

Some flight schools throw in a lavish package of extras, including books, materials, training CD-ROMs, and even a flight bag. They include the cost in the total package price, but you might get a wholesale price on the merchandise, which could save you money.

The Airplane

Think the costs are starting to add up? Frankly, we haven't started to scratch the surface yet. The cost of an airplane is where flying gets *really* expensive. Airplanes require much more maintenance than a car, use more fuel, are more expensive to insure, and have a far higher sticker price when they're new—well over $100,000 for even some of the smaller models (which is why I recommend *renting* your airplane).

That's all in order to prepare you for the economic reality of learning to fly. The least expensive flight school, including ground instruction, flight instruction, and airplane rental, will cost $3,000 or more. It's not unheard of for a quality program to cost as much as $6,000 or more. Most private pilot training packages include 20 flight hours with an instructor and another 20 solo. Don't count on finishing with the FAA minimum of 40 hours. It will probably take longer, so accept that and budget the cost from the very beginning.

But here's one area in which you can legitimately trim costs. Don't opt for the expensive training airplanes such as a Beechcraft or the larger Pipers and Cessnas. There will be time to fly them later. During your training, settle for the smallest, and least expensive, Cessna 150s, Cessna 152s, Piper Archers, or Grumman Cheetahs. If you're flying from a high-altitude airport, you may need the extra performance of a Cessna 172, Piper Cherokee, or Grumman Tiger, which cost more. As long as your FBO pays for high-quality maintenance, less expensive airplanes don't mean less safe airplanes.

Additional Training Options

There are some extras that you might want to add to your training. Some schools, though too few to suit me, offer pre-solo spin training, where you and an instructor practice entering and recovering from simple spins, a potentially hazardous condition that students can inadvertently create out of inexperience. (We'll talk about spins, a situation where the airplane loses lift and twirls downward like a spinning leaf, in more detail in the next chapter and in Part 4, "Meeting the Challenges to the Perfect Flight.")

I always recommend spin training because I believe students who can recover from them are more confident pilots. But this type of training adds another cost, perhaps extra $60 to $100 per hour. A single flight should be enough to adequately expose you to spins.

You may also want to pay for extra "hood time," where students don a piece of headwear that narrows their field of vision, blocking the view outside the plane and permitting them to see only the instrument panel. Instructors use hoods to simulate a flight into a cloud or a flight after sunset. This sort of training got extra attention after the death of John F. Kennedy Jr. and his wife and sister-in-law in July 1999. Many aviation writers, including me, believe his inexperience in flying without a clear view of the ground may have caused the accident. Extra training in this area could pay big dividends later.

Turbulence

When it comes to spins, one training session with an instructor does not an expert make. There are a lot of safety concerns your instructor knows about in order to make your flight safe and informative, but he might not tell you all of them for the purpose of a single familiarization flight. That means if you try spins on your own, you could be in real danger. Never practice spins by yourself until you are fully trained and competent.

Finally, some flight schools offer flight simulators that allow students to practice some cockpit skills from the safety of the ground. Simulators cost much less to practice in than an airplane, though instructor time is still a factor. Simulators aren't good substitutes for everything, however. For example, you can't improve your takeoff and landing skills in a simulator. But in case you want to become more familiar with the way flight instruments are used or you want to practice flying safely if you encounter clouds or bad weather, as JFK Jr. did, simulator training is the ideal way to learn.

Study Aids and Video Programs

Pilot shops are bursting with study aids and video programs to help student pilots pass their private pilot exams and help other pilots with their advanced certificates. The most valuable study aids I've found for the private pilot written exam are the Gleim study guides and the three-volume *Pilot's Manual* series by Trevor Thom.

The Gleim books help pilots prepare for the FAA written exam by reprinting the actual exam questions along with the correct answer and detailed explanations of the principle underlying the question. The Gleim series includes a preparation guide for the practical test, which is the portion of the FAA exam requiring the student and the FAA-approved check pilots to make a flight in order for the student to demonstrate his skill in a series of basic maneuvers.

The Thom books, published by ASA, are highly professional guides to ground-school material, as well as an excellent resource for studying the maneuvers and skills required for the practical test.

One other handy book for sharpening flying skills is a little treasure called *Visualized Flight Maneuver Handbook,* also published by ASA. Every instructor and student pilot should have a copy of this pocket-size gem, which depicts in full graphic detail the finer points of basic and advanced maneuvers.

On Course

Check out Appendix C, "Recommended Reading," for other books to get you started in your studies as well as materials for flying pleasure reading.

I find that the perfect supplement to study books are study videos, which can help pilots better visualize their study material. By far the best videos are those produced by King School. The series, which is frequently updated as regulations change and teaching methods improve, is renowned for boosting test scores far above the national average.

In addition to being unequalled learning tools, the King School videos introduce you to John and Martha King, perhaps the most engaging husband-and-wife pilot team you're likely to meet. They are excellent instructors, in part because they know better than anyone else what pilots should expect during a written exam and a practical test. That's because both have *every* certificate and rating the FAA can offer, including the airship and gyroplane. That's quite a distinction, and one that student pilots can take advantage of.

FAA Written Exam and FAA Flight Test

Before you earn your real private pilot wings, you'll have to take a multiple-choice written exam and an in-flight practical test.

Once your ground-school instructor feels you're prepared for the written exam—typically after you have passed a sample test to his satisfaction—he will give you a form that allows you to take the FAA test. He will also give you a list of approved test proctors or computerized testing sites that administer the test.

If you're taking the test in person, you'll have to bring along a fee of $60 or so. A proctor will give you a test book containing nearly 1,000 questions, and a list of 100 numbers. Those numbers tell you which of the 1,000 questions in the test book you'll be required to answer. In a room where several people are taking their private pilot written exam at the same time, no two of them might have the same list of questions, reducing the chance for cheating among the test-takers. Here are a few sample test questions:

What is the one common factor that affects most preventable accidents?

A. Structural failure

B. Mechanical malfunction

C. Human error

How many feet will a glider sink in 10 nautical miles if its lift/drag ratio is 23:1?

A. 2,400

B. 4,300

C. 2,600

When flying HAWK N666CB, the proper phraseology for initial contact with McAlester AFSS is …

A. "MC ALESTER FLIGHT SERVICE STATION, HAWK NOVEMBER SIX CHARLIE BRAVO, RECEIVING ARDMORE VORTAC, OVER."

B. "MC ALESTER RADIO, HAWK SIX SIX SIX CHARLIE BRAVO, RECEIVING ARDMORE VORTAC, OVER."

C. "MC ALESTER STATION, HAWK SIX SIX SIX CEE BEE, RECEIVING ARDMORE VORTAC, OVER."

The test will be graded later and your test results will be mailed to you.

If you're taking the test at a computerized testing site, call ahead for the fee. When you arrive at the location, either at a flight-training center or at an approved commercial site, you'll be instructed on how to use the computer screen, which is sometimes the touch-screen type. The computer program will allow you to change your answers or skip hard questions and come back to them later.

You'll have the same four-hour time limit, and when you're sure you've answered every question to the best of your ability, you formally end the test. You'll get an instant official score, something that gives computerized testing a definite advantage. Many a sleepless night has been spent by student pilots sweating out their written test score.

The flight test begins with an oral Q&A session with an approved FAA practical examiner, who will also charge a fee of well over $100. It's possible to fail the exam during this oral quizzing, though it's a rarity.

On Course

You'll be given four hours to take the test, which *is* more than enough time to finish it; use the extra time to double-check some of the answers you might not have been sure about.

Once past the Q&A, you and the examiner will begin the flight portion of the test, usually beginning with a cross-country flight that he has asked you to plan in advance. You'll conduct the flight without any help from the examiner, and perform any one of a number of maneuvers.

The practical test is difficult to predict. A great deal depends on the habits of the individual examiner; an elaborate grapevine develops among students at each airport about the quirks of the local examiners, who are in a small group approved by the FAA to administer practical tests within a particular geographic area.

If you're like me, you come away from each practical exam having learned a good deal from the examiner. Although they are not formally permitted to teach you anything, only to observe your skills, most of the better examiners pass along a few words of wisdom or a handy tip that they've learned during their many thousands of hours of flying experience.

Buying Into Sport Flying

It won't be long after you begin flying rented airplanes at your local airport that you decide you might like to buy one to call your own. You'll put aside a little bit each month and skimp a bit on the entertainment budget, and before long you'll have enough for a down payment on a little weekend fly-about.

Be prepared for sticker shock. Even a 25-year-old Cessna 172, a relatively low-power, low-speed airplane with few, if any, frills and options, will run you $55,000 or more if it's in good condition—and there's too much at stake to buy an airplane in less than good condition.

If you want to get a bit more sporty by buying into a trim, sleek Mooney, be ready to shell out $90,000 or more for a 20-year-old model. If you want to buy a new Mooney, the company's latest M20R Ovation, you'll have to slap down $407,000 just to fly if off the lot, and that's before you start paying for insurance, maintenance, more fees and fuel, all of which can cost thousands of dollars a year.

Wish somebody else would pick up the huge up-front cost while you just enjoy the flying? Somebody has, of course—the fixed-base operator at your airport with an airplane rental business. My advice, and probably the advice of any responsible financial planner, would be to rent your plane rather than buy one. The per-hour cost to rent is lower simply because the airplane will get used far more than you can possibly fly it yourself, and someone else is dealing with the hassle of federal registration, record keeping, and so forth.

Rent, my friends, and happy flying!

The Least You Need to Know

➤ Learning to fly can be costly, but there are ways to cut expenses while remaining safe.

➤ Get the best ground training and flight instructors you can afford.

➤ Take advantage of any extra training options your flight school offers, such as spin training.

➤ Unless you have an extra hundred thousand bucks lying around, you're better off renting your plane than buying.

Chapter 14

Navigation: Getting from Here to There Without Street Signs

In This Chapter

➤ Aviation maps: a sky-high view of earth

➤ The latitude and longitude of it

➤ Great circle routes: the shortest routes on earth

➤ The challenge of dead reckoning

➤ Navigating by radio

Navigation is the element that transforms flying into traveling. The pilot who loves flying for its own sake can take his airplane aloft and enjoy the sensations of flight, then return to land without ever wandering more than a few miles from his home airport. The pilot who wants to get from one airport to another, or make his way to a particular site that he wants to see from the air, must be able to navigate—to plan a specific course between departure point and destination and then put that plan into practice in the air.

Drawing a Map

Road maps don't need much explaining (unless we're talking about learning to fold them up again so they'll fit back in the glove box). They depict the features that are most useful to automobile drivers—things like roads, parks, churches, schools—anything that drivers can easily see and use to navigate.

Aviation maps follow the same principle. They depict the features that will prove most useful in helping pilots navigate. But the definition of "useful features" to a pilot means that aeronautical maps look far different from road maps.

The Chart

First, don't call an aeronautical map a "map." It's called a "chart." There's really no logical reason for the terminology, except that pilots always have to be different.

The differences between a road map and an aeronautical chart go much further than terminology. Most noticeable is the *scale* to which they are drawn. Aeronautical charts are designed to work for an airplane traveling a couple hundred miles an hour, not for a car traveling slowly and stopping at every corner. If aeronautical charts were drawn on the same small scale as a city road atlas, a pilot traveling at high speed would have to turn the page every minute or so.

Not only does the scale of an aeronautical chart differ from what we generally see on a street map, its features differ as well. When navigating by car, street names on corner signposts are critical to making your way to a particular restaurant, for instance. But in the air, the names of roads are far less important (and far less legible!) than the shape of the road against the terrain. A pilot compares the shape of a road with a distinctive pattern to a similar pattern on his *sectional chart* to find his way by air.

A third critical difference between the two maps is that road maps usually ignore all but the most heavily used airports. Sectional charts depict every possible airport and out-of-the-way landing strip, even some that are no longer usable. That's because landing strips make particularly noticeable landmarks when seen from the sky. A secondary benefit is that if something goes wrong with the airplane in flight, it's nice to be able to fly toward a landing strip as quickly as possible.

By the Book

The **scale** of a map can be thought of in terms of the size of the features on a map. In other words, a lake that appears large on a large-scale road map might appear miniscule when it is drawn on a small-scale aeronautical chart.

By the Book

A **sectional chart** is the most common aeronautical chart. Its 1:500,000 scale means that one inch on the map represents 500,000 inches, or about 8 miles, of ground terrain. Thirty-eight sectionals cover the mainland United States. Larger-scale maps show greater detail near major airports, and smaller-scale World Aeronautical Charts show less detail for high-altitude, high-speed jets.

On the Grid: Latitude and Longitude

Latitude and longitude represent a set of imaginary grid lines that give map makers, or "cartographers," a system for pinpointing any location on the surface of the earth. The horizontal lines on this imaginary grid are the lines of latitude; the vertical-running lines are the lines of longitude.

Latitude

Midway between the earth's North and South Poles is the equator. The equator is a line whose points are all at equal distances from both poles. It divides the globe into Northern and Southern Hemispheres and can be thought of as the starting point for latitude. The equator is the line of zero degree latitude, and every location north and south of the equator is measured in *degrees, minutes,* and *seconds* of arc.

Each degree of distance in a northerly or southerly direction from the equator is about 69 miles in width, meaning each minute of arc is a bit over a mile wide. That means you cross one second of latitude for every 101 feet you travel in a northerly or southerly direction.

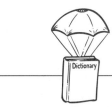

By the Book

Mathematicians and cartographers, following the lead of the ancient Greek inventors of geometry, divide circles into 360 equal divisions called **degrees of arc,** which are further divided into 60 **minutes of arc.** Each minute of arc is divided into 60 **seconds of arc.**

Longitude

But longitude is not quite so simple to explain. That's because lines of longitude aren't parallel to each other the way lines of latitude are. In the case of latitude, each line is parallel to the equator and parallel to each other. In fact, we sometimes call lines of latitude "parallels." But lines of longitude, or "meridians," as they are also called, converge at the poles. All 360 of them meet at the North and South Poles in a space that can theoretically has no distance at all. If you stood at one of the poles, you could walk around all 360 degrees of longitude in a few steps.

Lines of longitude converge at the poles because they were conceived as running north and south. Because every north-bound trip ends at the North Pole—going any farther would be a *south-bound* trip—the lines of longitude end at the poles, too.

At the equator, the degrees of longitude are 69 miles apart, as wide as degrees of latitude. When you move north or south, however, the degrees of longitude grow narrower, since they all have to meet at the poles. That's why aeronautical sectionals and other maps feature perfectly parallel latitude lines but curving longitude lines.

Though latitude and longitude form the fabric of our mapping and navigation methods, pilots don't often refer specifically to them. Instead, they refer to compass directions, or "azimuth," and the time and distance of flight. These terms suffice to convey the important aspects of navigation for pilots.

On Course

Pilots refer to directions using 360 degrees, from zero degree indicating straight north (usually meaning magnetic north, which we'll discuss later, rather than true north) to 180 degrees indicating straight south. Directly east is 90 degrees and directly west is 270 degrees. Pilots refer to courses by using three digits, and they usually omit the word "degrees." A typical reference among pilots might include the phrase, "When I reached Worcester from the north, I turned to a heading of zero-eight-two [degrees] toward Boston."

What's So Great About Great Circles?

If the earth's surface were flat, the shortest distance between two points would be a straight line. But when we're traveling on the curved surface of a globe, the shortest distance between two points turns out to be something else: an "equator."

Recall that the geographical equator is a line around the earth that splits the globe into two exactly equal halves. If we ignore the location of the poles and forget that the geographical equator is a line whose points are all at equal distances from both poles, we can imagine a multitude of possible equators circling the globe. In fact, we can imagine connecting any two locations by an equator—that is, the equator will run through both locations with exactly half the globe on either side.

Imagine an equator connecting two points—connecting Rome, New York, to Rome, Italy, for example. Another word for this line is a "great circle," and a great circle is the shortest distance between the two points—even if that means flying from Rome, New York, to the northeast and arriving in Rome, Italy, from the northwest.

Plane Talk

The principle of the great circle route holds the answer to a question that tantalized me as a youngster reading about the exploits of Charles Lindbergh. My rough knowledge of geography told me that when Lucky Lindy flew from New York to Paris, he should have pointed *The Spirit of St. Louis* in a general easterly direction and held a constant heading. But Lindy knew that fuel would be a deciding factor in whether he succeeded or failed. So he navigated his plane on a great circle route that took him northeast over Canada, then eastward across the North Atlantic, and finally southeastward over Ireland and toward the continent.

From a pilot's point of view, navigating across a great circle route is more difficult than flying a straight-line route. Great circles force pilots to constantly change course, while straight-line courses give us the luxury of pointing the airplane in one direction and holding it there.

But airliners and other planes gulping large amounts of fuel for hours at a time can save a lot of gas and money by trimming minutes off their flight times. So, with the help of computers and complex navigation equipment, they manage to fly a gradual great circle route.

When North Is Not Truly North

Navigating over the surface of the earth has other complications. One of the most fundamental is that there's no instrument on an airplane that can tell a pilot if he's pointing directly at the North Pole. After all, the North Pole is simply an ordinary point on the earth's surface with no special physical quality. It just happens to be the pivot location, one end of the spinning planet's axle, if you will.

Fortunately, there are a couple of points on the earth's surface that *do* possess a special physical quality. Near the North and South Poles, but still many hundreds of miles from the actual poles themselves, are points where the magnetic forces of the planet rise out of the earth's core. These points are called the magnetic poles. For pilots, directions are measured from the magnetic north and south poles (though in the Northern Hemisphere the southern pole is mostly irrelevant, and vice versa).

Inside an airplane's cockpit, the pilot has two instruments at his disposal to measure the direction to the magnetic north pole. The primary instrument is the simplest and most ancient—the magnetic compass. Compasses haven't changed much since the Chinese first conceived them, and the aviation version is a lightweight card attached to a magnetic bar that points toward the magnetic north pole. The whole thing floats in a bath of white kerosene to stop it from jiggling too much in flight.

Even with the stabilizing help of kerosene, the compass can be somewhat jiggly and difficult to read in flight. So early aviators built the directional *gyro,* or DG. The DG

On Course

Why not build roads and highways in orientation with the magnetic poles? Because the poles have a habit of wandering around Northern Canada in the north and Antarctica in the south. Geologists attribute the movement of the magnetic poles to changes in the movement of the molten rock far below the earth's surface, where moving currents help generate the earth's magnetic field. All in all, the magnetic poles are not reliably attractive.

doesn't point northward by itself, though, as the compass does. The pilot must set it before flight according to the magnetic compass. Periodically during flight, he must reset the directional gyro, which wobbles a bit due to friction in the stabilizing *gyroscope*. (We'll talk about the array of flight instruments in more detail later in this chapter.)

Plane Talk

Nowadays, magnetic compasses float in a pool of white kerosene, which is viscous enough to stabilize the compass and clear enough to see through. Legend has it that the white kerosene has come in handy for pilots who crash-landed their planes in cold weather and needed help starting a fire. But in the old days, pilots sometimes used a different fluid in their compasses—booze. The alcohol worked well in stabilizing the "whiskey compass," as they called it, and it came in handy after a crash landing, too—though old-timers didn't waste it on starting a fire.

Turbulence

Pilots are responsible for their own navigation. Air-traffic controllers don't provide much help, and pilots like it that way. Pilots use a number of navigation instruments and a network of ground-bound radio transmitters to help create electronic roadways in the sky; we'll talk about both of these in Chapter 15, "From Takeoff to Landing."

Dead Reckoning: Safer Than It Sounds

Armed with an aeronautical chart, a firm grasp of latitude and longitude, and a clear distinction between the true and the magnetic poles, it's time for a glimpse of the way pilots navigate.

Most modern planes come with sophisticated electronic navigation systems, called "inertial navigation," which use extremely sensitive motion detectors. Others use a network of space satellites to help the pilot determine his airplane's position around the globe. The cockpits of modern airplanes are becoming crowded with all sorts of "flight management" hardware, computerized gadgets updated electronically on occasion. Some depict the airplane's flight path in relation to a background that looks exactly like a sectional chart or another type of chart.

But the most "retro" navigational technique, and the one that demands the most skill from a pilot, is dead reckoning.

Dead reckoning was first used by the ancient mariners who plied the waters of the Mediterranean Sea. Those sailors knew that if they headed in a particular direction at a set speed for a precise amount of time, it would be easy to calculate how far they had traveled. For example, if a ship left shore and traveled at a speed of 10 *knots* in a northward direction, after one hour it would be 10 *nautical miles* north of port.

In theory, dead reckoning is a relatively simple form of navigation for a pilot to use. A pilot flying over the earth at a certain speed and direction for a specific time could, with a simple calculator, a protractor, and an aeronautical chart, easily deduce his position in, say, an hour. But, as in everything else, real-life conditions make such "simple" navigation a little more complicated.

By the Book

Gyroscopes are spinning wheels usually made of metal that, once they start rotating in a particular position, tend to resist disturbance. In obedience to Newton's laws of motion, a gyroscope that starts spinning in a north-south orientation, for example, will tend to remain lined up north and south. As the airplane turns, the directional **gyro** notes the difference between the direction the airplane is pointed and the gyro's north-south orientation, and depicts it on the face of the instrument as a heading.

Plane Talk

The origin of the phrase "dead reckoning" is lost in the mists of time, and there is still disagreement about it among pilots and navigation experts. The lamest explanation I've heard is that it derives from the nautical practice of navigating by referring to objects that were "dead in the water." The most likely origin of the phrase is from "deductive" reckoning, which means deducing your position based on a series of observations.

199

Airspeed and Groundspeed

Airplanes don't simply fly over the ground. They fly in air that is always moving in the form of wind. And wind at high altitude always blows from different directions and at different speeds than the wind on the ground. Not only that, a plane flying at an altitude of 10,000 feet might feel strong wind from the south while a pilot at 5,000 feet might have very light winds from the west.

In navigating, the wind can never be left out of the equation. A flight from Boston, say, to New York's Kennedy airport, which is toward the southwest, will arrive at different times depending on the wind speed and direction. A plane flying to the southwest will be pushed even faster by a northeasterly wind. For example, if an airplane is flying at 125 knots with a direct *tailwind* of 25 knots, the plane's speed over the ground will be 150 knots, the combination of the two speeds.

By the same token, a plane flying at 125 knots into a 25-knot *headwind* will have a total speed over the ground of just 100 knots. The effect of headwinds and tailwinds explain how an airline flight can take off late and still arrive at the destination gate early.

So, no matter how fast an airplane's "airspeed," the speed it travels through the air, what's most important is its "groundspeed," or its speed relative to the ground. Groundspeed affects all aspects of a flight. If a pilot must travel at 125 knots into a 25-knot headwind, and he wants to fly to an airport 200 miles away, he can calculate that the flight will take two hours to complete. From that, he can determine the amount of fuel he has to have on board to finish the flight plus have a safe reserve. The longer the flight, the more fuel a pilot needs. The weight of the fuel he must carry for the flight—about six pounds per gallon—will affect the number of passengers or the amount of cargo he can carry, or more likely how often he will have to land to refuel.

Steering the Course

Of course, headwinds and tailwinds are not all that complicate dead reckoning. They do enter into calculations of flight speed and time, but what about course, the direction a pilot must travel to get from one airport to another? In calculating course, we start to deal with crosswind. If we miscalculate the effects of *crosswind*, we will be blown off course and will run the risk of getting lost.

To understand the effects of crosswind on an airplane's course, imagine rowing a boat across a river. Let's say you want to row from a point on one shore to a point that is directly opposite. If you point your boat directly at your destination and begin rowing, you'll soon notice that you're not heading toward your destination at all. Instead, you're being carried slowly downstream as you make your way across.

A smart boatman knows that if he wants to track a course directly across a flowing river, he has to point his boat's nose upstream so that some of his energy is spent on counteracting the downstream drift. The downstream drift of the boat is exactly what happens to an airplane flying in a crosswind, or in any wind that is blowing even slightly from the side with a crosswind component. The strength of the crosswind and the amount of time the airplane spends in it will combine to push the pilot off course unless he points the airplane's nose slightly in the direction the wind is blowing from.

If you become a student pilot, you'll learn how to estimate the wind's speed and how to calculate which direction, or course, to steer to fly over a particular ground track. (The ground track is the direction you end up traveling when the airplane's direction and speed and the direction and speed of the wind are all taken into account. Think of the ground track as the direction the airplane's shadow travels.)

The Radio: All Navigation, All the Time

It wasn't long after people started flying that inventors began looking for ways to put radio waves to work in helping with navigation. Their inventions are still used in the form of a worldwide network of radio beacons. Those broadcast

By the Book

A wind that moves in the same direction as the airplane is called a **tailwind,** while a wind moving in the opposite direction of flight is a **headwind.** Wind from the side of an airplane's course is called a **crosswind.** Using basic trigonometry, wind from any direction can be divided into its headwind, tailwind, and crosswind components.

On Course

Don't be intimidated by the prospect of calculating course, track, or groundspeed. Over the years, pilots and seagoing navigators have developed all kinds of tools to simplify the process. The traditional circular slide rule, which is still the greatest test of old-fashioned navigating skills, has been replaced by battery-operated flight calculators that make the job of flight planning a snap. The old-fashioned "plotter"— a protractor that measures the basic course—is still in use, and takes only a few minutes to learn.

On Course

Airliners always carry far more fuel than the amount needed to get from start to destination. Regulations demand that airliners have to be able to fly not only to the destination, but to a specific alternate airport in case bad weather or something else forces the plane to divert its course. Once the plane gets to its alternate airport, it must be able to sustain a landing delay there before it runs low on fuel. FAA regulations make airline flying very safe.

stations send out signals in a range of frequencies that special airplane radios receive and translate into information about an airplane's track.

The most common radio navigation instrument is the VOR, or the very-high frequency omnidirectional range. Its name comes from the part of the radio spectrum it broadcasts on, the very-high-frequency portion, and the fact that it broadcasts an omnidirectional signal that can be received no matter which direction a plane flies in relation to the broadcast station. In essence, a pilot dials in a particular course—called a "radial" in navigation parlance—and the VOR indicates which direction the pilot should steer to get to that course.

Some cockpits have radios that rely on a miraculously precise form of navigational aid called GPS, which stands for "global positioning system." GPS uses a network of stationary satellites some 23,000 miles above the earth. Using precise clocks and complicated triangulation, GPS receivers are capable of pinpointing a location to within a few feet, and hold great promise to revolutionize the way we use radios to get around in airplanes.

Plane Talk

Because AM broadcast radio stations were so widespread in the Golden Age of Radio, back in the days of Jack Benny and Edgar Bergen, pilots began using a navigation device that homed in on ordinary broadcast radio signals. The instrument, called an automatic direction finder, simply points directly to the location of the radio station's broadcast antenna, which is also depicted as a symbol on an aeronautical chart. With a few mental gymnastics, ADFs can even be used to navigate a fairly accurate flight track. But to me the best thing about having an ADF in an airplane is that even if I don't need to use it to navigate, I can listen to some good music on AM radio stations, as long as there's nothing pressing to take care of at the moment.

I'm no Luddite, and I've been accused of going overboard in adopting new technologies, but the cockpit is one of my few refuges from the press of new technology. When I fly, I prefer to turn back the clock to the days of charts, slide rules, and a pencil behind my ear. I enjoy dead reckoning and using *pilotage* because it forces me to look closely at the ground below and to search for the tiniest details of topography.

For me, old-fashioned dead reckoning and pilotage are akin to driving my truck down the back roads of New England, while modern aviation aids seem more like racing down the interstate. Still, I am intimately familiar with all the navigation equipment in every plane I fly. Though I may prefer not to pay a lot of attention to them all the time because I'm busy enjoying the pleasures of hands-on navigation, electronic flight instruments add a degree of safety that pilots a few decades ago could only dream of.

By the Book

Pilotage is the art of being able to recognize on the earth's surface those features that are depicted on aeronautical charts. That includes distinguishing one hill from a similar one simply by a difference in the steepness of a slope or identifying a stream bed by its shape. Pilotage is one of the great forgotten skills, but one of the most rewarding that a pilot can learn.

So You Think You're Lost: Getting Back on Course

Once, while preparing a student for a test flight with an examiner, I reviewed with him the various methods of finding his course should he get lost. I knew it was a question he'd be asked, and he and I spent some time on it. At the end of the review, as a joke to lighten the pressure a bit, I said, "And if all else fails, land at the nearest landing strip and ask somebody on the ground where you are."

Now, under the pressure of a test flight, the mind can behave in funny ways. Sure enough, the check pilot quizzed my student on how to get his bearings if he's lost. "What's the first thing you'd do once you think you might be lost?" she asked. My student, obviously rattled, blurted out, "My instructor said I should land at a nearby airport and ask somebody where I was."

Fortunately, the check pilot recognized a case of jangled nerves when she saw it, and she drew the student out until he had laid out the full list of procedures. Later, he and I had a short briefing on how to recognize a joke when he heard one.

Getting lost is actually not that unusual for beginning pilots. The intricacies of navigation are only mastered after lots of practice, and that often means lots of getting lost. But to a seasoned pilot, getting lost should mean only a few moments of uncertainty before he identifies a terrain landmark on his chart.

Turbulence

On some flights—say, flights over the ocean or over uninterrupted forest—there are few prominent features that a pilot can rely on to stay on course. Such flights could be beyond the skill level of some pilots, who should plan their flight on a less direct but safer route. The John F. Kennedy Jr. tragedy might have been related to this, and Chapter 20, "John F. Kennedy Jr.'s Final Flight," is devoted to a discussion of his fatal accident.

If that fails, the pilot can turn to his on-board navigation radios for an almost surefire fix on his position. With the VOR, a pilot can find his direction from a specific navigation broadcast antenna, whose position is marked on the chart. The pilot can draw a line on his chart corresponding to that VOR direction, and he knows he has to be somewhere on that line. Then, he can tune in another VOR and determine his position relative to the second VOR. He can draw that line on the map. Where the two lines intersect is where he's positioned.

It gets even easier if the first VOR is equipped with distance-measuring equipment, or DME. Not only does the VOR provide a course line, but the DME tells the pilot exactly how many miles he is from the VOR broadcast station. By pinpointing that position on his chart, the pilot knows where he is and he can get his bearings.

The details involved even in the few navigational techniques I've described here require a good deal of classroom study and then practice in the airplane with an instructor. But the main thing to remember is that getting lost need not be a disaster, and pilots are equipped with a host of options when the terrain begins to look unfamiliar. Of course, if you still can't figure out where you are, just land at a nearby airport and ask somebody where you are!

The Least You Need to Know

➤ Aeronautical charts are tailored for the high speeds of aviation.

➤ In aviation, the shortest distance between two points is a great circle route.

➤ Headwinds, tailwinds, and crosswinds present a challenge to the pilot who navigates using dead reckoning.

➤ The combination of pilotage and dead reckoning is an honored flying tradition that owes much to seafarers.

➤ Getting lost doesn't have to turn into a crisis.

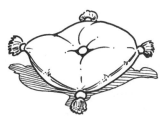

Chapter 15

From Takeoff to Landing

In This Chapter

➤ The preflight inspection

➤ Taxiing the airplane

➤ The specialized language of pilots and air-traffic controllers

➤ Landing the airplane

When a pilot puts together all the skills of maneuvering an airplane, understands how to navigate it from one airport to another, and has a sturdy understanding of the forces that affect the airplane in flight, he's almost ready to start a cross-country (airport-to-airport) flight.

Let's take a look at what happens in a typical flight, from the preflight checks to the landing.

Preflight: Keeping It Safe

There are a few things the pilot has to do even before the flight begins. First, he'll have to have planned the cross-country flight based on the weather conditions and the weight limitations of the plane (see Chapter 14, "Navigation: Getting from Here to There Without Street Signs," for details).

Second, pilots have to make sure that they are healthy and prepared to fly. Physical conditions that are only annoyances on the ground can be magnified by the effects of

altitude. Even some simple over-the-counter cold or allergy medications can slow down reactions and render a person unfit to fly until the medication fully wears off. Many pilots find it hard to admit to themselves that they are in no physical condition to fly, or that they lack the training and experience to make the flight safely. As we'll discuss in Chapter 19, "Emergencies in the Air," a better grasp of pilots' limitations would prevent a vast number of aviation accidents.

Third, the pilot must make sure the airplane's paperwork is in proper order. A plane can't legally fly without its paperwork on board. A student pilot flying solo is required to take along his logbook containing a short entry by his flight instructor giving permission for the flight. And of course, just as a car driver has to have a driver's license with him, all pilots must also carry their pilot certificate. For a student pilot, the student pilot certificate and medical certificate are one and the same.

A last item of paperwork is to check the maintenance condition of the airplane. Depending on the flight school or fixed-base operator, the maintenance logs will be stored in different places, but they should always be checked before starting out to ensure that the airplane has been inspected within the last 100 hours of flight time and that any malfunctions noted by other pilots have been repaired.

Turbulence

The most important preflight check a pilot can make is a self-assessment. From stress to the effects of alcohol to a bad cold, there are a number of reasons pilots should decline to fly.

Plane Talk

Even though a pilot is required to carry his pilot certificate with him when he goes flying, there's very little chance he's going to have to show it to an "air policeman." Aviation is regulated by the Federal Aviation Administration, which writes and enforces the rules. The FAA does not have a force of officers patrolling the skies and giving out tickets. That doesn't mean the FAA doesn't have sources of information, however, and misbehaving pilots who break the regulations or fly unsafely can expect a visit from an FAA inspector—and perhaps a suspension of their pilot certificate.

The Once-Over

Once he's out at the airplane, the pilot begins a preflight inspection. Following a checklist supplied by the airplane manufacturer and contained in the airplane's Information Manual, he first sits in the cockpit and checks the major electrical systems. He turns on the master electric switch, which turns on the juice to the instrument panel and the *avionics*.

In almost every case, the cockpit check will turn up no problems. So, with a checklist in hand to remind him of all the details, the pilot begins an exterior inspection. Often flight schools transcribe the checklist from the Information Manual onto a laminated card to make the checklist easier to handle and less vulnerable to fuel and oil spills.

For the most part, the preflight inspection is meant to make sure the mechanics have not made any serious mistakes and that other pilots who flew the airplane recently didn't cause any damage. It doesn't go much deeper than a surface inspection, but careful pilots can turn up some significant defects in time to get them corrected on the ground.

Depending on the model of airplane, the pattern and details of the exterior preflight will vary. In a small Cessna, for example, the preflight starts at the back of the left wing and progresses clockwise around the airplane.

After checking that the ailerons move easily, the pilot checks the wings' leading edges. Here, he looks for any signs that the plane might have bumped into something while moving around the airport. It's not uncommon to find small dents, called "hangar rash," that come from being moved around during maintenance, but the leading edges should be relatively smooth.

The most important check of the left wing of most small planes is the "stall warning horn." In a Cessna, this is a simple hole in the wing's skin that must not be blocked by insects or litter. In other planes, it might be a simple switch that must be free to move easily.

By the Book

Avionics is a word created just for aviation. It's a combination of two words—"aviation" and "electronics"—and it refers to the navigational equipment and two-way voice radios a pilot uses, as well as to the new generation of high-technology devices.

On Course

Birds seem to have a fascination with airplanes. I've seen bird nests in wheel wells where retractable landing gear are stored during flight, and I've seen them in engine compartments. I even saw a bird make a respectable start on a nest near the horizontal stabilizer of a twin-engine Piper Seminole, and she did it in the 45 minutes between two flights. Bird nests are perhaps the most common foreign object you'll find during preflight inspections.

Both of these devices trigger an audible warning to the pilot during flight if he is getting close to the critical angle of attack that could result in a stall (discussed earlier).

Also on the left wing is the fuel tank. The pilot will step up onto the wing for close inspection. Not only does he want to make sure the fuel cap is securely fastened, but he also has to make a careful check of how much fuel is in each tank. It isn't enough to rely on the fuel gauge in the cockpit to make sure there's enough fuel to finish the flight safely. The risk is simply too high to leave that up to a sometimes-faulty gauge. So airplane manufacturers provide a fuel stick—a graduated metal or wood stick that a pilot dips into the tank until it hits bottom. When it's pulled out, the pilot can see the line of liquid and check it against markings that indicate how many gallons are in the tank.

Plane Talk

It's not just pilots of small airplanes that have to perform preflight checks. The pilots of jetliners also do a "walk-around," usually armed with a flashlight that lets them peer into the holes and recesses of a modern jetliner. It's more than simply "kicking the tires and lighting the fires." Professional pilots know they can't rely solely on mechanics to keep the airplane safe. Everybody, even airline captains, have to play a role.

The pilot then checks the fuel in a second way. A small valve located on the underside of the wing allows the pilot to pour some raw fuel from the tank into a clear plastic sampling cup. Any particles of dirt or globules of water will be easy to see.

Finally, before moving on, the pilot unhooks the *tie-down* ropes or chains and inspects the tires and brakes.

Inspecting the Powerplant

At the front of the plane, the pilot carefully inspects the engine, making sure the oil is full and there aren't any leaks—the same sort of common-sense checks you might make on your car. But the airplane has something else up front, of course, that you don't find on many cars: a propeller.

The propeller is vulnerable to a lot of damage and has to be inspected carefully, even though the check only takes a few moments. The propeller's leading edge can become badly nicked and pitted from small stones that it sucks up. A large rock can even crack a prop blade. So a pilot has to check the leading edge for dangerously deep pits or for cracks that could cause part of the prop to break off in flight.

That could be a catastrophe for two reasons. First, the prop's thrust will decrease, maybe a lot, and that could mean the airplane can't sustain enough speed to maintain a constant altitude. In that case, the airplane will begin do descend and the pilot will have to plan for an emergency landing.

Second, the loss of a part of the propeller will throw it out of balance and could cause an extreme vibration of the engine. If the pilot doesn't respond quickly by reducing the throttle, the engine could be severely damaged or even damage the rest of the airplane with its shaking. Once the throttle is reduced to idle, or to whatever lower setting will cause the vibration to stop, the pilot will have to begin descending in order to maintain safe airspeed, and that means an emergency landing.

By the Book

When small airplanes are stored on the ground, even if it's only for a few minutes between flights, they are secured by **tie-down** ropes or chains. Because airports are wide open spaces, the wind at an airport can be stronger than on nearby residential streets or commercial districts; sudden gusts of wind can damage planes on the ground. Planes should always be tied down when there is no pilot at the controls.

No matter what happens during flight to damage the prop, the result is an emergency landing. What better reason to carefully check the prop?

While he's near the nose, the pilot will inspect the front wheel, or the "nose gear." The tire should be fully inflated, have a safe amount of tread remaining, and there should be no oil or fluid leaking from the shock-absorbing piston that's clearly visible just above the tire. Then, the pilot inspects the right wing in the reverse order he looked at the left one.

Finally, the pilot moves back over the empennage and around the stabilizers, checking that they are securely hinged and that they move freely. While he's back here, he'll disconnect the third and final tie-down.

By now, in the course of less than 10 minutes, the pilot has looked over the entire airplane, moving everything that moves, tugging on anything he can get a grip on to make sure it's securely attached to the plane. Now it's time for one last walk around the airplane. The pilot wants to make sure all the tie-down chains are removed, and the radio antennae are in place. And he wants to be darn sure the fuel caps are tightened all the way down. That completes the preflight inspection.

On Course

There's a bit of folk wisdom among pilots claiming that the quickest, simplest way to check a propeller for invisible cracks is with the flick of a fingernail. The theory goes that an undamaged propeller will ring like a bell, while a crack in the prop will cause more of a dull thunking sound. I've always found that a flick that is hard enough to "ring" the prop is also hard enough to cause a good bruise under the fingernail. What's more, I have a tin ear for a ringing prop, so I prefer to inspect the propeller visually.

Getting a Move On

Once the preflight inspection is finished, everybody settles into their seats and fastens their seat belts, something the law and common sense require.

The pilot follows the manufacturer's checklist for starting the engine, and with a turn of a key or the push of a starter switch, the propeller starts turning, slowly at first, then at an idling speed of about 1,000 revolutions per minute.

In order to keep the plane from moving too soon, the pilot holds the brakes by pushing on the top part of the rudder pedals. Each rudder pedal controls the brake on one wheel, so pressing them both holds both wheels still. When the pilot is ready, he releases the brakes to let the plane begin to roll forward.

Taxi!

Now, airplanes trying to maneuver on the ground aren't quite as ungraceful as a pig on roller skates, but almost. Obviously, airplanes are designed to work best in the sky. But because they have to move on the ground as well, designers have had to arrive at a compromise between flying and *taxiing*, as pilots call moving on the ground. (Why use the word "taxiing" when they could simply call it driving? Because, as you've heard me say many times already, pilots insist on being different.) Most small airplanes can be maneuvered by turning the nose wheel using the rudder pedals or by "differential braking," which means using one brake at a time to cause the plane to swing in one direction or another.

The pilot taxis the airplane along a network of "taxiways." To keep pilots from accidentally taxiing onto runways where they might find themselves prop-to-prop with another airplane in the middle of a takeoff or landing, taxiways are clearly marked. At airports with control towers, a controller watches taxiing airplanes like a traffic cop.

Liftoff!

The taxiing ends at a waiting area very near the beginning of the *active runway*. Before takeoff, pilots usually make one more safety check called a "run-up" just to make sure that it is ready to operate properly at high power.

Again, following the checklist, the pilot will check that all doors and windows are closed and secure and that his flight controls move freely. He once again checks his flight instruments to verify they are conveying the correct information, and that his fuel gauges show a safe fuel level.

Pressing the brake pedals firmly, the pilot then pushes the throttle forward until the engine is turning between 1,500 and 1,700 rpm, depending on the manufacturer's recommendation. This allows the pilot to check the engine's performance at a throttle setting similar to those used in flight. At this high throttle setting, flight instruments and engine instruments are put through one more check before the power is reduced to a more placid, and far quieter, 1,000 rpm or so that is generally used as an idle setting.

When the run-up is finished, the plane pulls up in line behind other airplanes waiting for takeoff, and makes a radio call to the control tower. An air-traffic controller makes sure the runway is clear of airplanes and that no other airplanes are close to landing. If all is safe, the clearance is announced over the radio: "Cleared for takeoff."

The pilot taxis onto the center line of the runway, pushes the throttle to full takeoff power, and the airplane surges ahead with a burst of acceleration. Small airplanes accelerate down the runway to speeds of 50 knots, or 58 m.p.h., or more. In the case of large jets, the wings don't produce enough lift for flight until groundspeed reaches far more than 100 knots, or 115 m.p.h.

Between the time the pilot pushes the throttle forward for takeoff power and the time he reaches liftoff speed, which pilots call *rotation* speed, the pilot has to use his rudder pedals very carefully. He moves his feet down to the lower part of the pedal so he doesn't press the brakes, which would slow his acceleration on the runway. At the very low speeds in the early moments of the takeoff the rudder won't have much effect, but at higher speeds it does. It takes a bit of practice to steer the airplane straight during the takeoff roll.

By the Book

Taxiing an airplane—moving it on the ground—can feel something like trying to pat your head and rub your stomach at the same time. That's because most of us are used to two pedals on the floor of a car that work far differently than the pedals in an airplane. Also, it's very tempting to grab hold of the control column and use it like a steering wheel. Actually, the control column has no effect on turning the nose wheel and turning the airplane on the ground. Our familiarity with cars works against us in the airplane.

By the Book

Pilots refer to the moment of liftoff as **rotation,** because the elevator control causes the plane to rotate around its lateral axis. If the rotation is abrupt, some airplanes can risk dragging the tail of the airplane on the ground. New airliner designs are required by the FAA to intentionally drag the tail on the runway during testing.

When the airspeed indicator on the instrument panel shows that the plane has reached a safe speed to fly, the pilot gently pulls the control column toward him, and the plane's nose wheel lifts off the ground as the tail drops. The wings' angle of attack widens, lift increases, and the airplane rises off its main gear into the air.

The pilot holds the nose at an upward angle that allows the plane to climb quickly and efficiently. The pilot will hold that angle, with some slight variations and maybe a brief period of level flight, depending on other air traffic around the airport, until he reaches his cruising altitude.

Cruising altitude differs depending on the type of airplane, the length of the trip, the capability of the airplane, and even which direction the flight is taking.

For small planes with relatively low power, such as training airplanes and many less expensive models, the low power production of the engine will limit the altitude a plane can climb to. That means pilots have to plan on a relatively low cruising altitude.

For very short trips, it makes no sense to fly at a high cruising altitude if the flight can be made at a lower one. After all, for a short flight, the plane might no sooner reach cruising altitude than it must begin its landing descent. In those cases, a pilot should plan as low a cruising altitude as he can.

Turbulence

Taxiing mistakes are one of the most common dangers at airports, including the big international jetports and the small community ones. At the largest airports, planners are starting to experiment with city-street–style traffic controls, from lights that resemble ordinary traffic lights to devices that resemble railroad signals. There's no consensus so far on what works best, but safe taxiing is a serious issue that lots of people are working on.

Some airplanes cannot be flown very high because of the FAA's oxygen requirements. Because the air is so thin above 12,500 feet above sea level, the FAA requires that pilots breathe supplemental oxygen from a special system installed in the airplane after 30 minutes of flying above that altitude. Above 14,000 feet, the pilot must breathe oxygen at all times, and above 15,000 feet, everybody on the airplane must breathe supplemental oxygen.

If the plane is not equipped with supplemental oxygen, and most small planes are not, the pilot has to plan a cruise altitude that allows him to remain below 12,500 feet most of the time. Of course, larger planes are often pressurized, meaning they are equipped with a system that keeps the air of the cabin and cockpit breathable throughout the flight, regardless of altitude. (We'll learn more about pressurization in Chapter 19.)

Finally, the FAA dictates which altitudes a pilot can fly at, depending on the direction of flight. For example, below 29,000 feet, if a pilot is flying eastward—that is, from a heading of zero degrees clockwise to 179 degrees—he must fly at "odd thousands plus 500 feet," meaning 3,500 feet, 5,500 feet, 7,500 feet, and so on. If he's flying westward—that is, on a heading of 180 degrees clockwise to 359 degrees—he must fly at "even thousands plus 500 feet," or 4,500 feet, 6,500 feet, 8,500 feet, and so on.

Above 29,000 feet, the FAA puts more altitude between planes. Heading eastward, pilots must fly at 30,000 feet, 34,000 feet, 38,000 feet, and so on in 4,000-foot increments. Heading westward the altitudes are 32,000 feet, 36,000 feet, and so on in 4,000-foot increments.

Some airplanes are like sports cars and have plenty of power to spare, allowing them to climb very quickly, maybe 1,500 feet per minute. Others are like old VW Beetles, with just enough horsepower to get the job done. These airplanes, which include some of the smaller training models, might climb at 500 feet per minute, and even less on a very hot day. (Later, we'll discuss the effect of hot weather on an airplane's performance.)

Either when the takeoff roll begins or when the pilot reaches a distinctive landmark near the airport, he will start a stopwatch to track flight time. As we've already seen, time is a crucial element in accurate dead reckoning navigation, and if a pilot forgets to click the stopwatch, he will find himself playing catch-up in his navigation.

By the Book

An airport, no matter how small, always has at least two runways, since any single strip of asphalt can be approached from either direction. A pilot can take off in one direction, say eastward on an east-west runway, or westward. Whether an airport is a single grass strip or a complex tangle of half a dozen concrete runways, the **active runway** is the one in use. Controllers determine the active runway based on wind direction, the noise concerns of nearby neighborhoods, and the demands of rush-hour air traffic.

On the Radio: Working with Air Traffic Control

During flight, pilots usually have to talk on the two-way radio with air-traffic controllers. For some reason, the idea of talking on the radio causes some pilots a lot of anxiety. Practice and experience usually calm their nerves.

Contrary to common opinion, by the time pilots have filled some pages of their logbooks with flying time, most understand that air-traffic controllers occupy a relatively small, albeit important, role in a typical flight. And with a little familiarity with the language pilots use to express themselves clearly, the give-and-take between pilot and controller becomes easy and friendly.

On Course

I've spent a great deal of time flying from high-altitude airports and experienced some nervous moments. Because the atmosphere gets thinner at higher altitudes, airplanes at high-altitude airports are slower to accelerate during takeoff and require longer runways. Once in the air, airplanes climb more slowly than they do at a sea-level airport. Still, some of the most beautiful airports in the world are at high altitudes, and pilots seldom regret the extra training and practice they need to fly out of them.

The typical radio call follows a basic pattern: Who is calling, where they are, and what they want to do. For example, here's what a pilot's radio call might sound like shortly after takeoff from Worcester airport in central Massachusetts for a flight to Portland, Maine:

> "Boston Center, Cessna four-five-zero-one-Charlie, over Worcester at five thousand five hundred feet en route to Portland, request flight following."

In a few words, the pilot, using the registration number of his airplane, Cessna 4501C, told a controller overseeing Boston-area air traffic that he was over the city of Worcester, he was flying at 5,500 feet above sea level, that his destination was Portland, and that he would like controllers to follow him on radar to his destination.

For some flights in good weather, controllers don't have to agree to the flight-following service. It depends on their workload. But if she can manage it, the controller will agree to act as a sort of second set of eyes for the pilot.

If the controller does agree to follow the flight, the pilot will be assigned a distinctive "squawk," or transponder code. A transponder is an on-board avionics device that amplifies the reflection of radar waves from an airplane. It makes the dot representing an airplane appear larger and brighter on a controller's radar screen.

The individual code also helps controllers distinguish airplanes from one another, which is particularly helpful in crowded airspace. The controller's radar screen automatically calculates the plane's groundspeed, which pilots can ask for to see how accurately they predicted their speed. What's more, some transponders tell controllers what altitude the plane is flying at, which helps controllers keep pilots away from other airplanes.

Plane Talk

Transponders, which were first used in World War II to help radar operators recognize friendly planes so they wouldn't shoot down an ally, have now been adapted to another life-saving duty. Some very new transponders are able to detect nearby airplanes, something older versions couldn't do. If that's not enough, the new transponders use a synthesized human voice to warn the pilot of an impending collision with a suggestion which direction to turn to avoid it. There have been some bugs in the system, but the new class of transponders promise to help make flying even safer.

Collision Avoidance: Keeping Your Head on a Swivel

In addition to controlling the plane, navigating on course, and communicating with air-traffic controllers, pilots are always on the lookout for airplanes flying nearby. In purely statistical terms, the number of midair collisions is incredibly small, although the risk goes up dramatically near airports, which serve as convergence points for a large number of planes.

Still, it doesn't take a near collision to get a pilot's attention. Even airplanes that are just a dot in the distance can loom large as a potential threat. That's because when airplanes are flying at sometimes hundreds of miles an hour, their head-on speed is so fast that pilots must have very quick reactions to stay out of danger.

Also, when airplanes are speeding through the sky, they lose a lot of maneuverability simply because of inertia. There's not much that designers can do about that, so pilots must detect possible collision threats early in order to avoid them.

On Course

Even when they're not flying, many pilots enjoy listening to the discourse between pilots and controllers. They use aviation-band scanners capable of picking up the frequencies that aviators use. These tabletop scanners, or the slightly more expensive transceivers that both receive and transmit, are good learning tools for students who can listen to the pattern of a typical radio call, then imitate it when they go flying.

Turbulence

Many pilots fall into lazy habits when they are being helped by air-traffic controllers. While radar is an excellent supplement that adds a margin of safety to flying, pilots must remain disciplined about watching out for other airplanes, some of which radar devices may fail to detect. The old-timers have it right when they lecture us to stay alert: "Keep your head on a swivel!"

The greatest threat posed by other planes comes from those flying at the same altitude, so pilots spend most of their visual scanning time looking for planes flying at about the same level. They scan systematically, starting from one side of the airplane, moving slowly around the front, and then ending on the other side. The eyes are better able to spot traffic if they scan a small patch of sky for a few moments, then move on to the next patch. A quick sweep of the eyes from one side of the airplane to the other will seldom pick up hard-to-see traffic.

In a typical flight, a pilot, or his passengers, might identify as few as one or two other planes when flying in an unpopulated area, to dozens when flying over large cities. If a pilot spots an airplane, he must determine how far away it is and which direction it is headed. If he decides it won't be a threat, he should continue to watch it anyway in case it changes course. If the "traffic," as pilots call other planes, is too close for comfort or seems like it might become a problem in time, the pilot must decide what the best remedy is. In most cases, he'll turn away from the other plane. In some cases he'll climb or descend, though this could cause him to become a threat to another flight at a different altitude.

Plane Talk

One near-collision will transform any pilot into a passionate traffic-watcher. While on a pleasure flight with a pilot cousin and some others from Santa Ana, California, to Catalina Island several years ago, bright sunshine filtering through Southern California smog significantly obscured visibility and forced us to squint into the light. One thing we did make out: a Cessna 182 flashing past us in the opposite direction only a few dozen yards away. The combined speeds of the two planes probably approached 300 knots, or 345 m.p.h. As I recall, once our hearts stopped pounding, we called off the rest of the flight to Catalina and turned back toward the airport, eager to be back on the ground where speeding Cessnas are less of a threat.

FAA regulations have a good deal to say about how to avoid collision threats. Pilots usually temper those regulations with common sense and a dash of help from air-traffic controllers.

Plane Talk

Many general aviation pilots put their passengers to work helping to locate other airplanes in the area. Before takeoff, a pilot can ask his passengers to lend a hand by looking for airplanes and bringing them to the pilot's attention. The more eyes that are at work looking for potential collision threats, the safer the flight will be. What's more, passengers enjoy the idea of being a part of the "flight crew."

Coming Back to Earth

At the end of each leg of a trip, a pilot makes his approach to his destination airport. If he has done his preflight planning correctly, he'll know something about the conditions at his destination airport. Airport directories published every few weeks by the FAA reveal any flight hazards at the airport and give pilots a sense of how local planes move around the *traffic pattern.*

While still a few miles from the airport, a pilot descends to the traffic pattern altitude, which is generally 1,000 feet above the ground. He radios the tower of his approach, and controllers alert him to other traffic in the area that could pose a collision threat. If there's no tower at the field—the vast majority of all airports are these "uncontrolled fields"—the pilot uses a local frequency, which is indicated on aeronautical charts, to let other pilots in the area know of his arrival.

By the Book

When they fly into or out of airports, pilots use standardized rules about how high to climb, which direction to turn, and which areas around the airport to avoid. Pilots call these rules the **traffic pattern.** Traffic patterns may differ slightly from one airport to another, but pilots from other areas study the local habits and abide by them.

There are some prelanding checklists the pilot goes through to make sure the plane is ready for landing. The checklists are contained in the airplane's Information Manual, but are frequently transcribed on a card that can be easily held in one hand. In a retractable-gear airplane, one of the most important is the checklist item that reminds the pilot

By the Book

On final approach, pilots follow an imaginary **glide slope** down to the runway. The glide slope, which can be an angle of descent as shallow as 3 degrees, is often indicated by a set of lights installed beside the runway. Depending on the airplane's height above or below that imaginary glide slope, the pilot sees varying color lights. It's a simple, easy-to-use system that helps pilots by displaying two red danger lights when the pilot is too low, two white caution lights when he's too high, and one of each when he's on the proper glide slope.

to extend the gear. There are few things more embarrassing—and potentially dangerous—for a pilot to do than land a retractable-gear airplane without dropping the gear.

The pilot also extends the wing flaps, usually by a few degrees at a time to progressively slow the airplane as it gets closer to landing. Finally, the airplane turns into final approach, the sloping descent to the runway that gives the pilot time to prepare his thoughts for the task of landing. During final approach, the pilot will make small adjustments to his throttle setting to stay on a steady *glide slope,* and he'll use the elevators, ailerons, and rudders to stay aligned with the center of the runway. In a small airplane, the pilot will hold a speed of about 60 knots, or 69 m.p.h., while in a jet, the speeds will be in the neighborhood of 150 knots, or almost 175 m.p.h.

When the plane gets to within 50 feet or so of the runway, the pilot gradually reduces the throttle setting and begins a smooth transition from a slight nose-down attitude to a slightly nose-up attitude. For a tricycle-gear airplane, it's very important that the pilot not land the plane nose-wheel first. The plane can be badly damaged, and it's even possible for the pilot to lose control of the plane.

Within a couple of feet of the ground, the plane will begin to settle to the runway. By this point in the landing, the throttle will be all the way off as the airspeed continues to slow. If the pilot has timed the landing properly, the plane will touch down on the runway just about the moment the wings begin to lose lift in a stall. Up to now, the pilot has been pressing the rudder pedals, but now that he's on the runway he will move his feet to the top of the pedals and begin to apply the brakes. After all, he's not flying any more—he's taxiing.

After landing and pulling off the runway onto a taxiway, the pilot will do many of the same things he did at the beginning of the flight, except in reverse. He'll read through his postflight checklist, contact the tower for permission to taxi, and head for the parking area to shut down the engine and attach the tie-down chains.

It's Easier Than It Seems—and Harder

In this general discussion, the newcomer to flying could be intimidated by the amount of detail and multitude of tasks involved in a simple flight. None of this should be off-putting to the would-be pilot. The aviation learning process is gradual and stair-stepped so that no new information or skill is added until each step is mastered. In fact, the vast amount of skill and knowledge required to be a good pilot is a major part of flying's appeal. We can spend years and thousands of hours flying and still be able to continue to refine our abilities toward the ultimate goal—flying the perfect flight.

The Least You Need to Know

➤ Preflight inspection of both pilot and airplane is crucial to staying safe.

➤ Taxiing an airplane forces a pilot to shift from the skills of driving a car.

➤ Radio communications are an important element of most flights, and has terminology that is easy to learn.

➤ Careful pilots must keep their heads "on a swivel" in searching the sky for other airplanes.

➤ Landing the plane is a simple concept, but it takes a good deal of practice to master.

Chapter 16

Cloud Dancing: Air Shows and Aerobatics

In This Chapter

➤ Aviation as entertainment

➤ The basic maneuvers

➤ The strain on plane and pilot

➤ If you want to learn aerobatics

If you're like me, you were bitten by the aviation bug the very first time you saw an ear-splitting formation of airplanes called the Thunderbirds. The U.S. Air Force's Demonstration Squadron was created in the 1950s to lure young men to join the youngest of the armed services, but for me, and I'm certain for millions of other youngsters and not-so-youngsters, the Thunderbirds fueled my interest in civilian aviation.

The Thunderbirds, and their Navy counterpart group, the Blue Angels, may have beckoned plenty of young recruits into the service, but I'll bet that half the cockpit seats in America's jetliners are filled thanks to the breathtaking air show performances of the Thunderbirds, the Blue Angels, and scores of thrilling air-show performers.

No Business Like (Air)Show Business

The part of the Thunderbirds show that thrilled me years ago and that continues to get my heart pumping today: Partway through the show, the five jets fly away into the distance after performing a series of maneuvers. It seems as though the show is over.

The Thunderbirds were created to inspire young men and women to join the Air Force, but with their thrilling formation aerobatics, they also serve as emissaries of aviation of all kinds.

(U.S. Air Force)

By the Book

The **Thunderbirds** are the younger of the two military demonstration flight teams. The Navy **Blue Angels** began recruiting and good-will tours in 1946, shortly after World War II ended, because Navy brass feared the public would lose interest in military flying and might permit defense funding to be cut. The Air Force's Thunderbirds took to the air in 1953.

But miles away, they turn back toward the airport in a tight arrowhead-shaped wedge and speed toward the crowd. With streams of smoke trailing behind, they get closer and closer while they fly lower and lower to the ground. Then, right at the center of the airport, the five jets pull sharply upward and split away from their tight formation, creating a starburst of smoke trails and an explosion of sound from the jet engines overhead.

For me, it was the mixture of roaring engines, beautiful airplanes, and a hint of danger that sparked my imagination. That potent mixture has made air shows one of the most popular summertime events in the United States, and a crop of daring, highly skilled pilots have emerged to showcase one of the most thrilling faces of aviation—aerobatics.

Every weekend from late spring to early autumn—air show "season" pretty much mirrors baseball season—airports around the country, large and small, play host to air shows featuring some of the most breathtaking flying stunts you'll see anywhere. From Patty Wagstaff, a slip of a woman who manhandles an airplane like no one in history, to Wayne Handley, who pilots the beefy, overpowered Turbo Raven, air-show pilots get up close and personal with aviation fans, often mingling in crowds and firing up enthusiasm in aerobatics.

Plane Talk

In 1982, the Thunderbirds suffered a tragedy that made some wonder if the boost to aviation was worth the danger of flying close-formation aerobatics. While performing a formation loop, the lead airplane suffered a mechanical failure. The formation airplanes, concentrating only on following the lead airplane, as they were trained, didn't realize what was happening until it was too late to recover, despite the fact that they are in constant radio communication with each other and are trained for just such an emergency. Despite the tragic loss of life, military pilots saluted the formation pilots for their unblinking discipline in the cockpit. Needless to say, the Thunderbirds team recovered from the disaster.

The Thunderbirds are famous for performing spectacular aerobatics at near-supersonic speed while only inches apart. Here's the incredible view of what it looks like to fly at 600 miles per hour at arm's length from another plane.

(U.S. Air Force)

On Course

When you watch the Thunderbirds and the Blue Angels fly through their routines, you're seeing actual military maneuvers and techniques that have been choreographed for your entertainment. The pilots are using the very same methods that their fellow pilots used to accomplish their missions in the Gulf War and during the Kosovo Crisis.

Turbulence

Aerobatics are a specialized form of flying and require special training by qualified pilots. Don't try to fly aerobatic maneuvers unless you have this training. Nothing in this chapter should be regarded as encouraging pilots to fly aerobatic maneuvers. Aerobatics can place enormous strain on airplanes and on the human body, and can be deadly if not done correctly.

Air shows aren't only about what's going on in the sky. Some of the most popular air show stars aren't the aerobatic pilots and planes, but the popular air show exhibits of the venerable war birds of World War II, which are still making the rounds thanks to dedicated mechanics and volunteers. Planes like the B-17 *Sentimental Journey*, and some of the memorable fighter planes of World War II, are on display at many air shows, as are exquisite antique civilian planes. Even the civilian classics are preserved so beautifully that they attract not only flying nuts but also antique auto buffs who appreciate historical vehicles that are lovingly maintained.

What Are Aerobatics?

When it comes to action and noise, the aerobatics are the centerpiece of the shows. Aerobatics are a sort of aeronautical acrobatics—two words that combine to give the sport its name. With specially built airplanes, aerobatics pilots can turn the art of flying on its head—literally. Flying upside down, in corkscrews, fluttering earthward like a leaf, even flying backward—all form a part of a sport that allows pilots to "spread their wings." For most pilots, flying means flying straight and level, so once we learn how to perform aerobatics, it is liberating for many of us to step into a high-powered, ultra-strong airplane and spend some time turning the craft of flying into art.

Aerobatics rely on four basic maneuvers that pilots combine and string together to create tens of thousands of subtle variations. In fact, the Aresti "dictionary," created by a Spanish aerobatics genius named José Luis Aresti, contains thousands of aerobatic diagrams that pilots use to sketch out their routines. But each of those diagrams is made up of a mixture of the five "letters" of the aerobatics alphabet.

Let's take a general look at aerobatics in order to make your next air show outing a lot more interesting. Refer to Chapters 7, "How Airplanes Fly, Part 1: The Parts of a Plane," and 8, "How Airplanes Fly, Part 2: The

Aerodynamics of Flight," for a description of how throttle, aileron, elevator, and rudder are used together to accomplish these maneuvers.

Turning Flying on Its Head

One of the fundamental skills that aerobatic pilots must master is inverted flying—flying upside down. Inverted flying is a challenge because it's not just the plane that stands on its head—the pilot does, too. When you're in the cockpit, your body protests all the blood that gravitates toward your head. (We'll talk more about the body's response to aerobatics later in this chapter.) Your instincts about how to use your controls are reversed, too.

Plane Talk

Although they might not enjoy it, most pilots can tolerate the discomfort of flying upside down. But not all planes can say the same. In fact, very few airplanes are capable of inverted flight for even a few seconds. That's because the systems that pump fuel and oil to the engine often rely on gravity to do their jobs, and when gravity is turned upside down—at least from the airplane's point of view—fuel and oil stop flowing, and that means the engine quits running until the plane is once again upright. Specially designed aerobatics planes are able to pull it off because their engines are equipped with fuel pumps and oil systems that keep the engine running and well lubricated regardless of the plane's attitude.

During inverted flight, every control movement a pilot makes in the cockpit with ailerons, elevators, and rudders has an effect different from what he'd expect in normal, upright flight. (For a review of the effects of the three basic control surfaces, turn back to Chapters 7 and 8.) The elevators provide the clearest example. In upright flight, the pilot pulls the control stick toward him to cause the elevators to make the airplane's nose move up. In inverted flight, the same control movement actually moves the airplane's nose toward the earth.

Entering inverted flight involves a highly coordinated series of control movements. First, with a little extra airspeed than usual in order to offset the high drag caused by the slightly steeper pitch attitude once it's inverted (after all, the airfoil is usually designed for upright flying, not inverted), the pilot turns the control column to begin a bank in either direction. When the bank angle reaches about 45 degrees, he begins to apply rudder in the opposite direction of the bank and begins to push forward on the control column. As he approaches inverted flight, he gradually reduces the rudder and bank angle, but maintains some forward pressure.

Until a pilot has practiced inverted flight for a while, everything the airplane does seems to be backward. But in order to be able to fly the full repertoire of aerobatics, a pilot has to learn inverted flying.

Putting a Spin on It

Spins are a key tool in the aerobatic pilot's kit. Think of spins as those maneuvers in which the airplane appears to be twirling downward like a spinning leaf. To execute the traditional spin, a pilot decelerates to a speed that is so slow the wings can no longer provide enough lifting force to keep the plane flying level. That's the speed where the pilot, using mostly rudder control, intentionally forces the plane to turn in one direction or the other, and the trademark downward spiraling motion begins.

Plane Talk

Although aerobatic pilots make the spin look easy, it is still a dangerous maneuver. Spins have claimed the lives of some of the best aerobatic pilots in the business, including the legendary Art "The Professor" Scholl, who was killed when he couldn't pull out of a spin maneuver while filming the Tom Cruise movie *Top Gun*. We aren't certain what made it impossible for Scholl to recover from the spin, but factors including disorientation, improper balance of cargo, or a malfunction with airplane's controls, and even the design of some airplanes can make spins impossible to stop.

Aerobatic pilots use the spin maneuver as the basis for performing a high-speed stunt called a "snap roll." The snap roll and the spin look very different and are executed at different speeds. What they have in common is how they are initiated—by a loss of lifting force, which the pilot causes and uses in different ways.

In the spin, the pilot eliminates the lifting force by decelerating to a point where the wings no longer provide lift. In a snap roll, the pilot doesn't bother to slow down to enter the spiral; he flies at a constant speed and altitude and may even be ascending.

How does he eliminate the lifting force in these circumstances? He uses a combination of full, even abrupt, left or right rudder control while pulling the elevator control sharply backward. This forces the plane to feel the same loss of lifting force that the wings experience in the traditional, slow-speed spin. But because of the snap roll's higher speed, the result is a startlingly quick rotation that thrills audiences.

Turning the Circle on Edge

The loop is one of the simplest aerobatic maneuvers to perform and one of the easiest for spectators to recognize. It was also one of the first aerobatic maneuvers to be mastered by early aviators.

Plane Talk

German fighter pilot Ernst Udet was among the first to make his fame by thrilling crowds with the loop maneuver. He added more danger to it than we see today. Instead of beginning and ending the maneuver from a few hundred feet above the ground, Udet would fly along the ground, touch his wheels on the ground, then pull up into his loop. As the loop was nearly complete, he rocketed toward the ground and pulled out just in time to touch his wheels on the ground again to end the stunt.

A pilot begins a loop by accelerating to a fast enough speed to carry the plane over the top of the maneuver, much as a roller coaster car must accelerate before speeding through the looping part of a ride. Then using mostly the elevator control, the pilot pulls the nose higher and higher until the plane is flying on its back. The pilot completes the loop by simply using the elevator to bring the nose "up"—up as seen from the cockpit, which is now upside down—until he recovers from the loop at the same altitude and speed he began at.

A pilot can use the loop maneuver as the basis for doing a number of other stunts. For example, at the top of the loop he can add a snap roll before continuing, a maneuver that pilots call an "avalanche." (See, we're already combining the basic aerobatic maneuvers to create complex ones!)

On a Roll

The ailerons, the controls on the wings that help the pilot bank the airplane right and left, can be used at the top of the loop to initiate the *aileron roll*. If the pilot

By the Book

When a plane's wings are vertical instead of horizontal, pilots say they are in **knife-edge** flight. Some aerobatic pilots stop the roll right at that knife-edge position and fly for several seconds that way. That means it is the body of the airplane, called the fuselage, that must act like a wing and produce enough lifting force to keep the airplane flying.

On Course

When you attend an air show, there are a few rules of common courtesy—as well as safety—that you should be sure to observe. First, don't touch any part of a display airplane, or for that matter any of the airplanes that are permanently parked at the airport. Also, remain behind all barrier ropes. They're there to comply with federal regulations. And the most important rule of all: Have lots of fun!

moves the aileron control, or stick, quickly to the left, for example, and leaves it there long enough, the plane will rotate toward the left so the left wing is pointed straight at the ground while the right wing is pointed to the sky. That "edgewise" position is sometimes called the *knife-edge* position, and if the pilot keeps the stick on the left, the plane will actually keep turning until it's upside down. The aileron roll can be stopped when the wings are level in inverted flight or it can be continued until the plane has rolled 360 degrees and is once again right side up.

Hammering the Point Home

The last of the fundamental aerobatic maneuvers is a funny little maneuver with a lot of names. Some pilots call it a hammerhead turn, others call it a hammerhead stall, still others a stalled turn. But it is commonly known as the hammerhead. For an aerobatic maneuver, it is unusual because of how slow the plane is flying when the hammerhead is performed. Here's how it's done.

At a relatively fast speed, the pilot pulls the nose up until it is pointed vertically to the sky. Keeping the engine at full throttle, the pilot holds the vertical flight path until the airspeed slows, then applies full rudder in one direction, let's say toward the left.

The left rudder will cause the nose to swing left toward the left wing, and will cause the left wing to slice downward toward the ground. The pilot holds the controls this way until the airplane's nose is pointed straight at the ground. As he descends and regains airspeed during a few seconds of being pointed straight at the ground, the pilot can gain enough speed from the combination of gravity and engine power to launch into other aerobatic maneuvers.

The hammerhead is a critical maneuver in competition aerobatics. Why? You can see that the pivot at the peak of the hammerhead has enabled the pilot to reverse his direction of flight. Part of the rules of international aerobatics contests is that pilots must perform their entire routine in an imaginary cube of only

1,000 meters (that's about 3,300 feet). From the ground, that appears to be plenty of space, but from the air, the aerobatic box can seem as small as a postage stamp. The hammerhead enables pilots to make full use of that tiny space.

An Intense "Headache"

Like artists in any medium, aerobatic pilots often go beyond the traditional boundaries—even beyond the maneuvers that can be created by combining the four fundamental aerobatic maneuvers above.

One of the most outrageous maneuvers doesn't just break the basic aerobatic rules—it shatters them. It's a wild, tumbling, cart-wheeling, out-of-control hodge-podge of a stunt called a "lomcevak" (pronounced *LOM-shi-vahk*), which is a Czech word meaning "headache." A lomcevak is one of the most violent things you can do in an airplane besides crash. From the ground, it looks as though the airplane is having a fit. One second, the airplane's flying along and everything seems fine. The next, it is tumbling chaotically, sometimes tail-first, sometimes wingtip first.

If it looks crazy from the ground, it's even worse from the cockpit. Some aerobatic pilots like to say that once they start the lomcevak (usually with lots of engine power, forward elevator, and opposite rudder and aileron controls), they don't have any better idea of how it will end than a spectator does. The question is whether the airplane will shake off its temporary madness with its nose pointed up, down, frontward, or backward. Once the in-flight flailing stops, the pilot has to gather his wits and decide how to keep the plane flying.

In actuality, there is a method behind the façade of chaos. There is also plenty of concern for safety. For a trained pilot and a strong airplane, the maneuver is a safe one.

The roll, combined with the spin, the loop, the hammerhead turn, and inverted flight, make up the basic elements of aerobatics. Add variations like the snap roll and the lomcevak, put these tools into the hands of a great pilot, and you have aerobatic maneuvers that make for dramatic and inspiring entertainment.

Of Aerobatics and "Comfort Bags"

Aerobatic flying is one of the few forms of flying that requires the pilot to be as fit as an athlete. For the most part, nonmilitary flying is a

On Course

If you want to see an excellent display of silver-screen aerobatics, see *Cloud Dancer*, a 1980 film starring David Carradine as an ill and aging aerobatics pilot. The plot is threadbare, but the flying is spectacular. Some of the best stunt pilots in the business, including Charlie Hillard, Leo Loudenslager, and Tom Poberezny, flew mind-blowing flying scenes that make *Cloud Dancer* a must-see, if hard-to-find, film.

relatively sedentary pursuit. But aerobatics are a big exception. Aerobatic flying puts enormous physical stress on pilots and takes a toll on the body during even a single flight.

The Pitts Special, with its distinctive biplane design and starburst paint pattern, has become synonymous with aerobatic flying. The plane's spectacular performance and strength has made it a favorite of fans and pilots alike.

(Guenther Eichhorn)

"G" Whiz!

To understand the demands on the body during aerobatics, you have to understand gravitational forces, or "g-forces," which is the nickname we give to the sensation of added gravity caused by centrifugal force. For example, if a pilot executes a loop that exerts 6 g's during a portion of a loop, he feels as though he weighs 1,200 pounds, or six times the normal force of gravity.

Acceleration comes in two flavors, at least for our discussion—linear acceleration and angular acceleration. Liner acceleration is the force that pushes you back into your car seat or that makes you feel heavier on an elevator going up. Angular acceleration, also called "centrifugal force," is what pushes you against the wall of the rotating carnival "tilt-a-whirl" ride or tends to fling you off a fast-turning merry-go-round.

Linear, or straight-ahead, acceleration is relatively easy to visualize, and is of concern to the aerobatics pilot—except when being launched from an aircraft carrier where a pilot is jolted with several g's when accelerating from a stop to almost 200 m.p.h. in a couple of seconds.

Centrifugal force is a bigger concern for the aerobatics pilot. Centrifugal force is what causes the g-forces that can feel as though the pull of gravity was magnified beyond the earth's 1 g force we live with every day. Centrifugal force during flight can turn up the g-meter inside an aerobatic plane to 10 g's or more.

Imagine holding a toy airplane on a string and spinning it around in a small circle. If you twirl it slowly, the plane goes round and round at pretty much the same distance from the ground that it was at rest. But if you really start spinning it quickly, the plane will move higher toward your hand and bring the string itself almost parallel to the ground.

Now imagine a miniature pilot inside your model plane. When you were spinning it slowly, if that miniature pilot dropped a pencil, it would not have dropped toward the floor you were standing on but toward the bottom of the airplane, which was slightly tilted because you were spinning it.

As you spun the airplane faster, a dropped pencil would still fall toward the bottom of the plane, even though to you the plane is flying sideways. And the pencil would drop much faster because of the increased centrifugal force caused by the faster spinning.

Now think of the pilot himself. The force that pulled the pencil to the floor more quickly is also pulling the pilot. The pilot can't fall like the pencil because he's restrained in his seat, so he begins to feel heavier and heavier. In other words, the pilot is experiencing more g's.

G-forces complicate an aerobatic pilot's life because the body is designed to function in the presence of about 1 g, the gravitational force the earth exerts on us. When a pilot makes a sharp pull-up, as entering into a loop, for example, the g-forces can spike up to several g's. Limbs feel heavy, skin sags, eyeballs flatten out somewhat in their sockets. Worst of all, the blood supply flows toward the pilot's feet and rear end, and can cause a *blackout.*

To prevent blackouts and grayouts, pilots use their chest and neck muscles to prevent the blood from leaving their heads. The concentration necessary for flying perfect aerobatic maneuvers, plus the muscle strength needed to keep the blood in the brain, where it belongs, make an aerobatic performance as strenuous as playing a set of tennis or running a 5K race.

By the Book

Blackouts are what happens when the brain *is* starved of oxygen, and they usually last only a few seconds. As soon as the heavy g-forces subside, the oxygen *is* able to return to the brain. Aerobatic pilots sometimes experience the less severe "grayouts" that can cause tunnel vision. Finally, even if a pilot doesn't black out during heavy g-forces, the gravity can pull the eyelids down over the eye, causing a "redout" (the blood vessels in the eyelid give the sunlight a reddish hue).

That Green Feeling

Ask pilots what the hardest part of learning aerobatic flying is, and most of them will tell you that it's overcoming airsickness.

Though it feels like it's in your stomach, airsickness is mostly in your head. Most flight physiologists agree that airsickness results from a psychological conflict between the extreme maneuvers of the airplane and the instinctive desire to be right side up. It comes down to a disagreement between the information the brain receives from two powerful physical sense organs—the eyes and the tiny balance organs in the inner ear. Basically, the eyes report one thing to the brain, and the inner ear reports another.

For example, in an aerobatic maneuver such as a loop, you are momentarily upside down, a radical change from the normal state of things for most of us and an unusual position for the brain to interpret. Yet the balance organs of the inner ear (which we will learn more about in Chapter 18, "Overcoming the Body's Limitations") sense g-forces that are similar to the normal pull of gravity. So the eyes say you're upside down while your inner ear says you're right side up (since g-forces are still pulling you into your seat). To further complicate things, a loop can put the body through a range of g-forces that might reach as high as 6 g's during entry and recovery and could approach zero near the top. The brain is forced to sort out and interpret some unusual and, frankly, potentially frightening signals.

But the fact that airsickness has its roots in the brain doesn't mean the physical symptoms aren't real. Even though the feelings are largely rooted in psychological reactions, the brain creates powerful bodily responses, including sweating, over-salivating, headache, nausea, and fatigue. The result is often airsickness.

Airsickness can be a formidable enemy. I once saw a young student climb out of an airplane after a simple training flight with a face that wasn't just pale, it was literally green—a waxy, translucent green. Unfortunately, that student and a few others I have known couldn't conquer airsickness and had to abandon flying. But a sensitive flight instructor using modern training techniques can almost always help pilots conquer airsickness.

On Course

Ginger might be an effective remedy for the student pilot who suffers from airsickness early in his flight training. Available in the form of a pill from health food stores or in the form of ginger ale, ginger is nature's airsickness tonic. Although drug stores sell over-the-counter Dramamine for airsickness, and physicians can prescribe drugs to calm the stomach flops, these should be left to the occasional traveler, not pilots. Dramamine can make you very drowsy and should never be taken before or during a flight.

What Does It Cost to Learn Aerobatics?

Aerobatic airplanes are among the most expensive small planes to rent, not only because they are meticulously crafted but because insurance companies think aerobatic flying is more dangerous than other types of flying, and thus charge higher premiums. Aerobatics may be slightly more risky than flying straight and level, but with proper training, a well-maintained airplane, and sound judgment, aerobatics can be very safe.

Renting an aerobatic training plane is far more costly than renting most of the small trainers you might fly to earn your private pilot certificate. For example, the popular Great Lakes aerobatic trainer usually starts at $140 per hour, including fuel costs and instructor fees. Typical aerobatics courses might require 10 hours or more of flying experience.

Another popular aerobatics plane, and one that is agile enough and powerful enough to fly in competition, is the Pitts Special. Pitts are eye-catchers because of their flashy starburst paint scheme and their striking biplane design. But they can carry a hefty per-hour charge of $230 or more.

You can even find schools that will train you in the ultra-high performance Extra 300, a German-made plane that has become famous for carrying American pilots to international competitions. But the extra performance brings extra cost— $270 per hour or more, including instructor.

But there's hope for would-be aerobatic pilots on a budget. Flying lower-performance planes such as the Standard Decathlon, a high-wing work-horse that is forgiving and docile enough for the beginner aerobatic pilot but capable of performing almost any maneuver you can imagine. The Standard Decathlon has another advantage: It's inexpensive to fly, at least compared to the Pitts. You can rent a Decathlon, and an instructor to tell you how to fly it, for $120 per hour.

On Course

If you suffer from airsickness, whether during aerobatics or not, you should consult a flight physician. She might be able to prescribe medication that relieves the most severe symptoms. But if you really want to be an aerobatic pilot, you should gradually get used to the g-forces and extreme flight conditions by beginning with short flights, then gradually increasing the duration of each flight until your body has adjusted.

Turbulence

Although aerobatic flying is spectacular and inspiring when performed by an expert, don't be tempted to jump into it too soon, if at all. First, earn your private pilot certificate, get some experience behind you, and gain some confidence in flying the airplane in normal circumstances. Then, when you have a couple hundred hours logged, it might be time to start looking for an aerobatics instructor.

Aerobatics are one of the most demanding aspects of aviation, but once you're in the select group, you're a part of a great flying tradition that includes the Navy's Blue Angels.

(U.S. Air Force)

The Least You Need to Know

➤ Air shows and aerobatics are a crucial tool to popularize aviation for the next generation.

➤ Aerobatics are complex, but every maneuver is a combination of four easy-to-learn basics.

➤ Aerobatics take some getting used to, but most pilots can shake off the physical roadblocks.

➤ It ain't cheap to learn aerobatic flying, but by now you've learned that nothing about flying is!

Part 4

Meeting the Challenges to the Perfect Flight

We've all heard that flying is statistically safer than driving a car. Yet there's no deny-ing that aviation can be hazardous. Tragedies like the 1999 deaths of popular golfer Payne Stewart in a gruesome jet mishap and of John F. Kennedy Jr. during a routine flight require careful examination if we are to understand the causes behind them and learn from them.

In this part, you'll learn about the possible barriers to flying the perfect flight—from the effects of bad weather to the limitations of the human body. You'll learn how pilots respond to flight emergencies. You'll also read a detailed analysis of Kennedy's final flight, as well as an examination of the decision-making factors that every pilot should understand.

Talking About the Weather

All pilots are students of the weather. From their very first flight, pilots begin to develop an instinct for weather. Weather affects all aspects of a flight, from the wind whose direction determines which runway you'll take off from to the make-up of clouds that signal the onset of stomach-turning turbulence.

Even pilots with a private pilot certificate in their pocket and hundreds of hours scribbled into their logbook keep a close watch on the weather. Without an instrument rating and special training in weather flying, private pilots are grounded by bad weather.

Weather is one of the most common factors cited as contributing to accidents, including the one in 1999 that killed John F. Kennedy Jr., his wife, and her sister. (We've dedicated Chapter 20, "John F. Kennedy Jr.'s Final Flight," to examining all aspects of Kennedy's accident, including tips on flying in clouds and in bad weather.) Even a rudimentary understanding of how the weather works can be a valuable tool for the pilot.

What Makes the Weather?

Weather on earth is created by two fundamentals of astronomy: The sun generates enormous heat, and the earth spins on its axis. All weather begins from those two simple conditions. Of course, from that simple starting point, weather can take many forms, depend-ing on many variables, and become a quite complex science—a science called *meteorology*.

Weather is generated when the sun heats different parts of the earth unevenly. The rotation of the earth complicates matters by adding a circular element to the movement of huge air masses that flow like liquid over the earth's surface.

But there's more—the interaction between water and air. Some of the ocean's currents transport cold water into the warm tropics and others move warm water into the chilly polar regions. The colliding boundaries between warm air, which holds large amounts of water vapor that evaporated from the warm ocean water, and cold air, which is comparatively dry, results in precipitation in the form of rain, snow, and ice.

Plane Talk

The sky is capable of putting on vivid color shows, as we will see, but the most enduring and comforting optical show is the deep, cerulean blue the sky robes itself in. The sky's blue color stems from a phenomenon called "Rayleigh's scatter." When light strikes an air molecule, the blue wavelengths of light are scattered, while the other colors continue undisturbed. The result is deep, cobalt-blue light coming at us from all directions.

Water is another major player in weather. In meteorological terms, the power of water lies in its ability to absorb and radiate heat when it changes state, going from liquid to vapor and back to liquid again. Water is a primary factor in the development of severe weather, such as thunderstorms, tornadoes, and hurricanes, which we'll discuss shortly.

The rotation of the earth is responsible for the circulation patterns of the atmosphere and for the spinning of air around *high-* and *low-pressure areas*.

Because of a phenomenon called the "Coriolis effect," high-pressure areas rotate in a clockwise direction in the Northern Hemisphere, while low-pressure areas rotate counterclockwise. In the Southern Hemisphere, high-pressure areas rotate counterclockwise, while low-pressure areas rotate clockwise. The direction of rotation around high- and low-pressure areas dictates the direction of wind flow.

The Coriolis Effect

Though its name might have a foreign sound, the Coriolis effect is familiar to anyone who has watched a spinning ice skater pull his arms inward. In the case of the earth's rotation, a parcel of air at the equator is farthest from the earth's pole-to-pole axis, and that means it's moving the fastest as the planet rotates.

When a parcel of air at the equator is nudged northward, it moves over terrain that is closer to the axis. Like the skater pulling his arms closer to his own rotational axis, the air parcel accelerates, pushing its rotational axis toward the right, or eastward. (The same rule holds true for a parcel of air moving southward toward the equator, except that the south-moving air is slowed like a skater extending his arms. That causes the air to slow, turning it westward to the right.)

The Coriolis effect turns everything to the right, and is partly responsible for causing wind to blow clockwise around a high-pressure area and counterclockwise around a low-pressure area. The rest of the explanation comes from the "pressure gradient force" that causes air to always flow from an area of high pressure toward an area of low pressure.

By the Book

High- and **low-pressure areas** are regions of air, sometimes covering an area the size of several states, where the barometric pressure is higher or lower than the surrounding atmosphere. In general, high pressure produces warmer temperatures, fewer clouds, and better weather. Low-pressure areas are usually cooler, have more clouds, and produce rainy weather.

Turbulence

Don't fall into the trap of believing that water in bathtubs and sinks always drains counterclockwise in the Northern Hemisphere. Over such short distances, the Coriolis effect has *no* effect, and the currents caused by washing our hands or stepping out of the tub—even the up-and-down movement of hot and cold water—exert a far greater force.

To start with, air in a high-pressure area begins to move toward a low-pressure area nearby. As soon as it begins moving, the Coriolis effect turns it toward the right, causing the clockwise flow around the high-pressure region.

As the clockwise-moving high-pressure air approaches the low-pressure region, the pressure gradient force begins to balance the Coriolis effect caused by the high-pressure area. Air that moves any closer to the low-pressure region will swirl inward in a counterclockwise direction under the influence of the pressure gradient force, which is stronger close to the low-pressure center than the Coriolis effect.

Reading the Clouds

To a pilot, clouds provide valuable clues to activity in the atmosphere. Although ideally a pilot should be armed with the latest weather reports, by scanning the clouds he can tell what sort of localized air movements may be transpiring that the most up-to-date forecast may not yet contain. Before we consider the different types of clouds and what a pilot can infer from them, let's take a look at how clouds are formed.

By the Book

The **dew point** is the temperature that a parcel of air would have to be chilled to in order to force the water vapor to condense into visible moisture droplets. When the sun goes down at night, the overnight cooling could reach the dew point, and the condensing liquid droplets will collect on any surface, including leaves and blades of grass. If the dew point temperature is below freezing, the vapor will condense directly into ice, forming frost.

A Cloud Is Born

Water takes one of three forms: ice, liquid, or vapor. Another name for vapor is humidity. There's a limit to how much water vapor the air can hold, or how humid it can be. The warmer the air, the more water vapor the air can hold. The cooler the air, the less water vapor it can hold.

All air, warm or cold, has a point at which it becomes saturated and can't hold any more water. When air reaches its saturation limit, any additional water vapor condenses, changing from invisible vapor to visible water droplets. We recognize these visible water droplets, in great masses, as clouds.

Because cold air is not able to hold as much water vapor as warm air, a moist parcel of air that cools below the *dew point* will also condense to form clouds.

To Name a Cloud

Clouds are classified according to two criteria—the amount of air movement in them and the altitude at which they typically form. Although one of the two criteria is often enough to designate a cloud type, a combination of the two is also sometimes used.

Clouds that feature air movement in the form of updrafts and downdrafts—vertical movement called *convection*—develop tall, billowy tops. They are called *cumulus* clouds, and can lend a bright, textured feeling to the sky. Convection is caused by the sun heating the earth's surface, or by cold air moving over a warm surface.

Clouds that form in relatively still air—air that has very little convection—are called *stratus* clouds, and are usually flat and slate-gray in appearance. As you might guess, cumulus clouds, to a pilot, signal the presence of unstable air, while stratus clouds signal the presence of stable air.

Clouds that possess little air movement but that form in high, cold altitudes are called *cirrus* clouds. Cirrus clouds are thin and wispy and are made entirely of tiny ice crystals.

Below the cirrus clouds are the middle-altitude clouds designated by the prefix "alto." If the midlevel cloud is unstable—that is, filled with convection currents—it is called *altocumulus*. If it is stable and is more horizontal than vertical, it is called *altostratus*.

On Course

What's it like inside a cloud? You've already seen it a hundred times—in the form of fog. Though we give fog its own name and pay a good deal of attention to it in local weather broadcasts, the insides of a cloud are identical to being in the middle of a fog bank. When flying in a cloud, the sensation ranges from featureless gray to bright white to intermittent flashes of blue sky alternated with white tendrils of cloud. It all depends on the type of cloud you're in and how close you fly to its upper boundary.

Plane Talk

High-altitude aircraft sometimes create their own clouds. Vapor trails, or condensation trails, form in the exhaust plumes of jet engines when the water vapor contained in the exhaust condenses in the cold air. The vapor condenses into ice crystals, which can last for hours.

Low clouds are simply called stratus, cumulus, or *stratocumulus*, meaning a scattering of lumpy, cotton-ball clouds across a wide expanse of sky, all at the same altitude, or stratum.

Turbulence

Think the study of weather is all about fluffy clouds and snow showers? Think again. Meteorology is among the most complex of all sciences, defying even the most powerful computers, which can't precisely predict weather beyond a couple of days into the future. As technology improves, forecasting gets a little better, but weather forecasting will always be a mixture of science and betting the odds.

Rain clouds get their own prefix—"nimbus." Any cloud that rains is designated with "nimbus," for example, nimbostratus and cumulonimbus. As you might guess based on the names, nimbostratus rain clouds are mostly flat and stable. Rain from these clouds can continue for hours or days at a time. Cumulonimbus rain clouds tend to have massive, dark-gray bodies, and can tower to heights of 50,000 feet or more. They rain in sporadic showers, and have powerful up- and downdrafts that can tear the strongest airplanes to pieces.

To the seasoned cloud-watcher, every cloud carries important information. I once ignored a telltale tendril of vapor, or virga, drifting downward from the base of a cumulus cloud, and it almost cost me my life. That seemingly innocent wisp of moisture, which signifies a rain shaft that evaporates before hitting the ground, should have told me of a potentially strong downdraft that almost always accompanies virga.

Because I didn't read the cloud accurately, I flew into a strong downdraft when I was just a couple hundred feet above the ground on approach to land. The powerful burst of air threw my plane almost into the ground, and if I were any lower, I would have crashed.

I was lucky that time and came away badly shaken but unhurt. Since then, I've become a much closer reader of the lessons the clouds can teach if we watch them closely.

Turbulence: Rocking and Rolling

Turbulence is a familiar phenomenon to most of us. Virtually everyone who has made an airline flight is familiar with the stomach-churning bumpiness caused by turbulence. But what causes turbulence?

Turbulence can be traced to a couple of main causes—heat and *wind shear.*

Heat-driven turbulence occurs primarily over regions such as the desert Southwest or the wide plains of the Midwest. Summer sunshine can boil up thick thermals that reach altitudes above 10,000 feet before losing upward energy and settling back toward the ground. Whether on their way up or down, they can buffet an airplane violently.

Wind-shear turbulence comes in several forms, including mountain waves that act similarly to the ripples in a stream formed as it flows around a rock. As with the water, winds flow up and over a mountain range, perpetuating ripples many miles long for a hundred miles or more.

Clear-air turbulence, or CAT, is a rare but potentially deadly form of turbulence. CAT occurs near a fast-flowing river of air called the jet stream, and has been blamed for serious injuries to airplane passengers and crew. In 1998, a Japan Airlines jumbo jet near Tokyo flew into CAT so severe that three people on board were injured.

These kinds of reports are not uncommon. Weather forecasters try to pinpoint the location of the jet stream, which in North America is found at the boundary between the high-pressure warm air over most of the United States and the low-pressure cold air over most of Canada. The jet stream ranges in altitude from 10,000 feet to 30,000 feet or more.

The jet stream can reach speeds of nearly 200 m.p.h. at its fastest. When an airplane flies through an area where the speed of the jet stream changes rapidly in a short distance, severe turbulence is possible. CAT is a good reason to wear your seatbelt throughout a flight, particularly because this type of turbulence is notoriously unpredictable.

By the Book

Wind shear is the turbulent air movement caused by a difference in wind speed or wind direction between two or more bodies of converging air—for example, between a region of northwesterly wind colliding with a region of southwesterly wind. In other cases, winds can blow one direction at one altitude, and a different direction just a few hundred feet higher. Between the two layers, the air roils in powerful currents that create turbulence.

Turbulence can be forecast by meteorologists based on measurements of atmospheric stability. But there's a second, more reliable technique—the informal exchange of information among pilots. Air-traffic controllers all over the country keep an informal tally of turbulence by polling airline pilots at high altitudes and small-airplane pilots at lower altitudes. What emerges is a mosaic portrait of turbulence in a region that other pilots can use to make their passengers comfortable and safe. It's not as scientific as the detailed meteorological charts, but it's first-hand and easy to use.

Severe Weather: Thunderstorms and Tornadoes

Once in a while, the atmosphere turns downright nasty. Thunderstorms, and their raging offspring, tornadoes, possess enough power to shred an airplane, and that includes large airliners and powerful military planes.

Thunderstorms

Thunderstorms grow best when the atmosphere is unstable and turbulent, and air temperature near the ground is hot and air temperature higher up in the atmosphere is cold.

Plane Talk

Lightning is the visible discharge of stored electrical energy created by friction between water droplets. Because air is a poor conductor of electricity, the electric charge builds up until it bridges the air between cloud and ground, setting off an upward moving flash of light and heating the nearby air to 43,000°F. The explosive heating causes the deafening thunder, which, if it occurs close enough, can create a bomblike concussion that can break windows. Because airplanes in flight are not grounded, lightning strikes rarely cause anything more than surface damage. Lightning has never been blamed for an airplane accident.

Turbulence

One of the most common forms of turbulence is the "wake turbulence" that trails back from the wingtips of very large airplanes. Most powerful during takeoff and landing, wake turbulence comes from rapidly spinning wingtip vortices that are an unavoidable by-product of lift. Though only a few inches across, wingtip vortices can spin dangerously for many minutes and seriously buffet any aircraft that follows too closely. Air-traffic controllers put plenty of space between planes to keep things safe.

Thunderstorms begin when warm, humid air is carried aloft by convective currents. A passing weather front can begin the process; so can thermals caused by very hot weather.

As the humid air rises and cools, the vapor condenses into clouds, releasing a small amount of heat as it does. Heat, which is released whenever water condenses, pushes the turbulent air even higher, for the same reason hot air inside a balloon floats. The higher the warm air goes, the more vapor condenses, which adds more heat to the air, sending it still higher. It's a cycle that stops only when the top of the growing cloud towers to heights of 50,000 feet or more. Some massive thunderstorm clouds have even approached 60,000 feet.

When water droplets inside the growing cloud become too large to be carried aloft any longer, they begin to fall. The falling droplets start pulling air down with them, initiating a downward draft of air. As the droplets reach warmer air below, they evaporate. Evaporating water cools the air around it, and cooler air is denser and heavier, making it descend still faster.

Not all the droplets evaporate, though, and some of them reach the ground in the form of a rain shower.

The cool air that accompanies the downward-rushing air of a thunderstorm explains the sometimes dramatic temperature drop as a thunderstorm approaches.

These two cycles—rising, condensing air and descending, evaporating air—take place simultaneously inside a developing thunderstorm for a time. After about an hour, the downdrafts begin to smother the updrafts, and the thunderstorm dies. However, the downdrafts from one storm can start nearby warm air rising, triggering another storm, which triggers still another storm, and so on for hours at a time, if conditions are right.

Thunderstorms can be dangerous, even deadly, to pilots. Pilots know that thunderstorms can throw massive chunks of *hail* as far as five miles away from the storm itself, and the violent shifts of wind inside a thunderstorm and for miles around it can send planes crashing to the ground. Pilots are warned to steer as far as 20 miles around a thunderstorm.

By the Book

Hail is formed when the updrafts inside a thunderstorm push upward into freezing air. An ice core forms in the cold air, but is prevented from falling by the force of the updrafts. Water droplets carried by the updrafts strike the ice chunk and freeze onto it. Depending on the strength of the updraft, a hailstone can grow as large as a grapefruit, though most are the size of rice grains.

Tornadoes

Tornadoes grow out of particularly strong thunderstorms. The updraft and downdraft of an intense thunderstorm cause a horizontal column of air to begin to rotate like a pencil rolling between your palms. When an updraft happens to push upward on a part of this horizontally spinning vortex, it is pushed into a horseshoe shape, with its bowed end upward and its two ends pointing downward. One or both of those spinning tubes can extend all the way to the ground, touching off a tornado.

Tornadoes are not often a hazard for pilots aloft simply because they accompany thunderstorms of such size and power that weather alerts and common sense would send pilots off in other directions in search of safer skies. But on the ground, tornadoes can cause massive damage to airplanes.

Winds as fast as 200 m.p.h. or more are common in and around tornadoes. The high winds and blowing debris can break apart airplanes on airport parking areas and demolish hangars that shelter others. What's more, the thunderstorms that give birth to tornadoes often pound the area with hail, causing thousands of dollars of damage.

Weather Charts

Pilots are well-armed with weather information before they go flying, or at least they should be. In this age of Internet access to massive databases of weather charts and forecasts, there's no excuse for being uninformed about the weather before setting out on a flight.

Even without the Internet, the FAA maintains a network of Flight Service Stations where pilots can look at charts and forecasts. With the help of an FAA specialist, pilots can get preflight briefings that include every important detail of weather that might affect a flight.

To be sure, local weather is highly changeable, often making a mockery of forecasts just a day or two into the future. That's why weather charts have life spans of just a few hours. Then, weather specialists publish updated ones that reflect changes in the atmosphere's variable currents.

If a pilot can't visit a Flight Service Station in person, a toll-free phone call will connect him to a specialist who will give the same weather briefing right over the telephone.

On Course

What do raindrops look like? They don't look anything like raindrops as we draw them in doodles. They begin as tiny, spherical globules, and as they combine with other raindrops, they begin to flatten on the bottom. When they grow larger than a quarter inch, they elongate and begin to get skinny in the middle until they are two drops separated by a thin tendril of water. The tendril eventually breaks, leaving two droplets half the size of the large one, and the process starts again.

Whether by Internet, in person, or by telephone, the preflight weather briefing is crucial for a safe flight. Here are a few of the charts and forecasts that pilots should become familiar with:

➤ **Surface weather observations.** These local weather reports don't attempt to forecast the weather, they simply report current conditions. In pilot shorthand, one might look like this: KBOS 202254Z 12008KT 11/2SM BR. After some basic training, pilots are able to translate easily: At Boston on the 20th of the month at 22:54 "zulu" time (as pilots refer to Greenwich time; that's 5:54 P.M. Boston time), the wind is blowing from 120 degrees, or the southeast, at 8 knots. The visibility is 1½ miles in smoke and mist, as indicated by "SM" and "BR."

➤ **Area forecasts.** These forecasts look at large regions the size of several states. They try to predict what sort of conditions are going to move through the region in the next 18 hours. These forecasts are meant to give a broad sense of weather rather than specific information about particular airports.

➤ **Surface analysis and weather depiction charts.** These maplike charts depict the locations of weather fronts and rain or snow storms across the mainland U.S. Major airports are represented by symbols denoting general weather conditions. These charts don't attempt to forecast the weather; they just report conditions in the past couple of hours.

➤ **Other charts,** including the significant weather prognostic chart, winds aloft chart, composite moisture stability chart, and constant pressure analysis chart challenge pilots to become weather forecasters. These charts are typically left to flight service specialists to interpret, but over time pilots can become remarkably adept at reading and understanding them.

The Visible Atmosphere

Despite the dangers of flying in rough weather, pilots who do so are privileged to experience some of the most eye-catching, breathtaking sights on earth. But be warned. As Mark Twain wrote, "We have not the reverent feeling for the rainbow that a savage has, because we know how it is made. We have lost as much as we have gained by prying into the matter."

With that caveat, here are a few of the strange and beautiful phenomena that meteorologists call "atmospheric optics" that the sky has in store for all of us. Pilots, however, have a front-row seat.

Mirages

When light waves pass from water to air, the rays are bent, yielding the impression that something in the water is closer to us than it actually is. The key to this bending phenomenon of light, called "refraction," lies in the difference in density between water and air.

When light passes through air masses of different densities, the same bending occurs, though to a smaller degree. Heat from the earth sometimes warms a layer of low-lying air, decreasing its density. The difference in density between the warm air close to the ground and the rest of the air above it causes light to bend and play tricks on our eyes.

Turbulence

Only pilots who have been fully trained and approved by the FAA for instrument flying should fly in or close to clouds. Regulations forbid it, as does common sense. Seemingly benign weather phenomena often hold hidden dangers and have to be regarded as hazardous.

Halos, Sun Dogs, and Sun Pillars

When light passes through tiny ice particles—smaller than about twenty-millionths of a meter—the crystals act like prisms that refract the light about 22 degrees. The result is a white halo circling the sun or moon. When the ice particles are slightly larger, with a hexagonal pencil shape, an arc at 46 degrees from the sun or moon can appear.

When large ice particles—about thirty-millionths of a meter—are flat and platelike, they tend to orient themselves horizontally as they fall to earth. Sunlight passing through them bends about 22 degrees, and when the sun is near the horizon, a person on the ground or in an airplane can sometimes see sun dogs, or "mock suns," on either side of the real one.

One optical phenomenon that is caused by light bouncing off of an object—reflection—rather than light bending an object through an object—refraction—is the "sun pillar." When the sun is low to the horizon, small platelike horizontal ice crystals sometimes reflect sunlight off their bottom surfaces. The result is a pillar of light that appears to rest on top of the sun.

On Course

If you're ever lucky enough to see a "tertiary" rainbow, the kind that have three distinct rings, you'll never forget it. The only tertiary rainbow I've seen occurred in New Mexico when my wife and I were driving from Albuquerque to Santa Fe. Against a backdrop of towering black clouds to the east, we saw a brilliant rainbow caused by late afternoon sun in the west. After a minute, a rare secondary rainbow appeared. Finally, a tertiary rainbow appeared. It was a vision of nature we'll always remember.

Rainbows

We've all seen plenty of rainbows, both the natural ones that appear during a rain shower and the artificial ones that appear in the spray of a garden sprinkler, for example. The brighter the sunlight, the brighter the rainbow. Really bright sunlight can cause a second, and even a third, rainbow to appear on the outside of the main one.

When sunlight enters a water droplet, it bounces around so much that it comes out almost the same direction it went in. Because each color of light bends at a different rate, each time the light refracts around the inner curve of the raindrop, the colors separate a little more. The result is a distinctive separation of the colors that always ranges from red on the outer edge, through orange, yellow, green, blue, indigo, and all the way to violet on the inner edge.

Coronas and Glories

These two phenomena are caused by a property of light called diffraction, which causes light to bend around objects.

Coronas are visible around the moon when moonlight filters through misty clouds. Moonlight bends around the tiny particles, creating a diffuse circle of white light with the moon at its center.

Glories are one of the phenomena that can usually be seen only from an airplane, though a hiker high on a mountain above a cloud layer might see one, too. That's because glories appear only on the top of a cloud layer.

When an airplane flies above a cloud, sunlight around the shadow of the airplane enters the tiny water droplets that make up the cloud. The light bounces around the inside of the droplet, as it does in a rainbow. But in the case of a glory, the light bends around the edge of the droplet. What results is a brilliant glow of light surrounding the airplane's shadow.

On Course

One of the most fascinating atmospheric optics is called heiligenschein, a German word for "halo." To see a heiligenschein, stand on a dewy lawn on a sunny morning. Turn to face your shadow. If the dew droplets are the right size, you'll see that your head seems to be ringed by a bright heiligenschein.

The Green Flash

This is perhaps the most elusive of all atmospheric optics, sort of the Loch Ness Monster of weather. It's so rare, in fact, that I've never met anyone who has ever seen it himself, and many meteorologists and active sky-watchers live a lifetime without seeing one. I never fail to look for the green flash when I can see the horizon at sunset.

Just as the sun's disk drops below the horizon, the blue light of the sky is mostly scattered, permitting green light to shine through. However, we usually can't see the green light—the sun's reddish light is so bright it "cancels out" the green. But if conditions are such that the green light is magnified—in very hot weather, for example—the green light will flash out for a second or so.

Sky-watchers who are pilots are particularly lucky. We have the best seat in the house for seeing the spectacular light show the atmosphere puts on every day.

Plane Talk

The aurora borealis of the North Pole (and *its* South Pole counterpart, the aurora australis) is an atmospheric light show that is born in space. The sun casts off tiny particles called the solar wind, some of which are swept up by the earth's magnetic field. When they all crowd together at the poles, they are heated up and emit bright ribbons of light that typically can be seen only by people close to the poles. Sometimes, though, they wander to the temperate latitudes (where they generate thousands of panicky 911 calls).

The newfound appreciation for weather is one of the greatest side benefits of learning to fly or becoming a close follower of aviation. Pilots look at the sky not as something far away but as a place they've visited and will return to soon. They don't see clouds as faraway places, but, as awe-inspiring works of nature that are almost as stunning from the inside as from the outside. Even raging storms take on a new aspect of strange beauty. The more we learn about the sky above us, the more enjoyable flying becomes.

The Least You Need to Know

➤ Atmospheric optics are not only awe-inspiring, they are accurate indicators of how the sky is behaving.

➤ Though the simple result of the sun striking the spinning earth, weather's complexity is unending.

➤ With a few simple categories in mind, anyone can become an expert cloud-spotter.

➤ Turbulence, either from heat or wind, holds dangerous potential that can cause damage and injuries.

➤ Thunderstorms hold dangerous secrets that can endanger a flight.

➤ Weather experts can help pilots interpret the weather, but many flyers enjoy doing their own forecasting.

Chapter 18

Overcoming the Body's Limitations

In This Chapter

➤ The body's trouble with high altitude

➤ Hypoxia goes by many names

➤ Airsickness: a common woe

➤ Flying phobias and their treatment

Although pilots sometimes pretend it's not true, the fact is that man has about as much business flying through the sky as a goldfish has playing the harp. It's obvious we're out of our element.

In the air, nature holds plenty of cards she can play against us, from weather hazards like invisible and dangerous clear-air turbulence to the thin air at high altitude that can rob a pilot of her ability to think and make decisions.

The human body is a poor match for the extreme conditions we encounter in flight. Fortunately, we've been pretty clever in designing safe airplanes that shelter us from the worst of the elements. Still, it pays to be aware of our bodies' limitations in flight and how we can live with these limitations.

How the Atmosphere Stacks Up

To understand how the atmosphere causes the body to function differently at different altitudes, we have to take a look at how the atmosphere is built.

The air we breathe is about four-fifths nitrogen and one-fifth oxygen. About 1 percent of it is argon, an obscure little gas called "inert" because it won't interact with any other element. There are a few other inert gases in our atmosphere, including neon, helium, and xenon. But after nitrogen, oxygen, and argon, the rest of the gases are so scarce they're hardly there at all. Of course, water vapor is part of the mix as well, helping to drive weather. (For the skinny on weather and the importance of water vapor in creating it, see Chapter 17, "Talking About the Weather.")

Air is heavier than you might think. The air in a room measuring 20 feet by 20 feet with an 8-foot high ceiling weighs about 237 pounds. The total weight of all the air in the earth's atmosphere is about 5,600 trillion tons!

Air possesses weight because each molecule possesses mass. (Helium and other buoyant gases also possess mass, but their molecules are lighter than the nitrogen and oxygen mixture in the air. That's why balloons filled with helium rise in our nitrogen-oxygen atmosphere.) We perceive air as weightless, however, because it presses on us from all sides. When we hold an arm out to our side, the air presses on it from above, but also from below, from the front, and from the back.

Turbulence

Each person's body responds differently to the extreme conditions we encounter in flight. It's not possible to generalize how each person will react to the rigors of high-altitude flight. A small number of altitude chamber facilities around the country offer training in actual high-altitude conditions, which is the best way to gauge each person's response.

A Lot of Pressure

Gravity pulls the atmosphere toward the earth. The air near the earth's surface compresses, creating greater air pressure near the earth and lower air pressure at higher altitudes. Because of the pressure exerted on the lower atmosphere, it is packed much more densely than the thin air at higher altitudes. In fact, of the roughly 180 miles–thick layer of atmosphere, fully 80 percent of it is packed into the lowest $3\frac{1}{2}$ miles.

At sea level, atmospheric pressure amounts to about 14.7 pounds per square inch. The higher we go in the atmosphere, the lower the pressure gets, until at the very top of the atmosphere, the air pressure diminishes to about zero.

> ### Plane Talk
>
> The air, like any gas, is composed of tiny atoms that speed through space bouncing into other atoms. Not only do atoms bounce into each other, they also bounce against every other surface, whether it's our skin, the walls of a building, or the body of an airplane. The combined force of these tiny collisions is called atmospheric pressure, or simply air pressure. We measure pressure by comparing the total push of all the little collisions over a certain surface area, usually in units of pounds per square inch.

Meteorologists measure air pressure using instruments called barometers, which measure pressure with long mercury-filled tubes. The higher the air pressure, the higher the mercury rises in the tube. Mercury barometers measure pressure in units called inches of mercury, the units pilots most commonly use. The equivalent of 14.7 pounds per square inch is 29.92 inches of mercury.

A cleaner and more compact barometer, the aneroid barometer, uses a small, flexible box with the air sucked out of it. High air pressure compresses the box, and low air pressure allows the box to expand. The changes in the shape of the box move a needle on the scale on the barometer's face.

A Little Pressure

In addition to its higher pressure, the lower atmosphere has a higher partial pressure, which is the amount of a gas that will dissolve into a liquid. In essence, the total pressure of the air is the sum of the partial pressures of oxygen and nitrogen. The greater the partial pressure of a gas, the more of it will be pushed into a liquid. In the case of the human body, we're most concerned with the amount of oxygen that dissolves into our blood, which transports the oxygen to the body's cells.

> ### On Course
>
> You'll find an aneroid barometer on every airplane instrument panel. Pilots use it to measure altitude. The altimeter registers the decrease in air pressure that takes place as the airplane climbs, then displays the lower pressure not as a measure of inches of mercury but as higher altitude.

Remember, oxygen, which the body uses to fuel most of its key physiological functions, represents only about 21 percent of the make-up of the air, while nitrogen, which the body hardly uses, comprises most of the rest of the atmosphere. So oxygen, which amounts to about a fifth of the gas in the air, exerts only about a quarter of the 14.7 pounds per square inch of the total pressure. (The reason a fifth of the gas exerts a quarter of the partial pressure is that oxygen weighs more than nitrogen.)

As air pressure gets lower, the partial pressure of the gases that make it up also decreases. In human terms, that means the oxygen that is so important to running the body has a harder time getting "pressed" into the bloodstream because of the lower partial pressure.

Plane Talk

In addition to providing the lifting force that permits us to fly, the atmosphere also acts as an effective radiation filter and a shield from falling objects. It helps destroy small stones and ice particles from space before they thump us on the head, and it filters out some of the sun's damaging rays that can cause cancer. Airline pilots and flight attendants are thought to have a higher rate of some types of cancer because they spend so much time in the high atmosphere, where the sun's rays are not fully filtered. Most passengers, though, don't need to worry because they don't spend enough time in the air for the radiation to have lasting effects.

By the Book

Hemoglobin is the molecule in red blood cells that picks up oxygen in the lungs and carries it to the parts of the body that need it.

When Air's Not There

The rare air at high altitude can take a toll on pilots. In extreme conditions, for example at altitudes above 10,000 feet, the thin air starts affecting the way the body operates.

The ability of the blood to carry oxygen to the body's cells, most importantly to the brain cells, is directly related to how much oxygen is carried in the blood's *hemoglobin*.

Doctors describe the lack of oxygen as hypoxia. Hypoxia is a catch-all term that is associated with a number of maladies and conditions, from dizziness to stroke. In the cockpit, we're usually concerned with four kinds of hypoxia: anemic, histotoxic, stagnant, and hypoxic. (Yes, I agree that hypoxic hypoxia sounds repetitively redundant, but that's what physicians call it.) Here's a brief description of each:

➤ **Anemic hypoxia** happens when the blood has too little hemoglobin. Even if anemia doesn't cause problems by itself, such as the shortness of breath and lightheadedness that a doctor might be concerned about, it can add to the problems caused by other types of hypoxia.

➤ **Histotoxic hypoxia** happens when another substance fills the hemoglobin molecule, robbing it of its ability to carry oxygen. Alcohol and carbon monoxide can bring on this form of hypoxia.

➤ **Stagnant hypoxia** occurs when a pilot pulls high g-forces that happen during steep turns or in aerobatic maneuvers. During high g maneuvers, the blood rushes away from the head and brain and pools in the feet and rear end.

Experienced pilots use the muscles in their neck and chest to try to prevent the blood from leaving their head. In what the military cryptically calls the "L1 maneuver," pilots strain their neck and chest muscles, which sometimes causes a grimacing facial expression. When they are contracted, the muscles pinch off the blood vessels that pass through them, preventing the blood from moving through too quickly and causing it to stay longer in the brain, where it's needed.

➤ The most threatening kind of hypoxia for pilots is the **hypoxic variety.** As atmospheric pressure drops, so does the partial pressure of oxygen. When the partial pressure can no longer fully saturate the hemoglobin, the body starts to slowly suffocate. The brain, which uses the largest proportion of oxygen, suffers the most.

Turbulence

Cigarette smoke contains carbon monoxide. In fact, pilots who smoke walk around in a perpetual state of histotoxic hypoxia. The poisoning of the blood makes the body feel as though it's 5,000 feet higher than it is, at least in terms of the amount of oxygen carried by the hemoglobin.

Turbulence

It's logical that too little air can be dangerous, but what about too much air? Yes, hyperoxia, or as it's better known, hyperventilation, can cause trouble in the cockpit. Rapid breathing, usually caused by anxiety and common among beginning student pilots, overfills the blood with oxygen and can cause fainting if it goes on too long. The cure is simply to consciously slow your breathing rate.

Plane Talk

I was fortunate enough to spend a day at Williams Air Force Base in Arizona experiencing the effects of high altitudes. Inside a sealed pressure chamber, technicians gradually pumped the air out of the chamber until we were at simulated altitudes that went as high as 20,000 feet or so. The purpose of the training was for pilots to recognize the individual patterns of symptoms. My first symptoms were a tingling in my fingers, numbness in my lips, a dimming of vision, and a sensation of anxiety. I also discovered that, although I was in excellent condition, my tolerance for high altitudes was far less than many of the less fit and older pilots who were with me in the chamber.

Hypoxic hypoxia is dangerous because the first symptoms are often difficult for a pilot to detect. To make matters worse, the first symptom is sometimes euphoria, a sensation that everything's just fine. In fact, unless the pilot descends to a lower altitude quickly, or puts on an oxygen mask that feeds pure oxygen, the hypoxia is likely to get worse. If something's not done to get more oxygen to the brain, hypoxia can be fatal.

Hypoxic hypoxia often causes blue lips, blue fingernails, tunnel vision, and shortness of breath. Pilots are taught to recognize these dangerous warning signs before disaster strikes.

It's Not Easy Being Green

Airsickness is one of the most common, and most hated, of all flight-related maladies. Many who've flown on an airliner or a small plane know the feeling: light-headedness followed by an increase in salivation, sweating and clammy skin, a ghostly pallor, and finally nausea and vomiting. Often, an attack of airsickness brings on a fit of sleepiness that can last for hours.

Airsickness is only one form of motion sickness that includes seasickness, carsickness, and trainsickness. I suppose you could even include "carnival sickness"

On Course

I once had a friend who managed, by flying mostly in the morning when the air was calm, to make it almost all the way through his airline pilot training despite the fact that he suffered from extreme, chronic airsickness. It was when he was in his final phase of training that an instructor put two and two together. My friend's airline hopes came to an end, all because of a case of incurable airsickness.

as another form, because of the feeling, maybe amplified by a stomach full of cotton candy and hot dogs, caused by riding on amusement-park rides.

Airsickness is caused by swinging, turning, rocking, and up-and-down motions. Of all these motions, the worst culprit often is the fishtailing of the plane caused by turbulence or a pilot with heavy feet on the rudder pedals.

Plane Talk

Passengers can thank airline engineers for a device called a "yaw damper." Yaw dampers were created to prevent dangerous "Dutch rolls" that cause airliners with swept-back wings to roll wildly back and forth. Fortunately for passengers, yaw dampers have the side benefit of reducing at least some of the sickening motion caused by turbulence.

Experienced pilots don't usually have much trouble with airsickness. But for student pilots, airsickness can stand in the way of a hobby, and even a career. With an attentive instructor and some ingenuity, many students are able to overcome this problem.

For a student pilot, a good flight instructor can mean the difference between a quick immunity for airsickness and a slow, painful cure. Smart flight instructors treat the first sign of airsickness by stopping the lesson and landing at the closest available airport. A short break from flying and a walk in the fresh air are often enough to beat back an attack of the "colly-wobbles."

After a few short flights, with breaks if necessary, most student pilots can develop a pretty good tolerance of airsickness. That's because the hypersensitivity to motion, which is typically brought on by nervousness about the new experience of flying, gradually eases. Once a beginning pilot feels comfortable in the air, it takes a lot of airplane motion to make her airsick.

Of course, passengers have the option of taking any number of over-the-counter antiairsickness

Turbulence

Here's a disturbing thought: Some of the pilots flying the jetliners you've flown could have been suffering from airsickness during the flight. A 1987 study by the International Federation of the Airline Pilots Association found that 29 percent of pilots couldn't complete a flight because of airsickness. Fortunately, airline flight crews always consist of two or three pilots.

medicines. Most of them are pretty effective, though they have some side effects. Pilots can't risk the side effects, which include drowsiness and sluggish reactions.

For pilots or student pilots who sometimes look green around the gills, there are a few folk remedies. Some sufferers swear by the stomach-steadying effects of ginger, either in form of ginger candy or ginger pills; others say ginger ale has the same effect. For the believer in alternative cures, there's acupressure. According to some, pressure applied about an inch below the wrist joint, on the same side of the wrist as the pinky finger, will cure a case of airsickness after about a minute.

The simplest solution could be watching your diet. Before flying, pilots or passengers who suffer from airsickness should stay away from high-salt foods like chips, as well as pork, beef, eggs, milk, and other dairy products. Also, don't eat for at least three hours before a flight, and eat small, carbohydrate-rich meals within 24 hours before the flight. Many pilots also bring along a small, energy-filled snack to eat during the flight.

On Course

According to some estimates, as many as one person in six suffers from a fear of flying that ranges from jitters to a fear so powerful that the mere thought of flying causes trembling.

On Course

One way to calm anxieties over flying is to meet the captain and co-pilot of the flight. Pilots are sensitive to the fears of passengers, and usually are glad to chat for a few minutes. Even if they don't say anything that directly addresses the fear of flying, their natural self-confidence comes through, and often that's enough to calm a jittery flyer's fears.

Fear of Flying

While pilots confront the physical effects of flying, passengers are often more concerned with the emotional ones. A phobia of flying can immobilize passengers and even keep them from traveling by air.

There are no simple solutions to treating a fear of flying. Many of the most frightening aspects of flying stem from not knowing how the airplane is controlled, combined with nervousness about being high up in the air.

Some of the sensations of flight cause discomfort. The sensation of being pressed back into your seat during takeoff, the steep tilting of the nose upward for the climb, the unfamiliar sounds of the landing gear and wing flaps being retracted or extended, the rolling of turbulence, the "elevator" sensations of growing lighter or heavier as the airplane climbs or descends during flight—any or all may cause uncomfortable sensations that lead to fear.

In "nervous flyers," even the slightest noise, vibration, or strange sensation can become magnified to a frightening degree. Cures, or at least treatments, for the fear of flying usually start with a greater understanding of how airplanes fly and how pilots operate them.

Though simple assurances will probably not calm the fears of every jittery flyer, problems in the air, whether caused by passengers, pilots, or with the airplane itself are, in fact, very rare. In the next chapter, we'll look at what to do when an emergency in the air *does* occur.

The Least You Need to Know

➤ Eighty percent of the air in the atmosphere is crammed into the lowest 18,000 feet.

➤ The gravity's pressure affects how much oxygen makes its way into the bloodstream.

➤ By any name, hypoxia could mean "lights out"!

➤ The simplest airsickness cure for beginning pilots is to take it slow.

➤ Nervous flyers usually benefit from a better understanding of how planes and pilots function.

Emergencies in the Air

Headlines seem to trumpet some sort of airplane emergency once a week, from the minor crack-up of a small plane to a passenger jet forced to make a landing because of smoke in the cockpit.

In fact, serious aviation emergencies that endanger lives in the air or on the ground are amazingly rare. When compared to the millions of miles people travel by air every year, and the thousands of flights that take place every day, aviation emergencies are very scarce.

The Rare Emergency

Don't take this the wrong way, but pilots are a strange breed. Every once in a while, they like a good old-fashioned emergency.

Turbulence

Most in-flight emergencies have very specific procedures that should be followed to provide the best margin of safety. Anything we discuss in this chapter, or in the rest of this book for that matter, is meant as general information. It isn't meant to take the place of an instructor's advice or any manufacturer's procedures.

Pilots train for years in handling emergencies, but almost never get to put that knowledge to the test. It's a lot like soldiers who, after training for war, are perversely curious about trying out their skills in battle.

That's not to say pilots like danger, but they do spend a good deal of their training time practicing how to respond to it. Airlines train their pilots using simulators so realistic that they feel almost exactly like an actual airplane—right down to the feeling of the landing gear rolling over seams in the concrete. In fact, after a few moments, everyone inside the simulator forgets they're actually in a two-story-high cockpit mounted on a set of hydraulic pistons that tilt and jostle to simulate the motions of flight.

No matter what happens during an actual flight, it's very unlikely that things could ever get as bad as the multiple catastrophes that a sadistic simulator instructor can inflict. I know of one airline simulator training session in which one of two engines on the plane failed, all airports nearby where closed due to heavy fog, a passenger suffered a heart attack, and a fire broke out in the storage well where the landing gear was hidden away during flight—all at the same time!

Plane Talk

Until the late 1960s and early 1970s, airlines trained their pilots in emergency procedures by flying in actual jetliners, with no passengers aboard. Later, simulators became good enough and cheap enough, and jet fuel expensive enough, to make simulator training the best, and safest, way to train.

Learning from the Past

Simulator instructors use their knowledge of real-life emergencies to get pilots ready for everything. For example, in July 1989, a United Airlines DC-10 piloted by

Capt. Al Haynes lost its hydraulic system, meaning that Haynes found himself flying a jetliner he couldn't steer. The tail engine on the three-engine DC-10 he was flying had suddenly blown apart, something that wouldn't have been terribly dangerous considering the plane had two other engines. But when it disintegrated, the engine happened to destroy the airplane's hydraulic system, leaving the pilots no way to move the ailerons, elevators, and rudder.

Capt. Haynes, with help from Dennis Fitch, an off-duty United Airlines pilot on his way home, managed to bring the jetliner down to a runway at the Sioux City, Iowa, airport, before the plane cart-wheeled and exploded into flames. The expert piloting of Haynes and Fitch saved the lives of 184 of the 296 people on board the plane.

In this case, Capt. Haynes and his crew had never practiced that specific emergency in the simulator, partly because the scenario they encountered was thought to be impossible to create in flight. Still, the discipline and skill pilots learn in simulators prepare flight crews to respond to any emergency with a cool head and practiced hand.

Plane Talk

One of the advantages of using computerized simulators is that instructors can program a simulator to reproduce the conditions that have led to a real-life tragedy. This allows new pilots to benefit from the painful lessons of fatal accidents, and if simulator pilots don't learn the lessons the first time, they can practice them again and again. One of the most common in-flight emergencies that pilots now practice in simulators is the "Dallas microburst," the weather-related disaster that led to the deaths of 136 people on Delta Airlines Flight 191 at Dallas in 1985. Now, pilots are routinely trained to deal with the exact conditions that doomed Flight 191, and thanks to repeated simulator training, they get it right.

Small-airplane pilots also make use of simulated training, but not to the same degree of sophistication the airlines do. That's because really good simulators cost tens of millions of dollars. Also, the cost of operating a small plane is relatively low, meaning that pilots and instructors can afford to practice emergency maneuvers in the actual airplane.

When the Engine Stops

The in-flight emergency most feared by pilots of single-engine planes is engine failure. Statistically, the number of times that airplanes lose power and have to make a forced landing is extremely low. And most of those cases end relatively happily, with a rough landing on a golf course or on a state highway, perhaps.

Airplane engines can fail for a number of reasons. Most of the time it's because the pilot failed to make sure she had enough fuel on board to complete the flight. True, airplanes have fuel gauges that display how much fuel remains in each tank, but as hard as it is to believe, some careless pilots manage to run the tanks dry, leaving no alternative but a forced landing. (Emergency landings go by many names, including "off-airport landing" and "unscheduled landing," but no matter how much pilots try to soften the tone, forced landings are emergencies.)

I should mention that, though it has happened on rare occasions, airliners rarely run low on gas, let alone completely *out* of it. Airlines and the FAA have strict rules that are meant to guarantee there's enough fuel to finish a flight with plenty of fuel to spare.

Airplane engines sometimes catch fire, and one of the prime culprits is the fuel system. If an engine catches fire, a pilot will shut it down and begin to plan for an emergency landing. Also, fuel systems are prone to all sorts of blockages caused by debris in the fuel or failure of the mechanical pumps that push fuel into the engine. In cases like these, if backup equipment such as a second fuel pump or a valve to switch to another fuel tank can't solve the problem, the airplane will lose power and probably won't be able to continue all the way to its destination.

On Course

In planes with two or more engines, one engine can fail in cruise flight without causing a disaster. Twin-engine prop-driven airplanes might be able to continue with only a slight decrease in airspeed and altitude, though the pilot has to pay a lot more attention to how she controls the plane.

What's important to remember, though, is that pilots are heavily drilled in the procedures and techniques for making emergency landings. Very few emergency landings result in a crash.

Training for Engine Failure

During flight training, instructors try to create the same sense of surprise that a pilot would feel if an engine actually failed unexpectedly in flight. The first few times a student hears the engine sputter or even die, he has a momentary fear response, but regular training turns a tendency to panic into a rational procedure of problem-solving—exactly the goal training is supposed to achieve.

When simulating a failed engine, an instructor reduces the throttle to idle. A real engine failure can include a power reduction that doesn't leave enough power to continue very far. The most urgent form of engine failure, however, is when the whole thing stops running. (Actually, in most cases, when an engine stops creating power, the propeller still continues to spin, being driven by the force of the wind like a big, metal pinwheel.)

The Unscheduled Landing

At the first sign of an engine failure, a pilot makes sure he's at a safe speed, then begins to plan a place to land. Depending on the terrain, coming up with a plan can range from simple to difficult. In the Midwest or desert Southwest, for example, flat terrain often lies on all sides, and most anyplace holds some potential as a landing strip. In mountainous areas or over densely populated cities, the options are far fewer.

Using well-practiced gliding techniques that are part of every sport pilot's training, the pilot circles the landing site and makes a surprisingly normal approach to the field. Because most engine failures or losses of engine power don't affect the plane's battery or electrical system, all the radios work, so the pilot can radio his location and important details to help rescuers find the plane.

Despite an understandably bad reputation, emergency landings are almost always safe, with no injuries to people and no damage to airplanes. Once the problem with the engine is fixed, many planes take off from the same open field they landed in.

Icy Wings

Wing icing is one of the most frightening sights the pilot of a small airplane can see during flight. In medium and large airplanes and jetliners, special on-board equipment such as heated wing surfaces or inflatable rubber bladders on the leading edge of a wing can get rid of ice. But in small airplanes, the situation can be life-threatening if it's not taken care of right away.

Turbulence

Because forced landings and other emergency procedures are complicated by remote, mountainous terrain, pilots who fly in those regions should get specialized training from experienced instructors. In desert areas, too, pilots should learn some fundamental survival techniques, just in case.

On Course

Do you think that once a pilot receives her certificate, she no longer needs to fly with a flight instructor? In fact, good pilots continue to work with flight instructors to hone some skills and to develop new ones that go beyond the basics needed to receive a pilot certificate. One of the most important skills to practice regularly with an instructor is responding to emergencies.

Ice accumulates on wings a couple of ways, either while flying in clouds—something only specially trained instrument pilots are allowed to do—or during a rainstorm in very cold weather.

265

Turbulence

Wings aren't the only part of the plane that can become covered with ice. Radio antennae can collect ice, which can block or distort radio signals, and even cause antennas to break off. The leading edge of propeller blades can build up ice layers, which can shake the engine violently because of unbalanced ice loads. Cockpit windshields can also collect thick layers of ice, blinding the pilot unless she acts right away.

Icing happens when the temperature is at or below freezing, with the water still in a liquid state. Contrary to common belief, water can remain liquid in temperatures as cold as several degrees below freezing, so-called "supercooled" water. As soon as something strikes a droplet of super-cooled water, it instantly freezes. Supercooled water in the form of tiny droplets in a cloud or supercooled water in the form of large raindrops, called freezing rain, can rapidly build up ice layers on the wings, tail surfaces, propellers, antennae and landing gear—virtually any structure on the airplane.

Icing creates two major problems: It adds massive amounts of weight to the plane, and it disrupts the smooth, aerodynamic flow of air over the airplane's lift-producing surfaces.

The solution is to quickly fly toward warmer air. Depending on the weather conditions, warmer air might be back in the direction you came from. In other cases, lower altitude might be the right place to go. And in some special circumstances, there might be a layer of warmer air at a *higher* altitude, even though air temperature typically decreases at higher altitudes.

Plane Talk

In spite of the complicated systems devised to get rid of it, icing has even been blamed for some commercial airline crashes. In January 1997, a Comair Airlines flight crashed and killed all 29 passengers and crew members aboard flight 3272 from Cincinnati/Northern Kentucky International Airport to Detroit Metropolitan Wayne County Airport. The airplane, a Brazilian-made Embraer propeller-driven plane, accumulated a layer of icing and began to lose control, perhaps before its pilots recognized the danger. Icing can happen on the ground, too, which is sometimes the cause of takeoff delays in cold weather as airport trucks spray de-icing fluid on the wings. The increased safety is worth the wait.

De-icing equipment is not common on small planes for a few reasons. Some de-icing equipment is very expensive and would send the price of the airplane sky-high. It also adds extra equipment that must be inspected and maintained, adding still more cost to the expense of flying.

What's more, most small sport planes aren't really meant for bad weather flying. They are sometimes equipped with the flight instruments and navigation radios needed to fly in clouds, but icing is something that pilots of small- and medium-size airplanes try to avoid, even if they are equipped with de-icing gear.

Microbursts

In recent years, microbursts have been blamed on a number of fatal airline crashes, including the crash of Delta Airlines Flight 191 in Dallas in 1985. They are part of the normal life cycle of thunderstorms, but they remained a mystery until the 1970s.

Microbursts are narrow flumes of cold air a half-mile to two miles wide that gush downward from the bottom of thunderstorms. When the air strikes the ground, it sprays outward horizontally in all directions.

Microbursts can be insidious. Airplanes run the risk of flying into them during landing, because most other times during flight, planes fly above the clouds rather than below them, where microbursts are found. Because the plane is so low to the ground and slow in a landing configuration, this is also the phase of a flight when a plane would be most vulnerable to a violent burst of downward-rushing air.

The first sign of flying into a microburst is often what looks like an increase in airspeed on the airspeed indicator. In fact, it's the horizontal rush of air at the bottom of a microburst that causes this phantom speed increase. Most pilots instinctively pull back the throttle to try to hold the airspeed close to a safe landing speed.

That is the wrong thing to do. Very soon the plane passes into the downdraft region of the microburst. With the throttle reduced and the power setting low, the plane can be pushed down very fast, and in a jet engine, the spool-up time can be several seconds. Flying low, slow, and with reduced power, an airplane can be in real danger if the microburst happens to be lurking near the runway, as it was in Dallas when Delta Flight 191 flew in.

For small-plane pilots, a safe practice when a sudden, unexplained airspeed increase occurs would be to "go around." During a go-around, a pilot adds full power, begins to climb to an appropriate altitude, and begins another landing approach. That option is always available to a pilot, and is almost always a safe way to handle a doubtful landing.

Plane Talk

In late 1999, one of the most unusual emergencies I've ever heard of took place at the Plant City, Florida, airport. A Cessna 152 trainer and a Piper Cadet were both on final approach to land, but neither saw the other. About 200 feet off the ground, the Piper's landing gear punched through the cockpit window of the Cessna and got stuck there. The Cessna pilot continued to the runway and landed, despite the airplane tire blocking his view. None of the four people in the two airplanes were hurt. Now *that's* a calm response to an emergency.

"Captain, the Passengers Are Revolting"

Ask many airline pilots the worst part of flying a passenger jet, and some will probably say, "the passengers." It's partly a joke, but many pilots find that the majority of the hassles of an airline pilot's job don't stem from weather, mechanical trouble, or the rigors of living out of a suitcase. Most of the woes that keep pilots awake at night come from passengers.

In the past couple of years, passengers have begun to openly revolt against what some say is a case of airlines taking passengers for granted and being callous toward complaints about safety, comfort, and on-time performance. The phenomenon has a name: air rage.

Some recent incidents of air rage:

➤ A woman whose job is to travel on airlines checking the quality of flight crews' performance allegedly slapped a British Airways flight attendant who tried to stop her from excessive drinking. The accused assailant also worked for British Airways.

➤ A college student reportedly had to be tied down after he got out of his seat during a flight, began offering passengers "eternal salvation," and insisted on visiting the cockpit to bless the flight crew.

➤ Pop singer Diana Ross was questioned in London in 1999 after she threw a fit, claiming that a female security guard at Heathrow Airport had touched her breast during a search. According to witnesses, Ross hollered at the guard, then touched her on the breast in retaliation.

➤ A banker assaulted a flight attendant and defecated on a food cart. He was fined $50,000.

➤ A passenger on a Hungarian airline flight paid the ultimate price for air rage. He was tied to his seat by other passengers, and a doctor on board injected him with a tranquilizer. He died before the airplane landed, probably from a bad reaction between the tranquilizer and alcohol or other drugs in his body.

The airlines behave as though they have a monopoly, because at some airports and over some routes, they do have a monopoly in practice, if not in law. And with monopolies comes a certain arrogance and disregard of passengers.

Plane Talk

Pilots may or may not have good reason to complain about passengers, but there are some occasions when passengers have legitimate gripes about the crew. In 1999, an airline captain was fired because he walked off the airplane, leaving a planeload of impatient passengers and a crew wondering what to do next. The reason the pilot left: He hadn't eaten for hours, and he was determined to get a bite to eat.

Quality and courtesy of service gets worse every year, airlines sell more tickets than the plane has seats, and planes get more and more cramped as airlines try to stuff more passengers on every flight. Air ventilation is poor, luggage is lost or delayed, food is sometimes unappetizing (when it's offered at all), inconsiderate parents let children cry and kick other passengers' seats, and alcohol is sold to passengers who don't handle it well. Some improvements are actually vetoed by airlines, who complain those improvements would cut into profits.

But the increase in air rage incidents, which British Airways alone says has risen 400 percent over the past three years, could be partly due to increased public attention. In other words, there's a "buzz" in the media about air rage.

Needless to say, neither the airplane nor the airport is the right place for passengers to act out their anger. For reasons of safety, the FAA and other agencies have clamped down on misbehavior in airports and on airplanes. Bad behavior on a plane or in an airport can carry felony charges and possibly years behind bars.

Whether we like it or not, the United States government is looking into airline shenanigans and the passenger rage they provoke. Some airlines have promised, on their honor, to make things better. Organizations supported by the airlines say they're satisfied with the promises, while passenger advocates remind us that we've heard these promises from airlines before. In the end, airlines will probably resist any attempt to force them to clean up their acts.

Plane Talk

Airline cockpits are pressurized to altitudes of about 5,000 to 8,000 feet, meaning the body only gets as much oxygen as it would if it were high on a mountain. The low air pressure has a magnifying effect on alcohol, making a small amount of wine, beer, or cocktails seem like a more potent drink. In other words, a slightly tipsy passenger on the ground can turn into a raging drunk in the air.

Here's some tips that will help fend off air rage:

➤ Call the airline before you leave home to make sure your flight will depart on time. If your flight is delayed, don't leave for the airport until later so you won't be stewing in the terminal.

➤ Write down your ticket confirmation number somewhere so that if you lose your ticket, airline computers can find your records easily.

➤ Get out of line. If your flight is cancelled or delayed, while your fellow travelers are boiling in line, get on the phone with your travel agent and get him or her to do the work for you.

➤ If you change travel plans a lot, carry a flight guide to help you make alternate plans.

➤ Bring your own munchies, so if the plane is late you're not going to starve, and you won't have to be robbed by exorbitantly overpriced airport restaurants. Besides, whatever you bring is bound to be better than any meal served in coach class.

Payne Stewart's Last Flight: Explosive Decompression

One of the eeriest aviation tragedies in history happened in the fall of 1999. The story received big headlines not only because of the macabre circumstances surrounding the deaths of six people aboard a *Learjet* 35, but because one of the dead was popular golfer Payne Stewart.

In October 1999 Stewart boarded a Learjet for a flight from Sanford, Florida (near Orlando), to Dallas, where he was scheduled to golf in a tournament. Everything about the flight appeared to be going normally until the jet reached Gainesville at an altitude of 39,000 feet. At about that time, just 20 minutes into the flight, the plane stopped communicating with air-traffic controllers and failed to make a westward turn toward Dallas. Silently, it continued northwest.

When controllers, who had been trying for an hour, still couldn't reach the plane, Air Force jets took off to intercept it and try to figure out what was wrong. The jet pilots caught up to the Learjet and watched it roller-coaster up and down, reaching as high as 45,000 feet at times. The inside of the jet's windows were frosted over, an indication that no one on board was alive, or at least not able to scrape the frost away. The jet finally ran out of fuel and crashed in a remote field in South Dakota.

The frost on the inside of the Learjet's windows tells most of the story. It points to an in-flight catastrophe that is the stuff of disaster films, but something very rare in real life—an *explosive decompression*.

Jetliners, and all high-altitude jets for that matter, are pressurized using excess air from the engines. Jet engines compress far more air than they can mix with fuel for burning and thrust. Designers put the excess compressed air to work, in part, to pressurize the cabin.

In order to provide a flow of fresh air and to give pilots a method for controlling cabin pressure, a valve in the cabin allows air coming in from the engines to rush out through a hole in the airplane. In the case of the Payne Stewart crash, investigators will look at the pressure valve to see if it somehow failed, causing the pressure in the cabin to plummet immediately.

By the Book

Learjet is a family of sleek, fast business jets that since the 1960s have been the trademark of the rich and famous, the "jet set," as they became known in part for their taste for the speedy Learjet. The Learjet 35 that Payne Stewart partially owned seated eight passengers, flew 510 m.p.h., and could travel 2,300 miles between refueling stops.

By the Book

Explosive decompression occurs when the atmospheric pressure inside an airplane changes rapidly from a comfortable pressure to a dangerously low one. The sudden pressure decrease can cause a high-speed wind inside the plane that sends papers, loose objects and, rarely, people flying around the cabin.

If the valve did fail to regulate properly, or something else caused the pressure to drop, the water vapor inside the cabin would have suddenly condensed into a fog, and the temperature at 39,000 feet, about 60 degrees below zero Fahrenheit, would have caused the fog to freeze instantly onto everything in the cabin, including the windows.

Turbulence

One cause of explosive decompression is bird strikes, particularly those involving large, migratory birds such as Canada geese. Migrating geese have been spotted by pilots at altitudes well above 20,000 feet, and they are difficult to see until it's too late. A goose hitting the windshield of an airliner at cruise speed can shatter the glass and depressurize the cabin, forcing pilots to make a rapid emergency descent.

More important for the passengers and crew, humans lose consciousness within 6 to 12 seconds at an altitude of 39,000 feet in case of decompression. The pilots were equipped with emergency oxygen masks, but if they were slow to react and put them on, they might have been knocked out within seconds and could have suffocated in a matter minutes. The same goes for Stewart and the other passengers in the cabin. Perhaps they were unable to see the emergency masks drop from the ceiling of the Learjet because of the fog. The point is, any delay in reacting would have been fatal.

Gruesome as it is to think of the "flying coffin" that Payne Stewart's Learjet had become, we must remind ourselves that such tragedies are incredibly rare. Airplane mechanics are some of the best-trained and safety-oriented people in aviation, and many regard any system failure on an airplane they are responsible for, regardless how minor, as a personal affront.

Some accidents are like bolts of lightning, completely unpredictable and, for that reason, not worth worrying about beyond taking reasonable precautions. Other accidents, unfortunately, occur because of human error. What pilots can do in either event, though, is to make sure they continue to receive the very best training so that when the rare emergency happens, they'll be ready to respond safely.

The Least You Need to Know

➤ Airplane accidents rarely occur, but grab headlines when they do.

➤ Ice on an airplane's wings adds weight and destroys lift—a dangerous combination.

➤ Airline passengers are taking out their frustrations with expensive tickets and cramped seats in "air rage."

➤ The macabre decompression disaster that killed Payne Stewart was caused by a very rare mechanical failure.

Chapter 20

John F. Kennedy Jr.'s Final Flight

In This Chapter

➤ A chain of decisions that led to disaster

➤ The radar records of Kennedy's last minutes

➤ The "graveyard spiral"—one of flying's most violent killers

➤ Night flight and the body's sense of balance

Flying is first and foremost a matter of managing risk. Beyond all the skills that must be mastered and the academic knowledge that must be learned, the practice of safe flying is an unending determination to discover hidden risk and prevent it from becoming a danger.

It happens all the time—a pilot has to balance the pressure he feels to make a certain flight against the risk factors the flight might have. Perhaps a pilot has to weigh the benefit of flying a particular route against hazardous weather conditions or the scarcity of emergency landing fields. And sometimes he has to assess his own skill level against the demands of a flight—the most difficult risk factor to judge objectively.

It was this sort of a balancing of risks that John F. Kennedy Jr. was faced with in the hours that led to a flight from New Jersey to Cape Cod in July 1999. He balanced the hazards of hazy weather and poor visibility against his skills as an eyeball-only pilot—a pilot who needed to be able to see the ground in order to fly safely.

As history shows, Kennedy made a deadly mistake in assessing the risks of that flight. He wasn't the first pilot to underestimate the power of the elements or to overestimate the skills he brought to the cockpit. Thousands of pilots have made similarly poor decisions. Although for most of these flyers, fate was usually more forgiving, the tragedy of JFK Jr. is an example of just how serious the consequences of a bad flying decision can be.

Still Another Kennedy Tragedy

When news reports that Kennedy's plane was missing were first broadcast on a Saturday morning in July 1999, the country held its breath. Yet again the Kennedy family was threatened with tragedy, and painful memories were reawakened.

As details of Kennedy's last minutes of flight began to emerge from the National Transportation Safety Board investigators whose job is to investigate fatal airplane accidents, pilots around the world felt an even deeper pain. Many could imagine themselves in the cockpit of Kennedy's *Piper Saratoga*, frightened and bewildered as events sped out of control. As days passed and details came to light about the plane's *radar track*, investigators, the press, and the public gradually acknowledged that John Jr., his wife Carolyn Bessette Kennedy, and her sister Lauren Bessette were almost certainly dead.

Before we look into the combination of circumstances and bad decisions that probably led, step by step, to Kennedy's crash, we should review how Kennedy and the Bessette sisters spent their last few hours. The chain of events that led to the crash started many hours before Kennedy's Piper Saratoga hit the waters of Rhode Island Sound.

The Last Few Hours

On Friday, July 16, the day of Kennedy's fatal flight, John Jr. spent the morning with a visiting publishing executive working on a plan to rescue his magazine, *George,* from financial problems. He spent the afternoon in Manhattan engaged in routine business duties and also visited a health club.

Kennedy had expected his sister-in-law Lauren Bessette to meet him at his magazine headquarters right after work. He, his wife Carolyn, and Lauren were planning to fly from Essex County Airport in Fairfield, New Jersey, to Martha's Vineyard to drop off Lauren. Then Kennedy and Carolyn would continue to Hyannisport for a family wedding the next day.

Lauren was late leaving work at the Morgan Stanley Dean Witter investment bank. By the time she arrived at the offices of *George*, it was 6:30 P.M., just a couple of hours before sunset. She and John Jr. drove from midtown Manhattan through Friday traffic to Essex County Airport, a drive that took an hour and a half.

At 8:10, John Jr. and Lauren stopped at a gas station convenience store across the street from the Essex County Airport for some fruit and a bottle of water. By that time, the sun was only 15 minutes from setting. That meant that while weather conditions for flying were technically classified as *visual meteorological conditions* (VMC), darkness would soon fall, and that would demand some "blind flying" skills. Blind flying skills come into play on very dark nights while flying over unlit terrain and when weather conditions are classified as *instruments meteorological conditions* (IMC). This kind of flying, also called "flight by reference to instruments," involves controlling the airplane solely by use of flight instruments, a specialized skill that Kennedy wasn't yet proficient in.

After Kennedy received an Internet briefing on the weather conditions, which included a warning that haze had reduced visibility to between six and eight miles, Carolyn arrived. John Jr., Carolyn, and Lauren boarded the plane, and at 8:38, more than 10 minutes past sunset and in deepening twilight, the Saratoga lifted off. Kennedy may or may not have known that other pilots who had just flown in from Long Island Sound, the direction in which he was headed, were reporting far worse haze conditions over the water than the six-to-eight-mile visibility being reported on the Internet.

The twilight was more than light enough for take-off, and during training for his private pilot certificate, Kennedy would have made at least 10 nighttime takeoffs and landings. So landings on Martha's Vineyard and then at Hyannisport would not have posed a serious problem. His training would also have included a cross-country flight of at least 100 miles. Night flying wasn't new to him, and in good weather, the flight would have been routine.

By the Book

Regulators sometimes define weather by the broad classifications of **visual meteorological conditions (VMC)** or **instruments meteorological conditions (IMC)**. Any pilot with a private pilot certificate can fly in VMC, which require visibility of three miles during daytime and five miles at night. Private pilots also have to stay away from clouds. Haze sometimes can meet the technical standards of VMC, though it seriously affects visibility.

Kennedy had a choice of a couple of routes to take. One would have taken him along the northern shore of Long Island, the other along the southern coast of Connecticut and Rhode Island. On previous flights to Hyannisport, the Kennedy family's home, John Jr. had flown the Long Island route, keeping the lights of the Connecticut shore to his left.

The lights of Long Island were bright enough to provide a semblance of a horizon, even on the haziest night. At about halfway along the route, the tip of Long Island would fall behind Kennedy, but in clear weather he'd have the darker but still light-speckled coast of Rhode Island to his left.

Plane Talk

The National Transportation Safety Board studied its general aviation accident records and arrived at a profile for a pilot most likely to be involved in an accident. He is between 35 and 39 years old, has logged between 100 and 500 hours of flight time, is on a personal flight, and is flying in reasonably good weather. John Jr. fit the profile exactly, and the weather during his last flight was technically acceptable for visual flight rules, meaning he wasn't required to have special blind flying training. Pilots are at highest risk of accidents between 100 and 500 hours of flight time because it is then that their confidence exceeds their experience, the NTSB says.

On that particular night, though, a menacing variable had been added to the familiar route—the hazy sky. Once Kennedy shot past Montauk Point, the last point of land on Long Island, he might not have immediately seen Block Island 12 nautical miles ahead. This is the first time in the flight when Kennedy might have felt uneasy.

With Long Island slipping behind him by three miles every minute, and the haze obscuring his view of Connecticut many miles northward over Long Island Sound, Kennedy would have had to be "on instruments" to control his plane in the deep darkness. His few hours of night-flying training would have taught him the simple basics of using his *flight instruments* to keep his wings level and his nose from rising into a climb or dipping into a shallow dive.

Kennedy's lessons seemed to serve him well. He remained on course until he reached Block Island, and then, as the radar track shows, he made a right turn for a new course toward Martha's Vineyard.

The Last Few Miles

Throughout the entire 50-odd minutes of flight Kennedy made no radio calls (none were mandatory), so we don't have any recording of his voice and demeanor that might give us an indication of his state of mind. But some speculation based on the way most pilots respond to stress and anxiety are safe to make.

The sight that met Kennedy's eyes after he passed Block Island must have been chilling. He would have been confronted with an utterly black sky. Every surface feature that in better weather would have been visible would have been, on that night, shrouded by the maddening haze.

Without a horizon—without even the barely discernible line that separates sea from sky—John Jr.'s concentration may have been disturbed to the extent that he could not completely focus on his flight instruments. Looking outside the plane for some kind of light or visual reference, as a pilot at his skill level is likely to have been desperate to do, he would gradually have lost a sense of whether his wings were level or banked and whether the airplane's nose was slowly rising into a climb or dropping into a gradual dive—a phenomenon called "spatial disorientation," which we'll examine later in the chapter.

One thing he didn't do, according to the radar track, was turn back toward the reassuring lights of Long Island.

By the Book

An airplane's instrument panel includes navigation instruments, engine instruments, and **flight instruments,** which help a pilot determine the airplane's attitude, including the bank of the wings and the pitch of the nose. Using these instruments, a specially trained "instrument" pilot can safely fly without ever looking outside the window. Student pilots must practice instrument flying for three hours before becoming private pilots.

Plane Talk

Pilots' radio transmissions during emergencies often betray their emotions very clearly. Some pilots in dire situations, usually inexperienced ones, can be heard shouting with excitement into their microphones, and sometimes their panicked voices rise to a shrill cry. But experienced pilots pride themselves in staying cool under even the worst conditions. The difference between newcomers and veterans is often most telling in how well they keep a cool head during an emergency.

Surrounded by darkness and growing uneasy, Kennedy probably leaned forward in his seat on the left side of the cockpit. He might well have pressed his face closer to the windshield in hopes of spotting the faintest light on the Rhode Island coastline to his left or a ship's light on the ocean 5,500 feet below—anything he could use to get a fix on his position.

Turbulence

Does haze sound like an inconsequential barrier to safe flying? Think again. Haze, which is caused by tiny particles of fine dust or salt scattering light to create a bright, milky blur, can almost blind a pilot with bright light in daytime and can block out much of the light coming from the ground at night.

On Course

Vision is about 90 percent responsible for giving us our sense of balance. Without our vision, including the peripheral vision that we call "seeing out of the corner of our eyes," we quickly lose an accurate sense of balance.

Carolyn or Lauren might have noticed already that the sky outside the plane was unusually featureless, and John Jr.'s increasing anxiety might have put them on alert. If they had a reading light turned on in the cabin, he might have called back to them to turn it off to reduce the glare on the inside of the Plexiglas windshield.

Up in the cockpit, the soft green and red lights that lit the instrument panel would have been reflecting a faint glow off the inside of the windshield, making visibility even worse.

Kennedy might have, very naturally, begun turning his head from side to side, first slowly and then faster, as he looked for lights that might help guide him. The instinctive turning of his head in search of a visual cue would have sent the delicate balance organs inside the inner ears spinning. As we'll see shortly, a distorted sense of balance could have contributed to the fatal maneuver that soon began.

Radar records show that when the Saratoga was about 34 miles southwest of Martha's Vineyard airport, it began a 700-foot-per-minute descent from its cruising altitude of about 5,500 feet. That descent rate is perfectly normal for a planned descent, but Kennedy had no reason to be descending over the middle of Rhode Island Sound so far from Martha's Vineyard, unless he was trying to slip beneath the haze layer.

Kennedy kept up the descent until he reached 2,300 feet, where he leveled the plane, still in the thick haze. Perhaps already growing disoriented, John Jr. rolled the airplane into a right turn combined with a slight climb to 2,600 feet. He may not have intended to make the turn, and with no visible references to orient them, John Jr., Carolyn, and Lauren might not have even noticed the turn taking place.

Radar records show that the right turn halted for about a minute, and the airplane leveled off at the same time, perhaps as Kennedy noticed on his flight instruments that he had been turning.

John Jr.'s Saratoga was now 16 miles from Martha's Vineyard airport and seven miles from landfall on the southwestern tip of the island. It was then that the plane rolled into yet another right turn—again probably the result of a faulty sense of balance caused by the impenetrable haze. This right turn became the final, fatal maneuver.

The Graveyard Spiral

At this point, the Saratoga's bank angle probably increased gradually, shrinking the amount of lift directed upward away from the ocean and causing the airplane's nose to drop and its airspeed to increase.

As the airspeed built up, the aerodynamics of the turn would have steepened the bank angle further, shrinking the upward lift vector even more. The cycle would have continued over a period of a minute or so, until the airplane was hurtling toward the sea in what pilots call a *graveyard spiral*.

A graveyard spiral, as its name suggests, is dangerous, but not necessarily deadly. An experienced pilot, in the unlikely event he would find himself in such a situation, would follow a precise procedure of reducing the throttle, leveling the wings, and gradually raising the nose to stop the descent. But if a pilot makes one wrong move and gets the steps out of order, the spiral can tighten and become lethal.

In fact, every student pilot is required to recover from this very predicament before they qualify for their private pilot certificate. But they usually do it in broad daylight by looking outside the airplane—not at night with nothing to refer to but their instruments, a far more difficult set of conditions.

Kennedy never recovered from the graveyard spiral. The Piper Saratoga struck the water of Rhode Island Sound in a 5,000-foot-per-minute descent, which would have felt like hitting a brick wall at 60 miles per hour. At that speed, in fact, water feels as hard as brick, and John Jr., Carolyn, and Lauren would have died before they knew what was happening.

By the Book

Graveyard spirals are often triggered by the smallest of air disturbances scarcely noticed by the passengers and crew. But because airplanes are slightly unstable when it comes to keeping the wing level—instability that designers create purposely in order to give the plane better maneuverability—a little bit of turbulence that lifts one wing farther than the other can set off a slight bank that, if it goes unnoticed, can deepen into a graveyard spiral.

All Signs Urged Caution

The factors that combined to work against Kennedy on his last flight seem nearly endless. A chain reaction of bad decisions and mistakes is usually what we notice when we examine any accident with the luxury of hindsight, and the Kennedy tragedy is no exception.

Had Kennedy better understood the complexity of the decision-making process, what pilots call *human factors,* he might have dissected his own decisions *before* they snowballed into tragedy. Even the pilots who understand them sometimes have a hard time making safe decisions.

Plane Talk

Much was made in the media of the fact that Kennedy hadn't filed a flight plan. Flight plans don't possess any mystical quality that enhance the safety of a flight. Though they should always be filed when appropriate, they are little more than a notice to the FAA of a planned route and expected time of arrival that helps narrow the search for a plane if it turns up missing. The fact that a pilot did not file a flight plan doesn't mean the pilot didn't plan his route. It simply means he didn't report the route to the FAA for search-and-rescue purposes.

By the Book

Human factors is a relatively new field of study that examines the collection of factors that can erode a pilot's performance, such as a pilot's emotional state of mind, his physical health, his relationship with other crew members, and his response to stress. Researchers hope to identify and help reduce hazards caused by human weaknesses.

Following are some of the factors that added up to tragedy for JFK Jr., his wife, and her sister. An experienced pilot—one who is sensitive to the vulnerability of the human factors involved in aviation decision-making—would have readily recognized them as warning signs.

Inexperience

Kennedy was not, by his own admission, a superb pilot. He was like most other pilots with a few months of experience—eager to learn, but immature in his skills and judgment.

Kennedy's sense of his own limitations might have caused him to look, with a growing anxiety, at the setting sun, whose disk was probably touching the horizon at about the time he was paying for his merchandise at the Sunoco convenience store. The sky was already becoming hazy, and Kennedy had many minutes of preflight preparation, weather checking, plane inspection, taxiing, and preflight engine check left to complete before takeoff. He must have realized at the gas station, and maybe as early as leaving his office, that he would have to fly in the dark over Long Island Sound to reach Martha's Vineyard, the most challenging leg of the trip.

Pressure

Kennedy no doubt felt tremendous pressure to get to his destination. The Kennedy family was gathering in Hyannisport for a Saturday wedding, and John Jr. must have felt pressure to arrive in time.

In flying vernacular, the pressure to get to the destination regardless of the risk is called "get-there-itis," and it's often a fatal disease. If Kennedy was feeling rushed, it would explain some of his decisions before and during the flight. A pilot in his position needed to rethink the notion of flying at all that night. In fact, other pilots with more experience than Kennedy had examined the persistent coastal haze that day and called off their flights.

Turbulence

Kennedy might have committed four out of the eight leading causes of airplane accidents during his last flight: loss of directional control, poor judgment, poor preflight planning and decision making, and poor in-flight planning and decision making. (The others are not maintaining airspeed, not staying far enough away from other planes or obstructions, inadvertent stalls, and poor crosswind handling.)

Challenging Weather Conditions

The weather conditions were perhaps the most difficult factor to deal with. Had conditions been better, Kennedy's visual flying skills would have been up to the task of making the flight. Had the weather been worse, FAA rules would have taken the decision out of his hands. As fate would have it, conditions that night fell into the gray area that forced Kennedy to make a difficult decision himself—and make the wrong one.

Personal and Professional Stress

Stress related to Kennedy's professional and personal life may have played a role in the disaster. The financial decline of his magazine *George* was well known, and was no doubt preying on his mind. Also rumored were his marriage difficulties with Carolyn. There is always a possibility that this combination of stress factors made it harder for Kennedy to concentrate solely on his flying.

Physical Discomfort

Kennedy was probably suffering some mild physical discomfort on this flight, too. He had broken his ankle, and the cast had just been removed a couple of days earlier. The press emphasized this factor a lot, but Kennedy's foot probably didn't play a direct role in the crash—he would hardly have been using the rudder at all when the accident occurred. But it's worth mentioning that physical discomfort, whether from illness or injury, can be a powerful distraction during a flight.

Route

Had Kennedy made a different choice of routes, the accident might never have happened.

There are two primary routes from northern New Jersey to Martha's Vineyard and Cape Cod—the familiar Long Island route that includes a lengthy overwater leg, and a second route that hugs the southern coast of Connecticut and Rhode Island.

Without adding any significant flight time (though it would perhaps have required a bit of additional planning time), Kennedy could have flown a brightly lit route over suburban Westchester County and into Connecticut. There, guided by the lights of Bridgeport, New London, and finally Newport, Rhode Island, which would have been more visible through the haze, he could have made a much shorter over-water hop to Martha's Vineyard. The short hop from there to Hyannisport would also have been relatively well-lit.

However, Kennedy seems to have succumbed to one of the most pernicious influences on decision making: opting for the familiar over the unknown, regardless of other factors. He chose the familiar route he had flown before, despite the fact that weather conditions for that route were *not* the same he had flown in before.

No Contact with Air-Traffic Controllers

Had Kennedy checked in with air-traffic controllers along the route, the outcome might have been different.

Air-traffic controllers don't dictate a pilot's route when the plane is outside the dense traffic areas around airports. On routes such as the one Kennedy flew that July night, controllers mostly help pilots identify the flight paths of nearby airplanes in order to prevent collisions. But controllers do have a subtle, steadying effect on pilots. They provide a firm voice and a connection to a world of resources at a time of crisis when a pilot might otherwise feel deserted and panicky.

For example, had Kennedy confided in a controller that he was having a hard time getting his bearings in the hazy night sky, a controller might have been able to put out a call to other pilots on that frequency asking if anyone had found clear sky, and if so at what altitude. Perhaps it would have been a simple matter of the controller's recommending that Kennedy climb from his 5,500-foot cruising altitude to 7,500 feet to get safely above the haze into clearer sky with a star- or moonlit horizon. That could have been the difference between disorientation and renewed confidence.

Plane Talk

Some controllers take a very protective view of the airplanes they track. After accidents of airplanes that a controller has been communicating with, particularly during an emergency that ends in tragedy, controllers often suffer severe emotional turmoil that has on some occasions ended in long-term depression or suicide. The FAA provides a variety of support services to controllers to ease feelings of guilt that can linger for months or years after an accident.

What's more, veteran controllers, many of whom are pilots themselves, often have a keen ear for the subtle indications of a pilot who's nearing his limit. A strain in the pilot's voice or a sudden rushing of words could betray a pilot's mounting fear. In some cases, the controller can make suggestions, such as a recommended direction of flight (known as a "vector"), that will guide the pilot toward a nearby airport.

To be sure, controllers can't reach into the cockpit and fly the airplane. In the end, the pilot is the only one who can do that. And often, controllers are overworked and not able to pay such close attention to every pilot. But Kennedy had one tool at his disposal that would have gotten a controller's full attention—he could have declared an emergency. Had Kennedy uttered that one word, "emergency," a controller would have given him priority treatment. After transferring the other airplanes to a colleague in the radar room, the controller would have worked with Kennedy to try to resolve the situation.

We can't help but wonder how the lives of the Kennedy and Bessette families, and the spirits of a nation, would be different now if John Jr. had reached out for help from the communications network that was set up for the sole purpose of helping pilots fly safely.

Dangerous Thinking

Setting aside the technical missteps Kennedy made that night, let's consider the possibility that he also might have been a victim of a more insidious danger—dangerous thinking. Kennedy might have fallen prey to some of the hazardous attitudes that can cloud judgment, sway decision making, and blur the clear view of risks.

One hazardous attitude is machismo, the attitude that makes pilots tell themselves, "I can do whatever I set my mind to, and I'll prove it." Another is a sense of invulnerability. Sometimes, the reasoning goes, "I've seen other pilots take off in worse conditions than this, and nothing ever happened to them." In other cases, it might sound like this: "I've always been able to get myself out of scrapes before." In any case, the pilot who feels invulnerable ultimately thinks "Nothing bad is going to happen to me."

Hazardous attitudes like these, and others that demonstrate impulsiveness, resignation to fate, and rebellion against authority, are as potentially dangerous as flying with an invisibly cracked propeller: It might not happen on this flight or the next, but eventually the hidden danger will become all too obvious—all too late.

Plane Talk

Some of the most challenging "intangible" lessons that instructors sometimes have to teach is the danger of hazardous attitudes. Many students take longer to break hazardous attitudes than they do to learn the most advanced flying skills. When it comes to hiring professional pilots at airlines or elsewhere, hiring officials may spend more time trying to detect potentially dangerous attitudes in a pilot than anything else. That's why airline job interviews include not only technical examinations but also questioning by experienced pilots and psychologists.

The Folly of Night VFR

We can find some of the seeds of Kennedy's tragic death in FAA regulations that allow relatively inexperienced pilots to fly under rules that permit visual flying at night, also called night VFR.

In essence, the FAA permits a private pilot with only a smattering of experience with instrument flying to fly at night as long as the sky is relatively free of clouds. Never mind the fact that in some parts of this country, as in the John F. Kennedy Jr.'s case, there are times when weather conditions that are technically acceptable are, in practice, daunting even to a trained instrument pilot.

Regulations in many nations throughout Europe and the rest of the world ground a private pilot at night—a rule that encourages many to get the extra training they need to be a safer instrument-rated pilot. Perhaps adopting similar guidelines would cause American amateur pilots to seek the extra training they need and take the difficulties of nighttime flying more seriously.

The Deceptive Sense of Balance

The accident that took the lives of Kennedy and his passengers was the result of some or all the factors we've previously described. We've talked a little about the graveyard spiral, and how pilots are susceptible to false sensations when flying in low visibility conditions at night. How, exactly, are these false sensations produced?

The Inner Ear

Deep inside the inner ear is a tiny, complex organ called the labyrinth that looks like a cross between a tuba and a toy gyroscope. The portion of this organ that we're concerned with is a set of three bony loops called the semicircular canals.

One loop of the semicircular canals is horizontal, lying flat like a bicycle inner tube on the driveway. The other two canals stand upright at right angles to each other. All three are connected in a structure called the vestibule.

Inside the bony exterior of the semicircular canals is a fleshy lining of hairlike fibers bathed in fluid. When you turn your head, the bony structure and the tiny hairs inside it turn with it, only the fluid is slower to accelerate. It's just like rotating the outside of a glass filled with an icy drink. The glass rotates in your hands, but the icy liquid inside begins to move only very slowly, creating a difference in velocity between the rim of the glass and the liquid just inside.

The tiny hairs in the semicircular canals are forced to sway in one direction or another from the difference in speed between the fluid and the bony structure, and nerves beneath each hair detect the degree of swaying. In our brains, this is transformed into a sensation of movement.

Without visual cues to help make sense of some of the sensations coming out of the semicircular canals, the vestibular system can relay completely inaccurate messages to the brain.

Disorientation

Let's imagine a pilot flying in complete darkness. If he enters a right-hand bank very gradually, the hairy fibers in the semicircular canals may not be sensitive enough to detect the movement of the fluid. Although JFK Jr.'s airplane was gradually entering a right turn, his vestibular system wouldn't have known it.

On Course

There are a couple of other tiny organs that contribute to equilibrium. Cristae have tiny jelly-like blobs that sense rotation, and maculae are bundles of nerves on a stem that tips downward when you bend down. Like the semicircular canals, both of these organs can be easily fooled in an airplane at a high altitude unless your eyes are working well.

Turbulence

One of the most dangerous things a pilot can do when flying in instrument conditions or in very dark skies like John Kennedy Jr. experienced is to make any rapid movements of the head. The jostling to the semicircular canals can set up a host of conflicting, and inaccurate, sensations of movement.

By the Book

Spatial disorientation is the catch-all term used to describe any situation in which a pilot isn't certain of the attitude of his airplane relative to the horizon.

Now let's imagine that the pilot glances at his flight instruments. He'd at least see a right bank indication on his attitude indicator and his turn indicator—two gyroscopic instruments. Surprised, he might move the aileron controls abruptly to the left to level the wings again. Now, that rapid control movement to the left would certainly create enough of a jolt to the hairy fibers to send a signal to the brain: We're turning *left*.

That left-turn signal is wrong in this case. The pilot is actually moving from a right bank to level flight. But because the semicircular canals didn't pick up the right bank and only noticed the left-hand movement of the ailerons to level the wings, the brain perceives a left turn.

The power of these sensations is hard to describe. In the scenario we've just described, the pilot might find the sensation of turning left so powerful that almost nothing would convince him he had done otherwise. He would be very likely to respond with right-aileron control to correct what his senses tell him was a left turn, even though his eyes told him a moment ago that he was correcting a mistaken right turn.

The power of these illusions was brought home to me some years ago during a training session on the topic of *spatial disorientation.*

I was placed in a contraption consisting of a simple chair mounted on a swivel. After an instructor told me to buckle myself into the seat (I thought this was an overprecaution), he had me lay my head on its side with my eyes closed. He rotated the chair with me in it, accelerating it so gradually that I had only a slight sensation of movement. In reality it was spinning quite fast at the end.

After about a minute of this, he gave me a signal to sit upright and open my eyes, while he simultaneously stopped the chair's rotation. What I felt was an overwhelming sensation of falling forward toward the floor. The feeling was so powerful that I yelled—an expletive, if I recall—and put my hands out in front of me to stop myself from falling on my face. What others in the room saw was a confused pilot sitting in a still chair, in the grip of a powerful balance illusion of falling that lasted for about a minute, and, I confess, turned my stomach.

Had I been in an airplane when this situation occurred—as when a pilot bends down to search for a flashlight or pencil on the floor while the airplane is turning—I believe that no amount of discipline and attention to my instruments would have prevented me from pulling the airplane into a steep climb. The illusion I experienced, called the Coriolis illusion, surpassed reason and went straight to the level of instinct and fear.

In this case, and in other balance illusions, the solution lies in prevention. Pilots must understand how these illusions are created and learn to avoid them. In the case of John F. Kennedy Jr., it's unlikely that his brief flying experience would have equipped him to prevent balance illusions or to correct them if they occurred.

Because the accident occurred in total isolation from air traffic control, and because human factors leave behind no evidence that can be examined in a lab, the cause of the crash that killed John F. Kennedy Jr. and his wife and sister-in-law will never be known with any certainty. Still, the sparse evidence we have of its last few minutes leaves us with a powerful lesson—that every pilot is subject to the same destructive attitudes and is saddled with the same unreliable senses. If any good comes out of John Jr.'s death, it will be a heightened focus on safety among general aviation pilots for decades to come.

The Least You Need to Know

➤ Kennedy's decisions before and during his last flight probably caused the accident that took three lives.

➤ Kennedy chose not to communicate with radar controllers, who may have been able to help him out of trouble.

➤ Like the spin, the graveyard spiral is a deadly situation for a pilot to find himself in.

➤ The vestibular system provides our body's sense of balance, but without sight it's easily fooled.

The Future of Aviation

Of all the forms of transportation humans have devised, none have progressed as far and as fast as aviation. If we consider the Wright brothers' flight in 1903 as the birth of modern aviation, it's taken just under a century for airplanes to evolve from a curious spectacle to a force powerful enough to send craft into space.

Indeed, the space shuttle—in effect a highly specialized glider—is capable of space flight for days or weeks at a time. It acts as a sort of ultra-high-tech ferry, rocketing people and material up to an international space station—a space station that, within a few years, will feature living and working pods for seven researchers and scientists who will stay in space for up to six months at a time.

It's nearly impossible to believe that the men and women who will soon spend parts of their lives skimming hundreds of miles above the earth can trace their legacy fewer than 10 decades back to the bishop's boys, Wilbur and Orville, and their experiments on wind-blown Kill Devil Hill.

Human Wings

Flying has always been a very personal means of expression. Even the most mechanized and regimented of all aspects of aviation, military flying, allows its pilots to express themselves with a flourish of skill or a touch of grace.

For years, airplane designers have been working on human-powered craft to bring man closer to the ultimate dream of flying as naturally as the birds. Human-powered flight, which, as its name implies, uses no power source other than human muscle, appears to be a reversion rather than a step forward in the technology of flight. But when considered as the realization of the centuries-old dream of taking to the air as easily as birds, it represents possibly the most sublime evolution in aviation.

Because humans are poor sources of power, creating only about ¼ horsepower at best, the goal of creating an airplane that can lift its own weight and that of its pilot was beyond most designers' abilities—and then ultra-lightweight composite materials were created.

At Dryden Flight Research Center at Edwards Air Force Base, pilot Glenn Tremml flew the human-powered airplane Daedalus 88.

(NASA)

Paul MacCready

One man, Paul MacCready, deserves credit for most of the advances in design and lightweight materials that have made human-powered flight possible. He also deserves credit for devising innovative ways to use old-fashioned material to bring out its hidden strength without adding weight.

Plane Talk

As proof that a talented designer doesn't have to shackle himself to any one pursuit, Paul MacCready's portfolio includes the design of General Motors' Impact automobile, which is solar powered. He also designed and flew the radio-controlled pterodactyl model that was featured in the IMAX film *On the Wing*.

For example, MacCready's first successful human-powered plane, the Gossamer Condor, used only cardboard and balsa wood as structural material, and weighed only 70 pounds empty, but it was able to carry a pilot that weighed more than the plane did. The Gossamer Condor, whose 96-foot wingspan was wider than a DC-9 jetliner's wings, was the first plane to maneuver around a mile-long figure-eight course powered only by human muscle.

In a photograph reminiscent of the photo of the Wright brothers' liftoff on December 17, 1903, Paul MacCready's Gossamer Albatross lifts off for a flight in 1980.

(NASA)

Daedalus and Icarus Redux

A few years later, MacCready's Gossamer Albatross flew the English Channel to win a £100,000 prize. And in 1988, a Greek pilot/athlete nearly duplicated the mythic flight of Daedalus and Icarus from Crete to Greece powered only by his own energy.

Kanellos Kanellopoulus flew 15 feet over the waves of the Aegean Sea for more than four hours, covering 115 kilometers. When he was within 10 yards of the beach, a gust of wind struck the tail, and the craft splashed down into the ocean waves, failing to reach its destination by a matter of seconds.

Plane Talk

The more things change, the more they stay the same. Some of the futuristic planes using the most cutting-edge materials and designs look strangely familiar. Just as the Wright brothers did in their early airplane designs, designers of next-generation airplanes are putting the horizontal tail up front, and moving the propeller to the rear of the plane in a "pusher" configuration. The Gossamer Condor even used piano wires to warp the wingtips to bank the wings, the precise design the Wright brothers used. The Gossamer Condor and the Wrights' *Flyer* now hang side-by-side in the Smithsonian Institution's Air and Space Museum.

If you're not convinced that human-powered aircraft represent an advance in design and construction, consider this statement by the designer of one human-powered plane: "We have an airplane that can be picked up in one hand, flies on the power needed to run a lightbulb, and has the wingspan of a commercial aircraft."

By the Book

Canards are wing surfaces that are positioned in the front of the airplane but serve the same stabilizing purpose as the tail surfaces of conventional designs. The word "canard" comes from the French for "duck."

Burt Rutan

Just as Paul MacCready dominated the movement in aviation design toward ultra-light human-powered aircraft, another man pioneered the movement toward *canard* designs—the legendary Burt Rutan.

Rutan runs a sort of "Skunk Works" for futuristic airplane designs out of his complex in the California desert. The original Skunk Works was a secretive Lockheed Aircraft factory that hired the best engineers and most rebellious thinkers in order to turn out, in the '50s and '60s, some airplanes that are still ahead of many companies' best efforts.

The Lockheed Skunk Works designed planes such as the U-2 spy plane, which flew so high it was thought to be impossible to bring down, until the Russians did just that in 1960, downing Francis Gary Powers. Later, the Skunk Works turned out another spy plane, the sleek SR-71 Blackbird, which flew so high and so fast that it would turn scalding hot from air friction. Its super-aerodynamic shape still sets the standard for what a fast plane should look like. The Skunk Works is still operating in the California desert town of Palmdale.

Skunking the Competition

Burt Rutan has become the Master Designer in his own desert Skunk Works. Rutan revolutionized airplane design, and he leaves a stylistic mark on his airplanes as recognizable as the architectural flourishes of Frank Lloyd Wright.

Most of his airplane designs include a canard in front of the craft and a pusher prop or a jet engine either on the back of the wing or behind the fuselage. Rutan's designs typically throw the idea of a rudder out the window and replace it with a number of smaller vertical surfaces spread around the airplane, from turned-up wingtips to twin stabilizers stuck out at the two ends of a horizontal stabilizer.

In the 1970s, Rutan designed a series of small, kit-built planes called VariEze, Quickie, and Long-EZ. These speedy experimental planes with outlandish designs quickly began turning up at airports around the country, and with relatively tiny engines, they were outracing other beefier, higher-horsepower conventional airplanes.

On Course

Rutan is able to defy many of the rules of conventional airplane design because he doesn't use conventional airplane materials. In place of metal, he prefers high-tech composite laminates, which are created by layering exotic fabrics one atop the other. These materials are strong and amazingly lightweight, and they can be formed to a designer's specifications without regard for the structural limitations of metal.

Around the World on One Tank of Gas

Rutan cemented his reputation in aviation history, and earned a spot in the International Aerospace Hall of Fame, with his design of the *Voyager*, the skinny-winged, ungainly looking "flying fuel tank" of an airplane that flew around the globe *without stopping for gas*.

Plane Talk

Voyager was piloted by the team of Jeana Yeager and Dick Rutan, the designer's brash and charismatic brother. Not long after *Voyager's* around-the-world flight, I happened one day to be flying into Ernest A. Love Field in Prescott, Arizona, at the same time as Dick Rutan. Throwing radio etiquette to the wind just as his brother ignores the conventions of plane design, Dick Rutan announced his presence on the radio to those of us who were also approaching Prescott. Rather than resort to the time-honored tradition of announcing his presence by referring to his airplane's registration number, as pilots have been doing since airplanes first got radios, the *Voyager* pilot keyed his mike and announced to the handful of us on the control tower frequency, "This is Dick Rutan, inbound for landing!"

In December 1986, *Voyager* lifted off from Mojave, California, in an attempt to do what no one considered remotely possible: fly some 25,000 miles, the circumference of the globe, on a single tank of gas. But what a tank it was! Rutan created an airplane so light and so strong that it was capable of carrying 10 times its own weight in fuel, crew, and cargo. Pilots Jeana Yeager (no relation to Chuck) and Dick Rutan, Burt's brother, kept cargo to a minimum in their cramped crew quarters so that fuel would make up most of the remaining weight.

Designed by Burt Rutan and piloted by Jeana Yeager and Dick Rutan, the Voyager *flew around the world in nine days on a single tank of gas.*

(NASA)

The flight was snake-bit from the outset. One of *Voyager*'s wings scraped the runway on takeoff, badly damaging a wingtip and causing a winglet to fall off. Worse, an autopilot, which Burt Rutan had installed in order to tame the wild oscillations of the inherently jittery airplane, failed early in the flight, making controlling the airplane difficult and tiring for the two pilots. But, fortunately, these problems didn't endanger the flight.

After nine days, *Voyager* touched down again in Mojave, having *doubled* the previous record for the longest nonstop flight without refueling, logging 28,000 miles.

Rutan is still turning out some remarkable designs, including the Boomerang, which defies the "rules" of design symmetry by creating a lopsided airplane with two fuselages and two engines, and seemingly only half a horizontal stabilizer. Unorthodox as it is, it's one of the most strikingly beautiful airplane designs I've ever seen, something like an airborne version of the Guggenheim museum.

On Course

As I watched the *Voyager* flight, I was unnerved by the slender wings' tendency to flap wildly in turbulence. When the air was bumpy, those 110-foot-long wings flapped so hard I was convinced they would snap off. But Burt Rutan knows how to build strength into his airplanes, as well as light weight, and the airplane held together for nine days.

Jetting Into the Future

Designers like MacCready and Rutan continue to draw the future of aviation on their drafting tables, creating aircraft that fly faster, higher, and even to the edge of space.

NASA is hard at work developing a line of X-planes that will carry people and cargo to altitudes that we only dreamed of a few years ago.

At Langley Research Center in Hampton, Virginia, designers and engineers are ready to launch a prototype of a hypersonic jet called Hyper-X. The Hyper-X is designed to fly at a speed of *Mach* 10, or 6,600 miles an hour, using an experimental "scramjet."

A scramjet, for "supersonic combustion ramjet," is a jet engine that has no moving parts. Air passes through the engine at supersonic speed, is mixed with fuel, and the mixture is then burned to create thrust. It's expected that the scramjet engine will be able to push future aircraft to speeds of about two miles *per*

By the Book

High speeds are often measured in units called **Mach** numbers, in honor of Austrian physicist Ernst Mach. Pilots also refer to one Mach as the speed of sound, because a plane flying at Mach 1 is flying as fast as sound travels through the atmosphere. Mach 1 is about 660 miles per hour, though the speed of sound varies with temperature.

second, or more than 7,000 miles per hour, as compared to 500 m.p.h. that is typical for passenger jets.

Whether they are scramjets or conventional jet engines, called "turbofans" in their most common form, jet engines compress air using a series of fast-spinning fanlike rotors contained inside a shroud that keeps the air from escaping once it starts to move through the engine. Once the air is compressed, fuel, usually kerosene, is sprayed into the dense air in a precise ratio.

The fuel-air mixture moves into a combustion chamber, where spark plug–like igniters cause the volatile mixture to explode. The heat and outward pressure of the explosion pushes on all sides of the combustion chamber, which is simply a cylinder with an exhaust opening at one end.

The pressure of the burning fuel-air mixture exerts a powerful force on every surface inside the combustion chamber including the front of the chamber, where in obedience to Isaac Newton's law of physics that says "every action produces an equal and opposite reaction," the combustion chamber receives a forward impulse. Because the engine is part of the plane, the impulse created inside the combustion chamber delivers a forward jolt to the entire airplane.

Once the volatile fuel-air mixture is ignited and delivers its thrust force, the spent exhaust gases rush out of the engine through the exhaust nozzle. But before the fuel-air mixture leaves the engine, it races past another set of fanlike rotors, called "turbines," set in the exhaust path. The force of the exhaust turns the turbines, which are connected via an axle to the compressors at the front of the engine, where the process began.

In other words, the force of the exhaust gas is harnessed to spin the compressor fans, creating a simple and self-perpetuating cycle that continues as long as the fuel and the ignition spark last.

Scramjets function in much the same way, except that the incredibly high speed of aircraft like the X-34 causes the air entering the engine to compress naturally. That means a scramjet has no need for compressor fans, not to mention the turbine fans to turn the compressor. The fuel system simply injects fuel into the compressed air, then ignites the mixture. In a scramjet operating at full speed, the airflow through the combustion chamber never drops below the Mach 1.

If NASA is successful at spinning off its technology into the private sector, we could one day be flying in airplanes that don't make any flights of more than two hours in length. After all, a trip halfway around

On Course

Sometime in 2000, a group of human-powered airplane junkies will try to break a distance record in the pedal-powered Raven, which is being designed and tested in Seattle. The 90-pound craft, whose 115-foot wingspan is wider than a 737's, will fly from Vancouver to Seattle, skimming over the waves of Puget Sound at an altitude of 18 feet. The project has been underway for more than 10 years.

the globe—the longest you'd ever have to make—is only about 12,000 miles long; at Mach 10, it would take just under 1 hour 50 minutes to make such a trip.

In aircraft traveling at speeds of Mach 3 to Mach 10 or more, travel would be revolutionized. For one thing, it will become far more expensive as scramjets and their kin evolve to power progressively larger jetliners. What could result is a class division even more stark than the one that separates first-class passengers from those in coach class: Wealthy travelers will enjoy the luxury of hypersonic speeds while others will settle for more sluggish 600-m.p.h. flights.

On board a hypersonic passenger jet, comfort and amenities will be less critical on a flight that is likely to take only 60 to 90 minutes. Today, when flights can drag on for 10 hours or more, comfort and entertainment are paramount. The hypersonic jets of the future will be technologically advanced, probably equipped with wireless communications and data links that are unimaginable today, but will not need to address the creature comforts that travelers consider of the new millennium so important.

Turbulence

The popularity, even the feasibility, of hypersonic passenger flights hinges on whether engineers can muffle sonic booms, the potentially damaging thunder-claps caused by airplanes breaking the speed of sound. Unless sonic booms can somehow be reduced or eliminated, something that has so far proven impossible, hypersonic flight will be limited to overseas routes that skirt populated areas.

But just as when airline travel gradually overtook rail travel during the 1950s and 1960s, hypersonic travel might spread to all classes of travelers as technology advances and fares drop. By 2030, virtually all travelers should be able to afford the price of a hypersonic flight across the country or around the world. At such speeds, many flights will be too brief for an airline meal—just one more advantage of the hypersonic age.

NASA's experimental Hyper-X is designed for speeds as fast as 10 times the speed of sound. If the technology makes its way into civilian jetliners, the most distant points on earth could be less than two hours apart by air.

(NASA)

A Seat in the Cockpit

While NASA tries to reach Mach 10, passenger jet manufacturers are trying to make movie headsets that actually work.

On Course

A St. Louis group interested in promoting space tourism put up a $5-million prize to the first design team to launch a spaceship carrying three adults at least 62 miles high, and then be able to do it all again within two weeks. One of the 20-odd entrants is Burt Rutan, with a design called Proteus, that is already flying. Based on his resumé, I'd put my money on Burt.

All kidding aside, jet makers continue to press technology to the limit in making larger airplanes that will carry more people at a lower fuel cost than other jets have been able to manage.

The first of the "jumbo jets," the Boeing 747, took the world by storm. When it was rolled out of the hangar in 1969, skeptics were sure a plane that big would fall out of the sky. Over the years, the 747 has grown even larger, and now a fully loaded late-model Jumbo weighs 875,000 pounds and can carry 568 passengers—though, at that capacity, not many of them will be flying in comfort.

Especially in its earliest days in passenger service, the 747 was a cruise ship in the sky. First-class passengers could climb a spiral staircase to an elegantly appointed upper level. In-flight movies, personal music systems—these became part of flying in a Boeing 747.

Now, the 747's top spot among the behemoths of the sky is being challenged by Airbus Industrie, a European consortium with a "we try harder" attitude. Airbus is preparing to roll out a model it calls 3XX— a two-level jetliner that will carry 555 passengers in comfort. That's less than the latest Boeing 747 can carry, but the 3XX-200 will be coming along right behind. It will be able to carry 656 passengers.

The future of jetliners, in the near future at least, seems to be pointing toward larger and larger planes with better and better safety features, although a single crash of one of these sky-ships could potentially be as deadly as the worst aviation disaster ever—when two 747s from Pan Am and KLM Airlines collided on the ground in Tenerife in 1977, killing 582 people.

But let's look on the bright side. Jetliners of the future will be connected to the Internet using satellite feeds, and the technologies now being developed to speed up the Internet will replace the golf magazines flight attendants pass out now with video and music on demand—for a price, of course.

Returning to Flying's Roots

There's a little company in California called Millennium Jet, and if Icarus could have gotten his hands on what they're making, he would have made it from Crete to Greece without hitting the drink before he got there.

Millennium Jet makes the SoloTrek XFV, or Exo-Skeletor Flying Vehicle. It's a one-person flying machine that looks like a cross between one of Leonardo da Vinci's helicopters and the jet-powered backpack that some daredevils flew around in during the 1960s and 1970s.

The SoloTrek XFV could bring pilots closer than ever to the ease and maneuverability of bird flight.

(Millennium Jet)

Here's how the XFV works: A pilot straps into it and fires up two shrouded fans above his head. Using hand grips, the pilot controls the speed and tilt of the fans to take off and maneuver above the ground. The XFV can stay in the air for 90 minutes and fly at 80 miles an hour.

The technology, which appears outlandish on first glance, has attracted NASA's interest, and it's sure to be one of the greatest toys for the wealthy since the DeLorean—and will probably cost about the same.

The XFV, Paul MacCready's human-powered flying machines, and Burt Rutan's visionary designs are all shades of a dream to fly higher, or faster, or less encumbered. Like the flyers of myth and the dreamers of antiquity, men and women with an itch to fly are still searching for their own wings.

The Least You Need to Know

➤ Human-powered flight continues to improve, thanks to research around the world.

➤ Burt Rutan's desert "Skunk Works" is inventing new rules for the way airplanes are designed.

➤ Hyper-X and other hypersonic planes could pave the way for super-fast passenger flights.

➤ Rival airline manufacturers Boeing and Airbus are trying to outbuild each other, and at least on the drawing board, Airbus has the advantage.

➤ Technology is close to enabling men and women to fly as high as, if not as gracefully as, the birds.

Glossary

aerobatics A specialized form of flying in which airplanes diverge from level flight and gentle banking turns in favor of maneuvers that combine loops, rolls, spins, and inverted flight.

aerodynamics A segment of the complex field of fluid mechanics that deals with the motion of air, including the forces it exerts on objects moving through it.

aeronaut Archaic phrase describing balloon pilots. Derives from Greek words meaning "voyager of the air."

aerostation Early French word for balloons.

aileron The hinged wing surfaces that are responsible for controlling the angle of bank. Controlled by the pilot using the control column.

aircraft Anything that flies under some kind of human control, including airplanes, helicopters, gyroplanes, gliders, hot-air balloons, gas balloons, airships, and other vehicles.

airfoil A surface whose shape helps create an aerodynamic force.

air pressure The force exerted by the air at a given altitude, produced by the collective collisions of air molecules on measuring devices.

air rage A newly created term describing outraged, sometimes violent expressions of passenger frustration over perceived misdeeds and maltreatment by airlines and on-board crew members.

airship Aircraft combining buoyant gas envelope with engines that permit control other than the simple movement of the winds.

airsickness A form of motion sickness brought on by air travel. Symptoms include light-headedness, increased salivation, sweating, clamminess, pallor, nausea, vomiting, and fatigue.

angle of attack The angle between the relative wind and the angle of the airfoil. Up to a critical angle where a stall occurs, a larger angle of attack translates into greater lift.

aspect ratio   An aerodynamics formula that measures how skinny or squat a wing is. It divides the wing's span by its front-to-back chord.

atmospheric optics   The large number of visual phenomena created by the sun's light reflecting, refracting, diffracting, or diffusing through or around airborne dust, water, and ice.

aviation   A catch-all term describing almost any sport or occupation that takes place in the air. Derives from the Latin word *avis*, meaning "bird."

avionics   A term of art in aviation, combining the words "aviation" and "electronics." Refers to the navigational and two-way radios, as well as new-generation high-technology devices.

balloon   A contained volume of air or gas that, due to its temperature or gas density, becomes buoyant and can transport a cargo of pilot, passengers, or equipment. The balloon's speed and direction are governed by winds.

barnstormer   The name given to itinerant pilots of aviation's early days who earned a living by selling passenger rides from farm fields and pastures.

barometer   A device for measuring air pressure. Variations include the aneroid type, which uses an evacuated container, and the mercury type, which measures the height of a column of mercury in an evacuated glass tube.

basket   The portion of a balloon where pilots, passengers, flight instruments, and fuel stay during flight.

blackouts   In aerobatic flying, the loss of vision or loss of consciousness caused by high g-forces.

canard   Wing surfaces positioned in front of the airplane, serving the same purpose of the horizontal stabilizer positioned on the empennage of conventional airplanes.

certificate   In flying terms, a certificate is a document that grants legal permission for pilots to operate an aircraft. Most certificates are issued without any expiration date, but pilots must practice certain skills on a regular basis to be able to legally exercise the privileges of their certificates. Certificates include private, commercial, flight instructor, and airline transport pilot.

collective pitch control   A control used in rotary-wing aircraft that alters the pitch of all blades simultaneously.

conventional gear   The configuration of landing gear featuring a tail wheel and two main gear located beneath the wings.

cyclic pitch control   A control used in helicopters to selectively change the pitch of rotors in order to tilt the rotor disk and produce thrust.

dew point   The temperature to which a particle of air would have to be chilled in order to force the water vapor contained in it to condense into droplets of visible moisture.

dirigible   Massive, rigid-frame airship. Early dirigibles used flammable hydrogen gas for lift and were popular in Germany as cruise vehicles and as wartime aircraft.

dog fight   The chaotic air battles between two or more enemy planes. Originally used during World War I, dog fights are still popular in aviation combat.

drag   One of the four forces of flight, drag is the retarding force that reduces the effectiveness of thrust. Drag is typically an undesirable side effect of the viscosity of the air, or an unavoidable by-product of lift.

elevator   In airplane, the hinged tail structure used to control an aircraft's pitch. Elevator is controlled by the pilot using the control column.

empennage   The airplane's structure that includes horizontal and vertical stabilizers and the aerodynamic elements that sustain smooth flow.

envelope   In a balloon or airship, a fabric or rubberized bag that is filled with hot air or buoyant gas to provide lift.

FBO   Fixed-base operator, the airport business offering aircraft for rent or sale, flight instruction, fuel, maintenance, charter flying service, and flight instruction. If there's only one business at an airport, it will probably be an FBO.

fixed-wing   Indicates a type of aircraft in which the main lift-producing surface is stationary, as in an airplane. See also **rotary-wing**.

flight instruments   Devices that measure parameters of flight, including airplane attitude, altitude, airspeed, rate of turn, direction, and rate of climb or descent. Flight instruments function using either gyroscopes or air pressure.

flight physiology   The field of medicine that studies the body's adaptability to flight and the maladies and injuries that flight can induce.

fuselage   The portion of airplane structure that contains the cockpit, passenger cabin, and cargo compartment, and provides an anchor for the wings, empennage and, sometimes, the engine.

glide slope   The imaginary slope, as shallow as 3 degrees, that pilots follow during descent to land. The glide slope is sometimes indicated by lights or electronic signals.

gliding   A form of aviation in which high-lift airplanes fly by exchanging altitude for speed. Requires a mechanical launch, typically behind a powered airplane or using an automobile tow.

gondola   See **basket**.

graveyard spiral   A potentially dangerous maneuver in which a cycle of increasing bank angle, lower pitch angle, and increasing airspeed result in rapid descent. Unless it is remedied quickly and correctly, graveyard spiral can result in structural failure or crash.

gyroplane   Also called "autogyro"; an aircraft that derives its lift from a typically free-turning rotor, and its thrust from an airplane-style propeller.

hangar   An airport building where aircraft are stored and protected from the elements. Often serves as a place where mechanics and pilots maintain aircraft.

hangar bums   Also known as "ramp rats," a mostly affectionate reference to the groups of pilots and aviation lovers who hang around the airport, often in a favorite hangar or at an airport restaurant or tavern.

hangar flying   The most daring, adventurous, and technically perfect form of flying there is—conversation usually carried on by pilots grounded by bad weather.

hour   The unit of time pilots use to measure flying experience. Usually measured from engine start to engine shut-down.

human factors   The study of the factors affecting pilot performance and judgment, including emotions, physical health, relationships to other crew members, and response to stress.

human-powered flight   Flight accomplished with no other power source of human pilots or crew members, requiring highly advanced, ultra-lightweight materials.

hypoxia   A catch-all term covering a number of conditions in which the blood is robbed of oxygen, or in which oxygen-rich blood is incapable of delivering oxygen to parts of the body that need it.

instruments meteorological conditions (IMC)   Combinations of visibility, precipitation, and clouds that, by federal regulations, limit flying to the pilots with instrument ratings and necessary recent flight experience.

Jenny   A popular World War I–era trainer that became familiar in the postwar years when pilots purchased thousands of them as surplus for civilian use.

knife-edge flight   Flight with a 90-degree bank angle (so that the wings are perpendicular to the ground), in which the fuselage becomes the major lift-producing surface.

knot   A unit of speed measuring the number of nautical miles traveled in a given time.

lift   One of the four forces of flight, lift is the pressure created by wings or other aerodynamic surface, or buoyancy, that counteracts the pull of gravity.

Mach number   The ratio of an airplane's speed to the speed of sound at flight altitude, density, and temperature; so called in honor of Austrian physicist Ernst Mach.

mass ascension   The ascension of a large number of hot-air or gas balloons in a brief period of time.

meteorology   The science that investigates the atmosphere, including its interaction with earth's surface, oceans, and life in general.

nautical mile   The unit of length used to measure distance in aviation. Longer than the 5,820-foot statute mile commonly used in the United States, the nautical mile measures 6,076 feet in length.

night VFR   Flying after sunset under rules that permit flying by pilots untrained in flying solely by instruments.

parachute   A fabric shroud that carries a payload, usually a person, and uses air resistance to reduce its rate of free fall.

preflight inspection   A thorough check of all aircraft systems made by pilots before each flight.

rotary-wing   Indicates a type of aircraft in which the main lift-producing surface rotates, as in a helicopter or a gyroplane. See also **fixed-wing.**

rotor   The powered or free-turning set of airfoils that creates aerodynamic force in helicopters and gyroplanes.

rudder   In airplanes, the tail structure that controls yaw. Rudder is controlled by foot-operated rudder pedals.

seaplane   Airplane equipped with floats in place of landing gear wheels, permitting takeoff, landing, and maneuvering on water. Some seaplane fuselages are designed like boat hulls and don't need landing gear at all.

scale   The size of features on a map.

soaring   Staying aloft without losing altitude. Requires an atmospheric boost from wind or sun-generated thermals.

solo   Technically, any flight time when a pilot is alone in the cockpit is considered solo time. It takes on extra significance when it represents the very first time a student pilot gets to fly the plane alone, without an instructor on board. The first solo is a memorable benchmark in a pilot's life.

spatial disorientation   A condition of the body's equilibrium organs resulting in pilot uncertainty over his orientation to the earth's surface.

spoilers   Panels or plates installed on the upper wing surface of airplanes and gliders in order to disrupt the lift-producing flow of air, having the effect of slowing the aircraft or increasing its rate of descent.

stall   In aerodynamics, the condition in which the smooth flow of air over the wing becomes turbulent, destroying lift force to a point that it falls below the force of gravity.

thrust   One of the four forces of flight, thrust is the force produced by an engine that works in the opposite direction of drag.

thunderstorm   A violent convective phenomenon that produces rain, hail, lightning, strong winds, and possibly more severe conditions such as squall lines, tornadoes, and waterspouts.

tricycle landing gear   The configuration of landing gear featuring a nose gear and two main gear beneath the wings.

visual meteorological conditions (VMC)   Combinations of visibility, precipitation, and clouds that do not limit flying to certified pilots only.

weight   One of the four forces of flight, weight is the force caused by tendency of any mass to move toward the earth; weight opposes lift.

wind shear   A change in wind direction or speed. Can produce swirling, turbulent air currents that can be hazardous to aircraft.

Glossary of Radio Communications

Pilots use their own peculiar radio vocabulary that many nonpilots find difficult to interpret. Part of the confusion comes from technical jargon, and part of it comes from the strange sound of the phonetic alphabet.

To overcome the poor transmission quality of early aviation radios, pilots and air-traffic controllers all over the world constructed the phonetic alphabet in which a word represents each letter of the alphabet, thereby sidestepping the similarity in sounds between letters like "b" and "v," for example. Also, because aviation is an international enterprise, the variety of foreign accents and dialects could be confusing without some unifying language rules.

The international phonetic alphabet features some familiar English words, though their proper pronunciations under the international rules are, in a couple of cases such as the numeral 5 and the word "Oscar," slightly different from how we might say them.

The alphabet is simple to learn and easy to remember. Once you know it, you'll find yourself using it to spell out all sorts of words, names, and street names that a listener doesn't understand.

Here's the phonetic alphabet, numbers, and a few key words used by pilots and air-traffic controllers.

Phonetic Alphabet

A   Alpha (*AL-fuh*)

B   Bravo (*BRAH-voh*)

C   Charlie (*CHAR-lee*)

D   Delta (*DEL-tuh*)

E   Echo (*ECK-koh*)

F	Foxtrot (*FAHKS-traht*)
G	Golf (*Gahlf*)
H	Hotel (*hoh-TELL*)
I	India (*IN-dee-yuh*)
J	Juliet (*DZEW-lee-ett*)
K	Kilo (*KEE-loh*)
L	Lima (*LEE-muh*)
M	Mike (*Miyk*)
N	November (*noh-VEM-bur*)
O	Oscar (*OSS-kuh*)
P	Papa (*Puh-PAH*)
Q	Quebec (*kay-BEK*)
R	Romeo (*ROH-mee-yoh*)
S	Sierra (*see-YEHR-ruh*)
T	Tango (*TANG-goh*)
U	Uniform (*YEW-nee-form*)
V	Victor (*VIK-tah*)
W	Whiskey (*WISS-kee*)
X	X-Ray (*EKS-ray*)
Y	Yankee (*YANG-kee*)
Z	Zulu (*ZOO-loo*)
0	Zero (*ZEE-roh*)
1	One (*wun*)
2	Two (*too*)
3	Three (*tree*)
4	Four (*foh-wuhr*)
5	Five (*fife*)
6	Six (*siks*)
7	Seven (*SEH-vin*)
8	Eight (*ait*)
9	Nine (*niner*)

Words and Phrases

Here are some of the words and phrases pilots and controllers commonly use in their radio communications—and sometimes even in ordinary conversation or in the airport tavern:

abort   To terminate a preplanned aircraft maneuver, for example, an aborted takeoff.

aerodrome   See **airport.**

affirmative   "Yes."

airport   The word most people use instead of aerodrome.

air taxi   Used to describe the movement of a helicopter above the surface, but usually not more than 100 feet above the ground.

air traffic   Sometimes called simply "traffic"; aircraft operating in the air or on an airport surface, not counting loading or parking areas.

air traffic control   A service operated by appropriate authority to promote the safe, orderly, and expeditious flow of air traffic. Also called ATC.

altitude   The height of a place or an object measured in feet above ground level (AGL), or above mean sea level (MSL).

ceiling   The height above the ground of the lowest layer of clouds or obscuring phenomena; ceiling can be reported as "broken," "overcast," or "obscured."

clearance   Authorization of an aircraft to proceed under conditions speficied by air-traffic controllers. For example, "cleared for takeoff" and "cleared to taxi."

distress   The condition of being threatened by serious or imminent danger.

emergency   A distress or an urgency condition.

expedite   A word used by ATC when prompt compliance is required to avoid the development of an imminent situation. In other words, "Get a move on!"

final approach   The part of a landing pattern that is aligned with the landing area.

flameout   An emergency condition caused by a loss of engine power.

"go ahead"   Proceed with your message. Not to be used for any other purpose.

"go around"   An instruction for a pilot to abandon his approach to landing, usually because of an obstruction or emergency on the runway, or because a distressed aircraft is making an approach to the runway.

handoff   An action taken to transfer the radar indentification of an aircraft from one controller to another if the aircraft enters the receiving controller's airspace and radio communications with the aircraft are transferred.

"how do you hear me?"   A question relating to the quality of the transmission or intended to determine how well the transmission is being received.

"immediately"   Used by ATC when such action compliance is required to avoid an imminent situation.

"I say again"   The message will be repeated.

known traffic   Aircraft whose altitude, position, and intentions are known to ATC.

light gun   A handheld directional light-signaling device which emits a brilliant narrow beam of white, green, or red light as selected by the tower controller. The color and type of light transmitted can be used to approve or disapprove of anticipated pilot actions where radio communications are not available.

lost communications   Loss of the ability to communicate by radio. Aircraft are sometimes referred to as NORDO (no radio).

"make short approach"   A command used by ATC to inform a pilot to alter his traffic pattern so as to make a short final approach.

"mayday"   The international radio distress signal. When repeated three times, it indicates imminent and grave danger and that immediate assistance is requested.

minimum fuel   Indicates that an aircraft's fuel supply has reached a state where, upon reaching the destination, it can accept little or no delay in refueling. This is not an emergency situation but merely a possibility of such situation should any undue delay occur.

"negative"   "No," or "permission not granted," or "that is not correct."

"out"   The conversation is ended and no response is expected.

"over"   "My transmission is ended"; "I expect a response."

"pan-pan"   The international radio urgency signal. When repeated three times, indicates uncertainty or alert followed by the explanation of the urgency.

"radar contact"   Informs pilots that controllers have received position information on radar read-outs.

"radar contact lost"   Informs pilots that controllers no longer receive position information on their screens.

"read back"   Means "repeat my message back to me."

"roger"   "I have received all of your last transmission." It should not be used to answer a question requiring a "yes" or "no" answer.

"say again"   Used to request a repeat of the last transmission.

"speak slower"   It's as simple as that. A recommended request for student pilots to make to controllers who speak too fast.

"stand by"   Means the pilot or controller must pause for a few seconds, usually to attend to other duties of a higher priority.

"taxi into position and hold"   An instruction to a pilot to roll on to the departure runway and hold until takeoff clearance is received.

"traffic in sight"   Used by pilots to inform a controller that previously issued traffic is in sight.

"traffic no factor"   Indicates that the traffic described in a previously issued traffic advisory is no longer a factor.

"transmitting in the blind"   A transmission from one station to other stations in circumstances where two-way communication cannot be established, but where the transmitting party thinks his transmitter is functioning properly.

"verify"   Request confirmation of information.

"wilco"   The contraction of the words "will comply," meaning "I have received your message, understand it, and will comply with it."

Recommended Reading

Books

Ahrens, C. Donald. *Meteorology Today: An Introduction to Weather, Climate, and the Environment, 3d ed.* St. Paul: West Publishing Co.

A must-read for any serious student of flying, this venerable text covers the gamut of weather, from atmospheric optics such as rainbows and sundogs to the most obtuse concept of vorticity—one of the most fundamental principles of meteorology. Don't miss the description of the "green flash," which is one of the rarest occurrences in the sky. Once you learn about it, you'll never stop watching for it.

Bach, Richard. *Jonathan Livingston Seagull.* New York: Macmillan Publishing Co., 1970.

Bach is one of the "Holy Trinity" of aviation writers, alongside Gann and Saint-Exupéry (see later in the appendix). This classic, Bach's best work, contains not a single airplane, nor a pilot. Yet it is the fullest, most transcendental treatment of aviation ever written. No pilot's bookshelf should be without his other greats, *Biplane, Stranger to the Ground,* and *Illusions.*

Bilstein, Roger E. *Flight in America: From the Wrights to the Astronauts.* Baltimore: The Johns Hopkins University Press, 1984.

Good "hole-filler" that bridges the gaps left in other texts, beginning with the birth of manned airplane flight and ending with the Space Race.

Brennan, T.C. "Buddy." *Witness to the Execution: The Odyssey of Amelia Earhart.* Frederick, CO: Renaissance House, 1988.

Another take on the Saipan theory, which trots out a purported eyewitness to the execution of the noted aviatrix by Japanese soldiers. Brutal in its premise, a single source of untestable credibility is far from a solid foundation to build a theory on. Still, for the conspiracists and Earhart cognoscenti, this is an entertaining take on the case.

Buck, Robert N. *Weather Flying, 3d Ed.* New York: Macmillan Publishing Co., 1988.

Robert Buck's book is in its second generation as an aviation classic. Buck doesn't stop at describing weather theory, though he deals with the science deftly. He goes on to bring the principles of weather straight into the cockpit, and adds a heaping helping of commonsense application.

Cole, Duane. *Conquest of Lines and Symmetry.* Milwaukee: Ken Cook Transnational, 1970.

This is one of a pair of books by the "father figure" of aerobatics, whose books have nurtured more aerobatic pilots than any other author's. Written in charmingly simple prose and designed with equally simple diagrams, this book should be a fixture in every aspiring aerobatic pilot's library.

Conway, Carle. *The Joy of Soaring: A Training Manual.* Hobbs, NM: Soaring Society of America Inc., 1989.

Devine, Thomas E., and Richard M. Daley. *Eyewitness: The Amelia Earhart Incident.* Frederick, CO: Renaissance House, 1987.

A well-researched, breathlessly conspiratorial essay based on the premise that Earhart and her navigator died on the Japanese-controlled island of Saipan after missing Howland Island, a refueling stop on the most dangerous leg of her globe-circling voyage.

Donahue, J.A. *The Earhart Disappearance: The British Connection.*

Almost addictive for its sheer wackiness, this could be regarded as the most out-landish Earhart disappearance theory, if only for its elaborate futility. The British are probably innocent as charged, but it's fun to go along for the ride.

Earhart, Amelia. *Last Flight.* New York: Orion Books, 1988.

With the eerie sense of impending doom, this collection of Earhart's own cable dis-patches traces her final flight from an aborted first attempt to circle the world to her Miami-Lae journey that, for some, has still not come to an end. The book was com-plied by her husband, publisher George Putnam, and features a foreword by aviation historian Walter J. Boyne.

Gann, Ernest K. *Fate Is the Hunter.* New York: Simon & Schuster, 1961.

Ernie Gann is to the aviation novel what Agatha Christie is to the parlor mystery. That is best exemplified by his novels *The Aviator,* which was turned into a powerful feature film, and *The High and the Mighty. Fate ...* is Gann's personal memoir of the power of fate—call it dumb luck—in determining life and death of pilots. Filled with haunting stories of survival told in Gann's unforgettable style. Every pilot should know this book, because it defines the shared pilot psyche.

Gibbs-Smith, C.H. *Flight Through the Ages.* New York: Thomas Y. Crowell Co., 1974.

A pleasant journey through aviation history with hundreds of drawings so quirky that they border on camp. Delightfully detailed.

Goerner, Fred. *The Search for Amelia Earhart.* New York: Doubleday & Co., Inc., 1966.

Thirty years after Amelia Earhart's disappearance in the Atlantic, radio broadcaster Goerner patches together an off-kilter theory in a fast-paced, readable book that makes it fun to join, at least for a moment, the conspiracist camp. His conclusions are probably wrong, but Goerner does know how to write an investigation adventure tale.

Harrison, James P. *Mastering the Sky: A History of Aviation from Ancient Times to the Present.* New York: Sarpedon, 1996.

An authoritative account of the high and finer points of the history of flight.

Holley, John. *Aviation Weather Services Explained.* Newcastle, WA: ASA, Inc., 1997.

This companion workbook to the FAA's *Aviation Weather Services* expands on the explanations of weather charts and forecasts included in the government publication. John Holley, a former professor of mine who planted a fondness for weather in me and hundreds of students at Embry-Riddle Aeronautical University, teaches pilots how to use the tools handed to them by the FAA's authors. With his characteristic humor, he brings a potentially dry topic to life and puts pilots on a first-name basis with weather services offerings.

Kalakuka, Christine, and Brent Stockwell. *Hot-Air Balloons.* New York: Friedman/Fairfax Publishers, 1998.

Like most books about hot-air ballooning, this one is heavy on the photography, all of which is high-quality and appealing. From the history of the sport to the nuts and bolts of how the bulbous behemoths function, Kalakuka and Stockwell have created a book that will satisfy both the coffee-table browser and the balloon enthusiast wanting a reminder of what makes balloonists so passionate about their sport.

Kershner, William K. *The Basic Aerobatic Manual.* Ames, IA: Iowa State University Press, 1987.

Bill Kershner is as familiar to many pilots as their Dick-and-Jane books. From student pilot to advanced aviator, Kershner, through his books, is America's aeronautics professor. In this book, he brings the same humor and clarity to aerobatics as he does to each of the subjects he writes about.

Langewiesche, Wolfgang. *Stick and Rudder: An Explanation of the Art of Flying.* New York: McGraw-Hill Book Co., 1972.

Though it was originally written in the 1940s, Langewiesche's classic is as pertinent today as it ever was. It should be required reading for every would-be pilot, every flight instructor who teaches beginning pilots, and anyone who enjoys graceful writing about flying.

Lester, Peter F. *Turbulence: A New Perspective for Pilots.* Englewood, CO: Jeppesen Sanderson, Inc., 1993.

For the first time, the subject of turbulence has been pulled out of the hurly-burly of general meteorology texts where it was often tossed in as an afterthought. Lester has given it the prominence it deserves with this exhaustive, readable, and well-illustrated guide to phenomena from dust devils to clear-air turbulence.

Longyard, William H. *Who's Who in Aviation History: 500 Biographies*. Novato, CA: Presidio Press, 1994.

A perfect browsing book for aficionados that captures in concise articles biographies of some of the rogues, rascals, and heroes of aviation.

Lovell, Mary S. *The Sound of Wings: The Life of Amelia Earhart*. New York: St. Martin's Press, 1989.

This is the best of the Earhart biographies. Lovell has her eyes open when she examines the life of an aviatrix who was more comfortable as an advocate for women and equality than she was in a cockpit. Exceptionally entertaining. Well illustrated and indexed.

Mason, Sammy. *Stalls, Spins, and Safety*. New York: Macmillan Publishing Co., 1982.

Sammy Mason has written the undisputed last word on stalls and spins, perhaps the most misunderstood and needlessly feared part of flight. Mason's essay is a classic of explanatory prose.

Milne-Thomson, L.M. *Theoretical Aerodynamics*. New York: Dover Publications, Inc., 1958.

This is a volume you'll be tempted to display in a prominent place in the front parlor in order to impress visitors. One thing you won't be likely to do with it is actually read it. True, there are some nuggets nestled in the ore, but most of Milne-Thomson's dense tome is closely reasoned formulas that defy comprehension and invite slumber. This book is on my list of the last book I'd want with me on a desert island.

Newton, Dennis. *Severe Weather Flying*. 1983.

Newton has written one of the best explanations of severe weather to reach the flying public. Newton's explanations of the fundamental elements of severe weather, and the ways they combine and interact to make bad weather worse, are readable and memorable.

Rabinowitz, Harry. *Conquer the Sky: Great Moments in Aviation*. New York: Metro Books, 1996.

A well-illustrated guide to aviation history, from ancient times to the present.

Roessler, Walter, Leo Gomez, and Gail Lynne Green. *Amelia Earhart: Case Closed?* Hummelstown, PA: Aviation Publishers, 1995.

This book provides the details behind the most likely explanation to a puzzling mystery. Forget the Japanese execution theory, the lady-spy theory, and all the other crank solutions that this book handily refutes. Sometimes the simplest answer is the best one.

Saint-Exupéry, Antoine de. *Airman's Odyssey*. New York: Harcourt Brace Jovanovich, 1984.

No writer evokes the mysterious union between plane, pilot, and sky like the Good Saint Ex. This volume contains his three best works: *Wind, Sand, and Stars; Night*

Flight; and *Flight to Arras.* Beyond his incomparable writing about flying, Saint Ex was a pioneer of early international aviation, a French resistance patriot, and a war hero who was ultimately shot down during an airborne reconnaissance mission. His poignant death in an airplane renders his timeless writing all the more powerful.

Serling, Robert J. *The Only Way to Fly.* New York: Doubleday & Co., 1976.

A masterful chronicle of Western Airlines, the national airline that traces its origins farther back in history than any other airline. Western Airlines helped blaze a trail for air mail, then became one of the most storied airlines in the world, and its tale is well-told by this veteran biographer of the great airlines.

Slepyan, Norbert, ed. *Crises in the Cockpit: Other Pilots' Emergencies and What You Can Learn from Them.* New York: Macmillan Publishing Co., 1986.

More than merely a collection of hangar stories—which it also has in thrilling, heart-pounding spades—this collection of real-life lessons in disaster and near disaster is readable and instructional from first page to last.

Slepyan, Norbert, ed. *Defensive Flying.* New York: Macmillan Publishing Co., 1986.

Sometimes it's not a pilot's actions that get him into trouble, it's the actions of a host of other people involved in completing a safe flight. From the fuel handler to the air-traffic controller, a defensive pilot is on the lookout for errors that can endanger a flight.

Smith, Hubert "Skip." *The Illustrated Guide to Aerodynamics.* Blue Ridge Summit, PA: TAB Books, Inc., 1985.

Smith takes the fear out of aerodynamics. Even those of us with a fondness for the arcana of the forces acting on an airplane can get overwhelmed by some of the standard texts. Smith doesn't shun the Greek alphabet that runs through aerodynamics, but the pace at which he motors through the subject allows us to follow him at a reasonably close distance. Clear and pertinent illustrations help immensely.

Spence, Charles F. *The Right Seat Handbook: A White-Knuckle Flyer's Guide to Light Planes.* New York: TAB Books, 1995.

Spence has put together an important instructional guide that will familiarize pilots' spouses and friends with the workings of the airplane, and even help them become part of an informal flight crew. There are plenty of things passengers can do to help out during a flight that will increase the safety of the flight and make it more fun for everybody. This charming little book opens up new adventures for passengers and pilots alike.

Trollip, Stanley R., and Richard S. Jensen. *Human Factors for General Aviation.* Englewood, CO: Jeppesen Sanderson, 1991.

The human element is almost always the weakest link in the safety chain, and until we replace human pilots with machines—which will be never!—pilots must continue to increase their awareness of how their decisions and physical condition affect the outcome of a flight. This book brings the frailty of the human equation home to roost.

Whelan, Robert F. *Cloud Dancing: Your Introduction to Gliding and Motorless Flight.* Highland City, FL: Rainbow Books, Inc., 1995.

Williams, Jack. *The Weather Book: An Easy-to-Understand Guide to the USA's Weather.* New York: Vintage Books, 1992.

If there's one thing *USA Today* newspaper is good at, it's explanatory graphics. This book is chock-full of them. Combine that powerful learning tool with Williams' wide-ranging curiosity, and the result is a book so instructive that it's almost addictive.

Williams, Neil. *Aerobatics.* New York: St. Martin's Press, 1979.

This is the best, most readable book on aerobatics ever written. Williams was a test pilot and aerobatics master who never forgot the soul inside the pilot and how aerobatics can be used in the same way that an artist uses color—as an expression of spirit.

Wirth, Dick, and Jerry Young. *Ballooning: The Complete Guide to Riding the Winds.* New York: Random House, 1991.

This soft-cover manual on the sport of ballooning reads as a celebration of the people who drag their gondolas out to the launch site before dawn and spend exhausting, rewarding hours working together to get a single bag of hot air into the sky for a few hours of breathtaking flight. Wirth and Young remind us that there's a lot more to ballooning than the balloons—more than anything else, it's a sport about people and camaraderie.

Aviation Magazines and Periodicals

Air and Space Smithsonian
The tender to the aviation culture. Photographically and editorially unsurpassed.

Airways
Airlines and commercial aircraft. Of interest to professional pilots and serious flying enthusiasts.

Aviation for Women
Published by Women in Aviation International mostly for female pilots and aviation hobbyists.

Aviation History
The planes and people that brought us this far.

Aviation International News
Corporate aviation.

Aviation Week & Space Technology
One of the most comprehensive of all aviation publications, providing very "inside baseball" content. This is what the experts read.

Balloon Life
If you like mixing your champagne and propane, this might be something you enjoy.

Flying
This publication is considered the standard by which others are measured, though that might be too high a pedestal. Still, a good magazine and widely available.

Pilot
Published by the Airplane Owners and Pilots Association, a powerful general aviation advocate, this is probably the best general aviation magazine on the newsstand.

Plane and Pilot
One of the best monthlies serving general aviation.

Professional Pilot
Serves the corporate and regional airline industry. A must-read for the aspiring professionals trying to crack into the business.

Sport Aviation
If you want to subscribe to this magazine, you have to join the Experimental Aircraft Association (EAA), which isn't a bad idea after all.

World Wide Web Resources

The World Wide Web is an aviation enthusiast's dream. It features hundreds of excellent Web pages that present credible, responsible information on every aspect of aviation. But the Internet is a freewheeling, evanescent medium that allows one person's ideas to be placed on a level ground with everyone else's.

That's why, no matter what pages I find interesting, you should regard their content with prudent skepticism. The content they presented when I visited them may have changed, even disappeared.

With those cautions and caveats, which are no more than common sense to those of us who turn to the Internet for more and more of our information, here are some Web sites I found interesting, even if I didn't buy into everything they had to say.

Aviation History

www.first-to-fly.com/

Here's the full story of the Wright brothers' historic first flight, told with the perspective and scholarship of the Wright Brothers Centennial Museum Online. For teachers and aviation history buffs, this is the Web's best Wright brothers' site.

aeroweb.brooklyn.cuny.edu/history/wright/first.html

This is the account, in Orville's own words, of what led up to the first flight of a man-controlled, powered airplane. From the glider test flights to the inevitable mechanical failures to the final successful flight, this is the account from the man who shared a place in history as the first flyer.

aerofiles.com/chrono.html

This site's designers say it's still being completed, and if so, we have something special to look forward to. This is a good, though not comprehensive, chronology. It skims over the last three decades, but makes up for it with an excellent store of entertaining, informative biographies. The Aerofiles home page (aerofiles.com) is also worth visiting.

www.aviation-history.com

This site is a treasure trove for fans of real-life histories, many of which are featured under the "Airmen" link. What's more, there are few sites anywhere else on the Web where you'll find such excellent photos of such obscure airplanes. It's the only site I've seen that includes a photo of Great Britain's vintage Bristol Beaufighter—not that I was looking for one. Still, this site features some serious history that's found in very few other places, on the Web or off. The sound file will drive you out of your gourd after a few "passes" of the war bird whose growling engine is part of the site's multimedia package. Wait a few minutes and it will stop, or just click the Stop button on your browser to silence it.

www.hq.nasa.gov/office/pao/History/SP-468/cover.htm

If you're a true student of aviation history, and not just looking at the pictures, here's a site worth your time. But bring a notebook, a No. 2 pencil, and one of those pink erasers, because this site can convince you you're going back to school. After a few minutes, you'll find that you're being rewarded with some of the best analysis of how aviation has steadily evolved into a sophisticated science. By the way, this is a government site, so don't expect any flash and glitz. It's all business, and very sound business at that.

members.tripod.com/usfighter/

Yes, this is one of those annoying Tripod member sites that insists on forcing pop-up windows down our throats. Simply minimize, but do not close, the first one and you won't be bothered any longer. Once past the pop-up, the site has its value. It features photos and histories of the aces of America's air wars and the airplanes they flew. The site is professionally presented, even though it is hosted by Tripod. By the way, if you have not gotten your fill of John Gillespie Magee Jr.'s maudlin verse "High Flight," you can read it here, along with a brief biography of the unfortunate author.

www.nationalaviation.org/inductee.html

Amateurishly constructed, this site can boast only one virtue: It features excellent biographies of some of the greatest figures in aviation. The write-ups of heroes range from aviation publishing giant Elrey Jeppesen to T. Claude Ryan, the man whose company built Charles Lindbergh's *The Spirit of St. Louis*. Aviation has some of the greatest and most courageous characters to be found, and these biographical sketches succeed in bringing them alive. This is a "don't-miss" destination for the aviation history buff.

www.thehistorynet.com/THNarchives/AviationTechnology

Here's a fair warning: Don't visit this site unless you have hours to devote to learning the history of aviation, and more. The aviation portion is excellent in itself, but it's part of an online history undertaking that will hold armchair historians in thrall for hours at a time. The tragic life of Ernst Udet, the World War I ace and partial inspiration for the film *The Great Waldo Pepper*, is one of the finest stories on the great pilot I've ever seen. All the content on this site is of the highest quality—a joy to visit.

www.airmailpioneers.org/

A good starting point for learning about the most daring of all pilots, I would argue—the air mail pilots who braved wicked weather, treacherous equipment, and callousness toward safety that causes modern pilots to blanche.

www.centercomp.com/dc3/

An excellent resource for information on the most important aircraft ever made. A case could be made that the almost indestructible DC-3 was the first airplane airline passenger trusted to carry them safely. Berliners, for their part, will never forget the C-47, as the military calls the DC-3, because during the long months of the Berlin Air Lift, its blunt nose and growling engines meant food, life, and survival. The site also serves as a meeting point for the community of airplane builders, pilots, and lovers of the airplane Gen. Dwight Eisenhower called one of the four most important weapons of World War II.

www.swizzle.com/panam.htm

This personal page by Rick Bollar is a good resource about all things Pan Am, from its heyday in the era of the great Clipper Ships to its darkest hours following the Lockerbie bombing and its ultimate demise in bankruptcy and disgrace. Now, the greatest name in airline history is making a comeback. If it pertains to Pan Am, you'll find it here.

www.tighar.org/

No other group has been as dedicated—or should I say obsessed?—with the mysteries surrounding the disappearance of Amelia Earhart as TIGHAR. This Web site lets us all wallow in the murky pool, though with more scholastic research and less wackiness than others might bring to the subject.

www.thehistorynet.com/AviationHistory/articles/1997/00797_cover.htm

C.V. Glines, the excellent aviation historian, beautifully spins a concise biography of Earhart. This is all you'll need to know to hold your own in a cocktail party debate over Earhart's fate.

www.pig.net/~stearman/airshow/wind.html

A delightful tidbit of barnstorming lore. Don't miss "Lisa's Rules for Wingwalking," with special attention to the first and the last rules.

www.deepsky.com/~mango/gustave/Pages/article8.html

Not many have the audacity to publicly confess a manic obsession with the first-flight claims of Gustave Whitehead, but the creators of this site do. Here you can find more testimony than you'd ever thought existed on claims that the Wrights were the second to fly—some of it compelling.

www.worldbook.com/fun/aviator/html/av6.htm

From the folks at World Book Multimedia Encyclopedia, this is a good reference site on the life and career of Charles Lindbergh.

www.lindberghtrial.com/

More concerned with the Lindbergh kidnapping than Lucky Lindy's life and career, this site nonetheless provides a comprehensive coverage of the greatest tragedy in the life of America's most famous flying hero.

www.pbs.org/wgbh/amex/lindbergh/index.html

As you'd expect, PBS is behind the best Lindbergh site on the Web. It's all here, and with authority.

www.richthofen.com/rickenbacker/

Here's the complete text of Eddie Rickenbacker's classic memoir, *Fighting the Flying Circus*. Rickenbacker knew better than anyone what World War I flying was about, and he tells it in his own words.

www.cfanet.com/mlewis/

A very rich, compelling resource for World War I aviation, though hamstrung by a clunky home page. Do the work required to dig into each category, because every vein yields a golden nugget.

www.richthofen.com/

Here's the complete text of *The Red Fighter Pilot*, by Manfred von Richtofen, the infamous Red Baron. Richtofen was a complex and thoughtful man who foresaw his early death and was haunted by it.

www.worldwar1.com/

This comprehensive site is a history text in itself, though more readable than most. It places the air war in its proper context in one of the deadliest conflagrations of the twentieth century.

www.mustangops.com/legends/yeager.html

Brief, photo-rich biography of Chuck Yeager, a war hero who went on to help pioneer modern aviation.

www.thehistorynet.com/AviationHistory/articles/1997/01972_cover.htm

Another C.V. Glines great going inside the cockpit and bomb bay of *Bockscar*, the B-29 that dropped the second atomic bomb on Nagasaki.

Aerobatics and Air Shows

acro.harvard.edu/IAC/acro_figures.html

Like a book that reveals the magicians' secrets, this site unveils the secrets behind aerobatics. Aside from Neil Williams' classic book, *Aerobatics* (see Appendix C, "Recommended Reading), this is probably the most clear and concise explanation of aerobatics maneuvers you're likely to find.

www.am-tek.com/WorldFederationOfAirshowCongress/airshowact.htm

For the incurable air show junkie, here's the lowdown on all your favorite performers.

www.airshows.com/

Presents still more air show lowdown.

www.blueangels.navy.mil/

This site covers the Navy's Angel Demonstration Team in more detail than you'd ever want to know.

www.nellis.af.mil/thunderbirds/default.htm

The Air Force's Thunderbirds Demonstration Team has a Web site that's almost as thrilling as their performances.

Ballooning and Blimps

www.launch.net/

From the basics of ballooning theory to weather to auctions where balloonists can buy their own bags of hot air, this site is the place—an excellent resource.

www.aibf.org/

The greatest balloon festival has the greatest Web site, with stunning, high-resolution photographs of previous fiestas and information about coming ones.

www.lakehurst.navy.mil/web99/hindenb.html

Going up in flames is not a major concern for modern balloon and blimp pilots, but it used to be. Here's a story of the worst aviation disaster the world had seen when it occurred in 1937. Listen to the chilling audio account if your nerves can stand it.

www.goodyear.com/us/blimp/index.html

The Goodyear blimp is the Granddaddy of airships, if only because it's been around the longest and has nearly universal consumer recognition. Here's the skinny on flying the blimp, and an explanation of why your chances of getting to ride in it are about the same as winning the Super Lotto.

www.ohio.com/kr/blimp/blimp.htm

Here's where the blimp yields its mystery. Find out what's inside that big bag of gas that bobs over the ball game every weekend.

Flight Safety

airdisaster.com/

There's no better aviation safety site on the Internet than this one. More readable than the National Transportation Safety Board's site, and more richly layered. As with any site whose focus is airplane wrecks, it can be unnerving at times.

www.ntsb.gov/aviation/aviation.htm

This site provides a fountain of flight safety information and statistics that the American aviation industry relies on. Dense but rewarding.

General Aviation, Gliding, and Helicopters

www.avweb.com/

AVweb is rapidly becoming the Web's best source of flying news and information. Sign up for the weekly e-mail newsletter.

www.aopa.org/index.shtml

The AOPA is one of the stalwarts of aviation. The organization tirelessly advocates for general aviation pilots, and they serve as one of the best conduits for information and education.

www.ssa.org/

The Soaring Society of America takes an active role in promoting the sport, including sponsoring clubs and hosting competitions. The result is a highly loyal membership. If soaring appeals to you, this site will give you all the information you need to get started, including a roster of training sites and plenty of information about soaring and gliding.

www.groenbros.com/

Groen Brothers company is working hard to develop a high-technology gyroplane, and it seems to be succeeding. Gyroplanes are regarded by some as a curiosity, but they have a lot of advantages over both airplanes and helicopters. Groen Brothers is adding a liberal helping of innovation to create what promises to be a remarkable family of aircraft.

Future of Aviation

www.aerovironment.com/

This company is onto something big, if you ask me. Nothing rings cash registers nowadays like a technology that is highly advanced while remaining earth-friendly. Combine all that with the fact that these aircraft are being used as airborne telecommunications platforms, and you have some serious potential.

www.geocities.com/CapeCanaveral/9334/

This page, called "Blackbird—Past, Present & Future," is enough to make some lovers of the "big iron" stand up and salute. The SR-71 is the biggest and baddest of a very tough breed. This site is the most complete and authoritative on the subject of the "Ablative Native" you're going to find.

www.moller.com/skycar/index.html

Moeller Skycars are one of the dandiest vehicles to come down the pike in a long time. I can see the Moeller Skycars becoming the playthings of the very rich, but I have my doubts if they'll be in most people's price range for a while. According to the manufacturer, this little beauty cruises above the madding crowd at a cool 350 m.p.h. at a gas-sipping 15 miles per gallon. Can anybody lend me a million clams?

spaceflight.nasa.gov/index-m.html

When it comes to a manned space station, the future is today. Though it's in its nascent stages in 2000, the International Space Station is growing one module at a time. For a tour of this "ultimate flying machine," check out this excellent site.

www.scaled.com/

Burt Rutan's company, Scaled Composites, is defining the leading edge of aerospace design. If you want to glimpse the airplane technology of tomorrow, snoop around this site.

www.solotrek.com/

I'd fly a SoloTrek in a New York minute, but something tells me this is going to be on the same list of dangerous luxuries as the Moeller Skycar. Still, we can dream, can't we?

Index

A

action-reaction forces, 107
active runways, 210
aerobatics, 224
    aileron rolls, 227
    costs, 233
    hammerheads, 228
    health of pilots, 229
        airsickness, 232
        blackouts, 231
        gravitational forces,
          230-231
    inverted flying, 225-226
    lomcevaks, 229
    loops, 227
    spin movements, 226-227
aerodynamics, 15
Aerofiles Web site, 321
aeronautical charts, 194
    scale, 194
    sectional charts, 194
aeronauts, 13
Aeroweb Web site, 321
aileron rolls, 227
ailerons, 99
Air Disaster Web site, 326
air mail, 42
    birth of airlines, 43-44
    pilots, 42
        Boyle, George L., 42
        Kelly, Fred, 43
Air Mail Pioneers Web site,
  323
air rage, 268-270
Air Shows Web site, 325

air-traffic controllers
    avoiding collisions,
      215-217
    navigation, 213-214
Airbus Industries, 297-298
airfoils, 107, 135
airlines
    history of, 43-44, 75-78
airplanes
    aerobatics, 224
        aileron rolls, 227
        hammerheads, 228
        inverted flying,
          225-226
        lomcevaks, 229
        loops, 227
        spin movements,
          226-227
    axes of motion, 105
        lateral axis, 106
        longitudinal axis,
          105-106
    cockpits, 97
        control columns, 98
        control panels, 97-98
    collisions, avoiding,
      215-217
    control columns, 115
        flight manuevers, 114
        turning, 115-116
    costs
        pilot certification, 186
        purchasing planes, 190
    designer, Burt Ratan,
      292-295
    drag, 110
        induced, 111-112
        parasite, 111

empennage
    horizontal stabilizers,
      99
    rudders, 101
    vertical stabilizers, 100
fuel regulations, 200
fuselage, cockpit, 97-98
inspections, preflight,
  205-211
landing gear, 101
    conventional, 102
    retractable, 102-103
    tricycle, 101-102
landing, 217-218
lift, 106-107
    action-reaction forces,
      107
    angle of attack,
      109-110
    limits, 108-109
    low-pressure, 108
manufacturers
    Beachcraft, 87-89
    Cessna, Clyde, 81, 83
    Cessna, 81-83, 85
    Millenium Jet, 298-299
    Mooney, 87, 89
    Piper, 85-86
powerplants, 94
    cowlings, 96
    engines, 94-95
    propellers, 96
radios, air-traffic
  controllers, 213-214
takeoff, 210-213
    run-up checklists,
      210-211
    taxiing, 210

B

C

337

X–Y